The Play of Reason

The Play of Reason

FROM THE MODERN

TO THE POSTMODERN

LINDA NICHOLSON

CORNELL UNIVERSITY PRESS   ITHACA, NEW YORK

Printed in the United States of America.

Cornell University Press strives to use
environmentally responsible suppliers and materials
to the fullest extent possible in the publishing of its
books. Such materials include vegetable-based, low-
VOC inks and acid-free papers that are also
recycled, totally chlorine-free, or partly composed
of nonwood fibers.

Library of Congress Cataloging-in-Publication Data
Nicholson, Linda J.
    The play of reason : modernism,
postmodernism, and feminism / Linda Nicholson.
        p.   cm.
    Includes index.
    ISBN 0-8014-3517-X (cloth : alk. paper).
    —ISBN 0-8014-8516-9 (pbk. : alk. paper)
    1. Feminist theory.   2. Postmodernism.
I. Title.
HQ1190.N53   1998
305.42'01—dc21   98-39167

Cloth printing
10   9   8   7   6   5   4   3   2   1

Contents

Acknowledgments

Over the years, Maureen MacGrogan and I have worked closely together, initially when she was my editor at Columbia University Press and then for many years when she was at Routledge. Our collaboration spawned many volumes, some of my own and others through the "Thinking Gender" series. Before Maureen left Routledge, she encouraged me to produce a collection of my own essays. By the time her arguments had begun to convince, she had left Routledge. Thus, although she was not the editor of this volume, she truly "birthed" it. I extend to her my love and deep appreciation for all she has given me.

I also thank Alison Shonkwiler for her work as editor on this collection. The combination of excitement, wisdom, and patience that she has brought to this collection is exactly what I needed to bring it together in its final form. Once again, I have been blessed with an excellent editor.

I would like to thank Bert Lapidus for his intelligence and effort in assisting me with the index.

Finally, I thank Steve Seidman, to whom this book is dedicated. I have acknowledged him in many places over the years, but this is the first time I have dedicated a book to him. It is fitting that this volume should be dedicated to him. The first essay in this collection, "Women, Morality, and History," was initially published in 1983, the year Steve came to Albany and our friendship began. Our friendship has been of central importance to me during the years when these essays were written. Steve, this one is for you.

The Play of Reason

Introduction

Beginning in the late seventeenth century, the idea of historical change began to play an increasingly important role in European social theory. The idea of "the past" was recast from that whose similarity with the present could be used to justify the present to that whose difference from the present could be used to valorize the present. Employing the idea of "progress," European theorists of the eighteenth and nineteenth centuries claimed the new as desirable precisely because of its difference from the past.

Thus the invocation of historical change to justify the new and different was linked with the idea of progress; however, the idea of progress contains at its core a key tension. On the one hand, as follows from the above, it is dependent on the idea of historical change; progress demands movement. On the other hand, it also assumes that beneath this change, there are certain historical constants—ideals that express what is best about being human. Without underlying values to give such movement meaning, history cannot be understood as representing progress; it remains merely change.

A tension between a commitment to historical change and universals of human existence exists within many of the social theories of the modern period. This tension has during the twentieth century increasingly become the object of attention. Twentieth-century social theorists have cast doubt on the idea of progress and its underlying premise that there are constants of human existence that give historical change meaning. They have also made suspect the idea that the diversity of human societies can be captured through concepts or analytical frameworks allegedly transcendent of such diversity. Thus, since the early 1960s, debates have flourished within anthropology and the philosophy of the social sciences around the question of whether social scientists can usefully understand the social behavior of others through concepts not familiar to those they are studying.

I came of age intellectually in the middle of these discussions. Educated by philosophers and intellectual historians in a department called "The History of Ideas," I came to see "How do we understand the cross-cultural adequacy of our own categories and frameworks?" as one of the central theoretical questions of our time. In my view, the most interesting theoretical work revolved around this question, and social theory inattentive to it I saw as riddled with problems. Politically, I was also coming of age as first a Marxist and, soon after, a feminist. The combination of my interest in this meta-theoretical question and my commitments to Marxism and feminism led me to think about the cross-cultural adequacy of Marxism's and feminism's own categories.

In relation to feminism, this concern occurred within a particular intellectual/political context that requires elaboration. Supposedly, in the early days of feminism's second wave, feminist scholars were inattentive to differences among women. Gradually, as lesbians, women of color, working-class women, and others became increasingly vocal, second-wave scholarship became more attentive to differences among women and less focused on the white, heterosexual, middle-class concerns that had previously dominated feminism.

I have come to believe that this story, like most simple stories, leaves out a great deal. In my own memories of feminist scholarship and the politics of the 1970s, for example, lesbians and women of color began speaking out very early in this period. Moreover, even many feminists who were otherwise privileged were talking about the need to stress differences among women. Anthropological theory played a key role in feminist theory during the 1970s, and many feminist anthropologists were sensitive to the issue of differences among women.[1] Many feminist theorists influenced by Marxism were also keenly aware of race- and class-linked differences among women. Certainly, among white, heterosexual feminists, Marxists and anthropologists tended to be more sensitive to issues of difference than many others. Even among the majority of those who did not fit within such categories, however, the issue of difference was recognized enough to be given a certain amount of acknowledgment. What was lacking was either the motivation, or the knowledge of how, to integrate this acknowledgment into the theory that was being produced.

The consequence was an acknowledgment of difference in some contexts and a marked failure of recognition in others. How was this discrepancy possible? How could scholars of that period both know that differences among women affected their lives in important ways and often incorporate so little about differences into their theory? The only explanation for this contradiction is by reference to understandings of theory that were operating then. Theory was seen as *having to* unify—having to pick out what was common. Thus, theorists typically mentioned differences among women but claimed that the differences necessitated only modifications to the core element of the theory, for example, in the degree to which the commonalities held true.

The problem seemed to stem from feminist scholars retaining traditional (i.e., modernist concepts of theory), despite the developing genuinely radical thinking about gender. The contradictions of modern social theory appeared to linger in feminist theory as feminist theorists replicated many of the modes of theorizing that they had learned from their teachers.

The first essay in this volume, "Women, Morality, and History" elaborates on this point. Although this essay has often been cited to note my criticisms of Carol Gilligan's *In a Different Voice,*[2] the bulk of the essay really is devoted to criticizing Lawrence Kohlberg, the theorist at whom Gilligan's book was primarily directed. When I do turn my attention to Gilligan, it is to argue that she takes over too much of Kohlberg, even as she criticizes him. Particularly, she inherits too many of his beliefs about how one theorizes. As I argue, it was this inheritance that not only led Gilligan to minimize differences among women but also kept her from replying adequately to some of Kohlberg's responses to her work.

From my perspective, Kohlberg's theory of children's moral development clearly embodied the problematic legacy of modern social theory.[3] Kohlberg, a late–twentieth-century psychologist, obviously was aware of the differences in children's orientations toward moral decision making both within and across cultures. Yet, he wanted to give this diversity some direction and meaning and did so by constructing an allegedly universal theory of children's moral development. Highly influenced by Piaget and Kant, Kohlberg's theory stressed a certain type of cognitive change as indicating "progress" in moral decision making. To develop morally was to base moral decision making on increasingly abstract principles.

Kohlberg's position raised the following two questions: 1) is the movement toward increased abstraction in children's and adults' moral thinking a universal phenomenon? and 2) even if this movement is empirically always present, should we assess it as that which should be prized? Kohlberg's response to the first question was that in a wide range of contemporary societies one could find instances of children's moral thinking moving from lesser to greater abstraction but never in the opposite direction. In answer to the second question, he argued that the description of increased abstraction in moral thinking as an advance was compatible with a wide range of moral philosophies.

Against these responses, I argue that the steady dominance of a modern western separation between private and public spheres of life across many otherwise different contemporary societies explained Kohlberg's finding of movement from concretė to abstract modes of thinking. I also argue that all of the philosophical theories that he appealed to were of the modern west. Consequently, whereas Kohlberg might be able to support both of his claims using evidence from many contemporary societies, he had not justified such movement as either universal or necessarily desirable.

In short, the major problem I have with Kohlberg's theory is that it selected a certain type of thinking—what Susan Buck Morss, in speaking of Piaget, has called "abstract formalism"[4]—from the historical context that not only fostered this way of thinking but also construed it as desirable. As I argue in this essay, however, Gilligan, in her critique of Kohlberg, committed a similar theoretical mistake. Although Gilligan rightly criticized Kohlberg's theory for failing to consider the moral reasoning of girls and women, her theory inadequately considered the moral reasoning of diverse groups of women. Furthermore, the reason for this failure was that, like Kohlberg's, it similarly abstracted one type of moral reasoning—most notably, that found in many contemporary girls and women—from *its* historical context. Gilligan, unlike Kohlberg, disclaimed the idea that her description of women's moral development could be assumed to be true of all women; but, because she did not explicitly frame her claims historically, the theory was silent about which girls and women her claims addressed.[5] Gilligan's silence led many readers to interpret her work as making universal claims about girls and women and also provided her with no obvious response to Kohlberg's finding that in some contexts girl's moral thinking was identical to that of boys. Thus, both Kohlberg's and Gilligan's theories ultimately assigned ideas specific to one society, to all societies, or to an indefinite range of societies. For Kohlberg, what was being assigned was a certain idea about progress in moral thinking and, for Gilligan, it was an idea of female morality. The problem, however, was not only in the ahistoricity of both theories; but it was also that moral progress and female morality were being discussed in singular terms. At the time I wrote "Women, Morality, and History," I did not have explicitly available the poststructuralist and Foucauldian insight that the attempt to make the indeterminate determinate is a political act that is geared to the accomplishment of certain political ends and is exclusionary of others. Now, looking back on this essay, I realize that I was approaching a similar idea: in both Kohlberg's and Gilligan's theories, the meanings of moral thinking and female moral thinking were being circumscribed for the sake of certain goals. In Kohlberg's case, the goal was to justify the idea of moral development as a cross-cultural phenomenon; for Gilligan, it was to counter the masculine nature of Kohlberg's description of that development. In both of their constructions, while certain political goals were achieved, others were excluded: Kohlberg neglected the idea that moral thinking may take different forms, whereas Gilligan ignored that women's voices are multiple in nature.

This poststructuralist insight can also help clarify an underlying theme of the other essays in Part I. In each of these essays, I cite an unrecognized historicity in meaning of some concept or idea, such as the economy, production, labor, woman, the family, or the political. In each case, this lack of recognition leads to the identification of one aspect of the concept or idea as its only possible meaning. Although the identified "meaning" of the concept or idea might reflect a dominant meaning within the identifying theorist's culture, the identification serves to exclude other meanings, either as legacies from a previous era or as newly emergent possibilities. In all cases, because the act of exclusion serves to further certain political goals and impede others, we might describe this kind of theoretical move as a "strategy." To elaborate on these points, I turn to "Feminism and Marx: Integrating Kinship with the Economic."

In this introduction I have discussed the tension within modern social theory toward, on the one hand, recognizing the importance of historical change and, on the other hand, understanding such change as meaningful through the use of concepts or analytical frameworks supposedly transcendent of history. The work of Karl Marx represents one of the great examples of this claim. While reference to the idea of historical progress can be found in the works of late–seventeenth- and eighteenth-century social theorists such as Locke and Smith, this idea appears to have reached its fully developed expression in the efforts of nineteenth-century writers such as Hegel, Marx, and Spencer. In the case of Marx, social theory *is* the study of social change; however, for Marx, it is the study of not just any type of social change but of that type of change that is behind all other types. As is widely known, Marx believed that underlying all historical change is change of the "mode and relations of production"—in other words, changes in "the economic."

Marx's idea that changes in the economy were the underlying causes of other changes led him into a crucial contradiction. On the one hand, Marx, an insightful historian of social change, was very aware that the growth of the economic as a separable and dominant sphere of social life was an historical phenomenon. On the other hand, in Marx's metatheory, he assumed that one could speak about such a sphere of life and its dominance in all societies. But in what sense could a phenomenon specific to one society be used to explain all other societies?

Independent of the adequacy of Marx's cross-cultural framework for analyzing societies without such a separated and dominant economy is the adequacy of this framework for analyzing societies with such a sphere. What happens when we make assumptions about the society we are analyzing in the very terms of our analysis? In Marx's case, the assumption of the separation and the dominance of the economic enabled him to highlight features of capitalist society that other social theory overlooked. By stressing the dominance of the economic, Marx highlighted the importance of wage labor in capitalist society. Politically, he could conceptualize a particular social group—wage laborers—as central figures in overcoming major inequalities in contemporary society. However, Marx's metatheory, in its assumption of the necessary separation and dominance of the economic, obscured other aspects of capitalist societies. No society is ever homogeneous. Even when certain patterns become dominant, older patterns linger and interact with the newer patterns to form hybrid phenomena. Earlier I claimed that the separation and dominance of the economic has been an important feature of capitalist societies in contrast to its predecessors. But, even in capitalist societies, the separation and the dominance of the economic has not been complete. It is in women's lives that older principles of social organization have lived on, generating forms of oppression not ascertainable by attention to uniquely capitalist patterns. Marx, in assuming the capitalist pattern of the dominance and the separation of the economic within the terms of his theory, was therefore unable to shed much light on many aspects of women's oppression. His theory neglected forms of social interaction that are governed by older principles of patriarchal kinship, such as sexuality. Nor could his theory account for the effects on women of the interaction of such principles with the growth of capitalist economies, such as women's assignment to certain occupations within a capitalist economy.

It is not only that Marx's theory could not account for aspects of capitalist society that are the effects of prior forms of social organization. Because in capitalist societies the economic has become relatively dominant and autonomous, there has also developed the ideology of the necessary dominance and autonomy of the economy. This ideology itself becomes a form of oppression in the face of phenomena that belie it. Thus, while women are assigned to certain places within the capitalist economy, they are also told that the economy is an autonomous, self-perpetuating system governed only by the laws of supply and demand. In so far as Marxists also believe in the necessary autonomy and dominance of the economic, they similarly cannot account for the specific ways in which women's labor is undervalued in the capitalist economy, and they put too much trust in the idea that once women join the paid labor force their oppression will cease. In other words, Marx's use of the economic has replicated dominant ways in which this concept has been understood within capitalist societies and consequently has reinforced forms of oppression linked to these understandings. From a feminist perspective, the point was not merely to reiterate these understandings within one's analytical framework but to deconstruct them.

My understanding of "deconstruct" is not to "throw away" or "destroy." Rather, it is to undermine the authoritarianism behind the idea of the determinateness of the meaning of concepts in general by delineating their histories, identifying their multiple meanings in the present, and attempting to foresee the possible political consequences of employing or elaborating any of these meanings in specific ways in the future. It is, in short, analyzing how power operates in diverse uses of such concepts and trying to understand how such uses make possible certain forms of human interaction and suppress or marginalize others.

"Feminist Theory: The Private and the Public" presents this kind of an analysis of the concepts of "private" and "public." The motivation behind this essay was a realization that feminist scholars seemed caught in a bind regarding the use of these concepts. On the one hand, it seemed apparent that some form of a separation between a private and a public sphere could be found in contemporary western as well as many other forms of societies and seemed a key element in many forms of women's oppression. The reality of this separation meant that feminists needed to acknowledge its existence. On the other hand, also involved in women's oppression has been the widespread belief in the necessary separation of these spheres, manifested for example in the widely held view that the personal is *not* political. Thus, feminists also needed to stress the ways in which the separation did *not* exist. In this essay, I argue that the way out of this theoretical dilemma is for feminists to make explicit both the historical emergence of these spheres as separate and their changing meanings and relationships to each other over time. For example, only by seeing the emergence of both contemporary personal life and contemporary political organizations out of societies where kinship relations govern what we now call "politics" can we understand both the gendered aspects of contemporary political life and many of the power dimensions of contemporary familial life. In other words, by constructing genealogies of contemporary understandings of the private and the public, we undermine dominant understandings of these concepts, which have construed these spheres as universally and necessarily separate.

If the goal of these last two essays was to deconstruct dominant understandings of the concepts of the economic, the private, and the public for feminist purposes, then my goal in "Interpreting Gender" was to deconstruct dominant understandings of two concepts central to feminist analysis itself—"gender" and "woman." Much of post-1960s feminist scholarship has relied on the distinction between "sex" and "gender." Although this distinction has served many useful purposes, particularly that of allowing feminists to challenge the idea that many observable differences between men and women are biologically based, it has also enabled feminists to preserve a type of dualistic thinking about women's identity. In brief, it has allowed feminists to think of women's identity as having both a "common part," as a consequence of all women possessing a common biology, and a "difference part," as a consequence of the diverse cultures women are part of. But such a dualist way of thinking allows feminists to think of differences among women as separable, or able to be bracketed out, from that which women share. In short, differences can again be marginalized; but, I argue, across cultures there is no single meaning of "woman" linked to specific biological traits. The meaning of "the biological" itself has varied and, therefore, so have cultural understandings of what it means to be a woman or a man. In other words, differences go all the way down, even to cultural understandings of the meaning and the importance of the body. Certainly, highly polar conceptions of the body and of the male/female distinction are dominant in many contemporary societies. And, therefore, as in Marxism, employing the dominant means of thinking in one's society as part of one's analytical framework can make certain insights possible. Such a polar framework has enabled feminists to stress the deep differences between women's and men's culture-generated experiences. But, because the polar framework of contemporary society neither is completely stable or hegemonic nor links perfectly male and female experiences with male and female identified bodies, employing it as an unquestioned element of one's analysis also leads to problems. This framework fails to capture the gender deviance of many of us, reinforces cultural stereotypes of the meaning of female and male experience, and acts politically to suppress modes of being that challenge gender dualisms.

The final essay in Part I, "The Myth of the Traditional Family" advances a similar type of argument, now not so much to feminists as to those with whom feminists often must struggle. In this essay, the "conceptual authoritarianism" I am wrestling against is that which asserts a singular and unchanging meaning of "family." I claim that the contemporary meaning of family as closely related kin who live together is a relatively recent cultural construction that emerged out of older meanings different in content. I show how the norm of family life as nuclear and exclusive of non–kin-related members became a mass phenomenon in the United States only during the 1950s in conjunction with specific economic changes of the period. As many people, particularly those of European descent, moved into a new "middle class," so did a particular form of family structure made possible by this expansion become idealized as representative of a truly "American" way of life. The irony, however, is that the "traditional" family of the 1950s was already in the throes of deterioration even as it was being newly constituted as traditional. Such phenomena as rising rates of divorce and the increased participation of married women in the paid labor force were, even in the 1950s and increasingly later, drastically changing the ways Americans lived. Such changes, however, have not prevented the persistence of exclusionary understandings of the "family," albeit with subtly changed criteria of "traditionality." The task is to undermine the support that invocations of "traditionality" give to such exclusionary understandings while also insisting on the need to assess the diverse consequences of different family forms on all of those affected by them.

Underlying my arguments in all of the essays in this volume is the belief that modernity has bequeathed us a problematic legacy. Although from modernity we have come to recognize the importance of historical change and cultural diversity, we have also inherited the belief that theorists can create analytical frameworks that transcend such diversity. In short, we have inherited both the idea that culture changes and the idea that constructs that rise above such changes are possible. This belief in the possibility of transhistorical theory, however, seemed to represent merely the false glorification of perspectives that were themselves historically limited. The political costs included not only a diminished understanding of societies different from those of the theorist constructing the framework but also the foreclosing of new possibilities for social interaction in modern western societies themselves. To extend the political democracy that was itself part of the legacy of modernity seemed to require the abandonment of that tendency to understand meaning ahistorically and monolithically and to look to transcendental analytical frameworks as the means for constructing social theory.

And yet, I also needed to come to grips with those who were pointing to the possibly dire consequences of such an abandonment. As various "postmodern" and "poststructural" theorists were articulating positions similar to mine, others were raising a variety of concerns about the wisdom of this stance. Did not the abandonment of the belief in such encompassing frameworks really entail the abandonment of theory altogether? Was not any analysis that went beyond particular descriptions of particular events likely to suppress alternative ways of understanding? How were social theory and criticism possible without such frameworks? Moreover, without such foundational frameworks of analysis and value, would we have any means for grounding cognitive or moral judgment?

The essays in Part II attempt to respond to these concerns. In "Social Criticism Without Philosophy: An Encounter Between Feminism and Postmodernism," Nancy Fraser and I argue for a form of social theory that does not see itself as foundational but that provides direction for social criticism. Against Jean François Lyotard, who claims that the rejection of metanarratives of social theory leaves us only in the position to create small, local narratives, we argue that social criticism sometimes demands large-scale accounts. Because sexism seems to be a phenomenon with a long history and global manifestations, theory that analyzes its causes and transformations must be on a large scale. Rejecting Lyotard's assessment of size as the source of the problem and smallness as the means to a solution, we point to ahistoricity as underlying many of the problems in the metanarratives Lyotard attacks. Explicitly historical social theory—that which sees its own categories as emergent from a particular social location and is therefore sensitive to the points at which such categories cease to be useful—can be on a large scale and politically efficacious. The problem with much feminist social theory of the 1970s and early 1980s, we argue, was not with the size of its object of inquiry—sexism in all of its historical and global manifestations—but in its attempts to provide monocausal accounts and to analyze sexism through categories, such as sexuality or mothering, which had biological associations. Because of these associations, feminists too often assumed that these categories had transhistorical meaning and failed to recognize sufficiently the ways in which their own use of these categories reflected their class, culture, and so forth. Social theory that understood its terms as rooted in history and was accordingly sensitive to its potential limits could indeed provide the basis for social criticism.

There was still, however, a deeper problem to be addressed: what about the question of relativism? Did not many of the metanarratives that Lyotard attacked attempt to provide a foundation for knowledge of the social? And was not the purpose of the metanarratives that philosophy in general saw itself as developing to arbitrate among claims about the social, the natural, the good, and the beautiful? Did not an abandonment of the belief in the arbitrating functions of such metanarratives leave us with only our own isolated views and criteria? These were serious questions that I, in echoing Lyotard's incredulity toward metanarratives, had to address.

My attempt to grapple with these questions is expressed in "Bringing it All Back Home: Reason in the Twilight of Foundationalism." Before elaborating on the specific themes of this essay, I will present some of the thoughts that led to its creation.

During the last several years, I have come to believe that modernity left us with an ambiguous legacy concerning not only the relationship between change and stasis but also the meaning of reason. Reason in modern western societies has been understood in what might be described as a continuum between, on the one hand, an "elitist" and "monological" understanding and, on the other, a more "democratic" and "dialogical" one.

At the elitist end of the spectrum, reason has been understood as a faculty exercised only by some, some of the time, when achieved by proper training, disciplining of the emotions, and exposure to specific kinds of information. Ideally, one individual who is trained, disciplined, and appropriately informed could practice reason in its pure form. This individual would then be in a position to access truth or to attain, at that point, "a god's eye view." According to this understanding of reason, that which distinguishes human beings from each other, the specificities of historical location that lead us to see the world differently, operate as an impediment toward attaining such a position. So, too, does the influence of any nonrational part of the psyche, such as the emotions.

At the other end of the continuum exists a view of reason as a much more mundane faculty, as that which, like the lungs or the heart, is exercised not all that differently by most human beings most of the time. According to this view, the biases that reflect the specificities of our respective locations, rather than necessarily operating as an impediment to the exercise of reason, can sometimes function as a resource, providing a diversity of perspectives that cumulatively advance humanity's storehouse of knowledge. Similarly, the other non-rational parts of the psyche, such as the emotions, are seen as only sometimes operating as an obstacle to reason; at times, they even improve its use. Moreover, whereas the former understanding of reason tends to view it as that which can, in principle, be embodied in one great mind operating on its own, the latter tends to think of it as a faculty that is dependent on human interaction. Thus, whereas the former tends to think of "truth" as that which is attained when any one individual manages to achieve "a god's eye view," the latter portrays "truth" as that on which human beings manage to provisionally agree in their respective bumpings against the natural world and each other.

My sense of what characterizes the present era is that although many aspects of the latter understanding have become more compelling to many, elements of the former remain. Certainly, with the decline in the attractiveness of correspondence theories of truth and in the belief in foundationalist positions, the idea of "a god's eye view" has become less attractive. Still lingering, however, is a type of "quasi-foundationalism"—the idea of reason as composed of a relatively limited set of rules whose adherence is necessary to move us toward the "true" or the "right" and whose justification transcends reference to any context more specific than that.

In "Bringing it All Back Home: Reason in the Twilight of Foundationalism," my goal is to undermine this lingering form of foundationalism. This goal does not commit me to a wholesale rejection of the distinction between the rational and the irrational. Rather, I suggest that we think about the criteria constituting "rationality" as diverse in relation to contexts and as always open to contest. Such a way of thinking about rationality makes the philosophical task one of arguing for the appropriateness of particular criteria in relation to specific contexts as well as over the boundaries of such contexts, rather than one of "uncovering" the meaning of reason across contexts or within contexts, understood as nonproblematically given.

Such a model is, of course, subject to the following objection: without an overarching set of rules defining rational argument, how are disputes to be ultimately mediated? To forsake the idea that some rules are context independent seems to invite relativism. Does not a reading of rationality as always potentially contestable leave us with no means of arbitration when it is precisely agreement about the criteria defining rationality that is itself required to arbitrate a dispute?

I respond to this objection in a variety of ways. First, I claim that although argument does require some points of agreement, these points can be understood as local and contingent—as themselves potentially debatable when other sources of agreement can be called on. In other words, an understanding of rationality as constituted by multiple criteria makes credible the idea of rationality's open-ended nature. Second, I claim that even if one acknowledges the possibility of scenerios without agreement, the invocation of this possibility need not be understood as a *reducto ad absurdem* conclusion to a philosophical argument. Rather, it can be understood as a depiction of a real-life possibility from which only real-life resources, such as our abilities to be creative and our willingness to keep trying, might save us. In other words, if we understand by "relativism" the situation in which the possibility of mediation breaks down, then relativism becomes not a philosophical position one does or does not endorse but a potentially real situation that one might or might not want to or be able to avoid.

At bottom, therefore, the kind of postmodernism I endorse in the essays in Part II is thoroughly pragmatic. In response to lingering views we inherit from modernity of reason as transcendent to the diversity of human practice, I suggest that we extend alternative legacies that construe reason as immanent to the diverse practices in which we engage. This very pragmatic elaboration of postmodernism has, however, implications for how we think about the relationship between reason and emotion. If one rejects a model of rationality as constituted by a single rule or set in favor of an idea of it as constituted by multiple sets overlapping and differing in varied contexts, then the emotions can no longer be depicted as necessarily standing apart from reason. Rather, how various emotional states interact with specific acts of judgment and discourse must be assessed in relation to the act's specific context. In the last two essays of Part II, the question of the emotions and their relationship to a postmodern understanding of reason is an explicit concern.

In "To Be or Not to Be: Charles Taylor and the Politics of Recognition," I discuss the relationship between reason and affect in the context of assessing Charles Taylor's defense of multiculturalism. Taylor defends multiculturalism by arguing that any culture that has persisted over time demands a presumption of worth by those who are considering the value of its contributions. Taylor differentiates this defense from a stronger one that would accord merit on the basis of considerations of justice. In making this differentiation, Taylor depicts the practice by which judgments of worth are made as one in which affect or interest should play no role. In short, behind Taylor's defense of multiculturalism appears an understanding of reason that is modernist in the sense that reason is viewed as ideally functioning independent of emotions.

I question on a number of grounds the utility of this understanding of reason in discussions of multiculturalism. First, even if one thinks that an affectless reason can be employed to make judgments of worth, there is no basis for a belief that this kind of reason underlies the judgments that currently inform any existing culture's understanding of "worth," including those of modern western societies. In current discussions of multiculturalism, the primary effect of exiling interest and power from discussions about judgment seems to be to discredit consideration of these factors as possible contributors to existing and prevalent judgments of worth.

But, second, a model of reason that assumes that interest and affect should, and therefore can, have no role in judgments of worth seems strange. One of the unfortunate aspects of many of the current discussions around postmodernism is that it is often posed as a battle between those who portray reason as always at its best when dispassionate and those who portray it as always a cover for power. If we think of reason as varying across contexts, however, then the idea of reason as always best when dispassionate seems as problematic as the idea that there are no differences in the degrees and ways in which "the force of the better arguement" operates.

But, here again, I do not see such issues as usefully discussed outside of an historical context. As the word "reason" does not describe that which persists across contexts, so too does not "the emotions." How we describe and carve up the operations of our psychic life seems deeply tied to our ideals of the good life and what it means to be a human being. As these ideas change across historical contexts so, too, do the ways in which we describe the structures of our psyche.

In "Emotions in Postmodern Public Spaces," I attempt to carve out shifts in twentieth-century U.S. culture that have resulted in some of the changed understandings of the relationship between reason and the emotions I have earlier described. In brief, I see during the course of the twentieth century a growing sense of connection between reason and the emotions in the construction of the popular idea of "feelings." As the term "feeling" is often used in popular discourse, it has come to signify an individualized cognitive orientation toward the world that is also partly affective. This psychic construction must be understood in the context of a growing individualistic sense of the self in relation to the world and an increased view of psychic satisfaction as a legitimate basis for action. This changed context has both positive and negative implications. Positively, the idea that feelings are legitimate grounds on which to base life decisions has made possible sustained attacks on older constructions of morality that legitimated inequality between women and men, stigmatized certain racialized groups, and organized sexuality in limiting ways. Negatively, such a viewpoint has contributed to an increasingly self-oriented understanding of the goals of human life.

I offer this kind of study as an example of how we need to think about reason today. To the extent that we recognize reason not as an ahistorical faculty or set of principles but as that which we construct to organize and evaluate judgment and communication for diverse purposes, we can assess how we wish to construct it in contemporary settings. It means examining, as this type of study does, the kinds of social phenomena that the creation of an idea such as "feelings" has made possible and assessing their worth. The last essay focuses only on changing understandings of the relationship between reason and the emotions in the contemporary United States. But thinking about reason as our own construction opens a host of questions beyond those concerning the relation of reason and emotion. To what extent does the construction of an idea of reason *as* a faculty preclude our exploring the relationship between processes of judgment and communication and the concrete circumstances that facilitate or preclude such processes? What ends of judgment and communication do we wish to promote—democracy, technological control, intersubjective understanding? In what balance and in what contexts should they be promoted? In short, to see diverse understandings of reason as human constructions that make some ends possible while precluding others seems most beneficial for making possible greater reflection and communication about such ends. It extends modernity's own promotion of reflection and communication about reflection and communication into postmodern times.

Part I

Modernity and the Problem of History

CHAPTER ONE

Women, Morality, and History

When women's studies first emerged in the early 1970s, many people expected it to bring forth some very basic challenges to the existing academic disciplines. Because it was clear that gender has been a basic organizing principle of all known societies, it was sensed that a perspective that made gender itself the issue would produce a potentially powerful new lens for viewing our past and our present. That sense has been vindicated. Women's studies has produced novel and indeed sometimes revolutionary means of viewing the subject matter of a variety of disciplines.

One such example is recent feminist scholarship in moral theory. Moral theory, as it traditionally has been taught in most British and American philosophy departments, has consisted of the writings of such men as Plato, Aristotle, Hume, Kant, Bentham, and Mill. Some feminist scholars have begun to make the increasingly convincing argument that the content of the theory produced by such men has been influenced by the almost universal masculinity of its creators. Whereas some might counter with the argument that the predominant masculinity signifies only that it has been men who have been given the resources for discovering that which is universal to the human condition, many feminists have responded that the masculinity of the authors has affected the content of the theory. Thus, in so far as these theorists claimed to be articulating that which is universal to the human condition, they were mistaken.

I agree with the feminist argument. The point I want to make in this essay is that the feminist argument needs more careful formulation and elaboration than it sometimes has been given. In particular, there needs to be more stress on the point that gender has been an important factor in influencing moral perspective and moral theory because gender has significantly influenced the concrete circumstances of people's lives. Thus, in elaborating how gender has shaped moral perspective and moral theory, we need to examine in depth the nature of such circumstances rather than relying too heavily on such shortcuts as "feminine" and "masculine."

For specific reasons, such shortcuts, though often helpful, can be misleading. For one, they incline us to overlook the point that although gender is and has been a fundamental social organizing principle, it is not the only such principle. Other factors, such as race, class, and the sheer specificity of historical circumstances, also profoundly affect social life and thus a moral perspective. Insofar as we talk about a feminine or masculine moral point of view, we risk not seeing how what we are describing reflects the gender viewpoint of a certain race or class at a certain time. We thus tend to commit the same kind of error of false generalization that motivated the initial feminist rebellion.

Kohlberg's Masculine Bias

To illustrate these points, I begin by examining some of the feminist scholarship that has emerged in moral theory. One of the major contributors to this discussion has been Carol Gilligan, who responded to Lawrence Kohlberg's moral development theory. Kohlberg claimed to discover certain universal structures of moral development that underlie all human moral perspectives. These structures were viewed by Kohlberg as formal—that is, as compatible with a wide variety of specific moral positions. He also described them as possessing an invariant internal order such that movement among the stages follows a certain unilateral direction. Kohlberg and his associates steadily revised the exact specifications of the stages in light of empirical findings. In spite of such revision, there remained one general characteristic of the sequence as a whole—that movement through the stages is marked by greater abstraction. Thus, according to Kohlberg's model, as moral reasoning progresses toward the higher levels, it is influenced less by reference to the consequences of actions on specific persons or communities and more by reference to abstract, universal principles. This idea is clear in a definition Kohlberg once gave of his highest stage, stage 6, "The Universal-Ethical Principle Orientation":

> Right is defined by the decisions of conscience in accord with self-chosen *ethical principles* appealing to logical comprehensiveness, universality and consistency. These principles are abstract and ethical (the Golden rule, the

categorical imperative); they are not concrete moral rules like the Ten Commandments. At heart, these are universal principles of justice, of the reciprocity and equality of human rights, and of respect for the dignity of human beings as individual persons.[1]

Because of a lack of empirical confirmation, stage 6 has occupied a controversial place in the theory. Even stage 5, however, which concerns the protection of individual rights, is more marked by appeals to nonparticularistic concerns than stages 3 and 4, which are characterized by reference to conventional norms. Similarly, reference to what is conventionally acceptable is itself more general than the perspective found in Kohlberg's lowest two stages, which emphasize the personal consequences of individual actions.

An obvious question that can be raised about this position is whether it describes a sequence universal to humans per se or represents a culturally biased perspective. Kohlberg, to deal with such a question, empirically tested his model in a variety of divergent cultures. He found that even in cultures as diverse as the United States, Great Britain, Mexico, Turkey, Taiwan, and Malaysia, the predictive capacity of the stages and their sequence was confirmed.[2] Kohlberg did note that not all societies or groups within a given society did as "well"; in other words, they did not progress through the stages at as fast a rate or reach in as great a number, if at all, the higher stages.[3] Kohlberg addressed this type of divergence by arguing that not all social experiences are equally conducive to moral development.[4]

If we ignore for the moment the ability of Kohlberg's model to predict successfully movement along the stages, the fact of divergence of rate and extent of moral development across cultures does speak in favor of the possibility of cultural bias. The point could be made that those who score low do not suffer from a lack of opportunity to reach the highest possible level of moral capacity but possess a type of moral reasoning poorly captured by Kohlberg's model. Thus, those who are classified by Kohlberg as "failures" might, from an alternative perspective, be viewed as "counterexamples." Gilligan raised this type of objection against Kohlberg.

Specifically, Gilligan argued that Kohlberg's model of moral development evidenced a masculine bias; its notion of development is skewed in favor of certain values more central to male than to female orientations. In part, Gilligan based her argument on the work of Nancy Chodorow, a sociologist heavily influenced by psychoanalysis and object-relations theory. Chodorow has drawn attention to a seemingly universal difference between early female and male child rearing: that the first and primary caretaker for girls but not for boys is a member of the same gender as they. According to Chodorow, one consequence of this difference is that young boys, to develop their own identity as masculine, must negate their early identification with their mothers. As a result, young boys tend to see social relationships as potentially threatening to their sense of self; protection against threats to their sense of autonomy acquires a high value in their lives. Young girls, on the contrary, incline toward defining themselves in terms of their connection to others. Thus, whereas men tend to fear engulfment by others, women fear abandonment. Chodorow also argues that because of the predominance of early parenting by women, young boys acquire knowledge of masculinity in a much more removed and abstract manner than young girls acquire knowledge of femininity; the role models of young boys are more frequently absent and distant figures. A consequence here is that abstract norms and rules play a greater role in the development of male gender identity than in the development of female gender identity.

Gilligan supplements these arguments with certain empirical studies. She draws on the work of Janet Lever, who notes one interesting difference in the games of young boys and girls: boys' games are more marked by conflict resolved through the creation of rules, and girls' games tend to involve smaller numbers of people imitating patterns of interaction of adult life. The girls' play, Gilligan notes, leans less "toward learning to take the role of 'the generalized other,' less toward the abstraction of human relationships" than that of boys. In contrast, "it fosters the development of the empathy and sensitivity necessary for taking the role of 'the particular other' and points more toward knowing the other as different from the self."[5]

From such studies as those of Chodorow, Lever, and others, Gilligan notes certain general differences in masculine and feminine personality structures that tend toward general differences in types of moral reasoning. Boys and men tend to evidence strong concern with issues of rights and autonomy; noninterference is a highly valued good. They are inclined, more than females, to be comfortable with rules that abstract from the particularities of situational concerns; they are more at ease than females with resolving hypothetical dilemmas. Girls and women, on the contrary, evidence a stronger orientation toward relationships and interdependence. Their moral judgments tend to be tied to feelings of empathy and compassion and to be situationally rooted. Their moral thinking in general tends to be contextual rather than categorical, to evidence in higher frequencies than males a response of "it depends."[6]

Following from such arguments, Gilligan claims that Kohlberg's model, with its emphasis toward abstraction from the particular, evidences a masculine bias. This bias, she argues, was made possible by his earliest empirical study from which he derived his model. That study used only boys as subjects. She claims that, given the bias within the theory, it is not surprising that girls tend to score significantly lower than boys on Kohlberg's scale.

Kohlberg responded to Gilligan's argument in a variety of ways. He noted studies that show no significant difference in the results of men and women.[7]

Kohlberg claimed to incorporate components of Gilligan's critique in the model; he also argued that although Gilligan's points have relevance to certain aspects of moral reasoning, those about content and orientation, they become irrelevant for the more formal issues of structure with which he is concerned.[8]

The "Masculine" in Western Moral Theory

At a later point in this essay, I deal with these responses. For now it is sufficient to note that even if there are elements of Kohlberg's model that remain untouched by Gilligan's argument, her argument remains important in and of itself. Much of western theory, independent of Kohlberg, has evidenced many characteristics that could be labeled "masculine" along the lines suggested by Gilligan.

This position is argued by Lawrence Blum. Blum focuses particularly on a certain tradition within moral philosophy that he calls "moral rationalism," which is best exemplified in the thought of Kant and Hegel. Blum notes that, within this tradition, many features viewed as distinctively moral parallel those features traditionally thought of as masculine. Thus, for both Kant and Hegel, the following qualities define that which is moral: rationality, self-control, strength of will, consistency, acting from universal principles, and adherence to duty and obligation. Moreover, these philosophers define the morally good "man" as specifically lacking the following qualities: sympathy, compassion, kindness, caring for others, and human concern—in short, those qualities associated with the emotional component of human nature that has also been linked with feminity.[9]

Blum relates this association between qualities of gender and qualities of morality to the differences in the kinds of worlds in which men and women have been expected to operate. Thus, whereas large-scale public institutions such as the state must abstract from the needs of particular persons and govern through the creation of universal laws, the family as bonded through intimacy and love, is concerned with the particular and concrete. Blum argues,

> The male world of work in corporate and governmental bureaucracies requires a certain kind of "universalist" outlook (though this outlook is ultimately compatible with serving private or parochial interests), a suppression of personal emotion, an adherence to procedures which abstract from personal attachment, inclination, concern for particular others. Similarly love, personal attachment, emotional support and nurturance are appropriate to the distinctive tasks of the family. To the extent that men are allotted to the former realm and women to the latter, different sorts of attributes and characteristics will be required of the different sexes. And society will have to provide a form of sex-differentiated socialization which prepares men and women for these societal roles.[10]

This idea that the separation of such attributes as rationality, impartiality, and abstraction from compassion, feeling, and a sense of connectedness might have something to do with a contingent modern western mode of thinking allied to a separation of domestic and nondomestic spheres of activity, can also be helpfully elaborated through the work of Roberto Mangabeira Unger. According to Unger, a modern, liberal-world view structures our experience around the following dichotomy. On the one hand stands the order of reason, thought, form, rules, and means. On the other hand exists the order of desire, feeling, content, substance, and ends. Similarly, the order of ideas stands opposed to the order of events as objectivity is opposed to subjectivity. Unger expressed this basic polarization in the following:

> Second, the estranged and the resigned share a common view of the relation of thought to life. They both believe that there is a public realm of factual and technical discourse and an intimate world of feeling. Within the logic of private emotion all religion, art, and personal love is arrested, and from it all rational thought is banished. The narrow conception of reason as a faculty addressed to the public rather than to the private life, to means rather than to ends, to facts rather than to values, to form rather than to substance, is necessarily accompanied by the cult of an inward religiosity, aesthetic, and morality that thought cannot touch, nor language describe.[11]

This mapping of reason, form, means, and so forth, with a public sphere and desire, content, ends, and so on, with a private one has the important manifestation that only the sphere of the former is seen to unite us, whereas the latter sphere is believed to constitute our particularity. Thus Unger notes that, following from this view, it is only when we are reasoning that we are seen to "belong to a public world because knowledge to the extent it is true, does not vary among persons. When desiring, however, men are private beings because they can never offer others more than a partial justification for their goals in the public language of thought."[12] What is eliminated from such a perspective is the possibility of objective value and subjective reason.

Reason and Desire

Unger's framework provides us with a helpful means for explicating modern western moral theory. The two major traditions in that theory are the deontological, exemplified in the theory of Kant, and the teleological or naturalistic, represented in utilitarianism. Unger describes these respectively as a "morality of reason" and a "morality of desire." He argues that both express this polarization. Whereas a utilitarian position accepts the validity of concrete desires being "factored" into moral judgments, it attempts to overcome the privacy and therefore incomparability of such desires through the use of an arithmetical calculus. The problem, however, is in trying to make public and comparable that which has already been constituted as private and incomparable. Given such a premise, arithmetical tools must prove worthless, for, as has often been pointed out, how can one measure the intensity of a desire? The deontological tradition similarly breaks down on its acceptance of the separation of the private and the public. Unlike a morality of desire, which accepts the validity of incorporating concrete desires into moral judgment, a morality of reason denies the validity of making reference to desires. It is reason alone, apart from motivation by any particular desire, that legislates morality. The traditional problem here is that such a position must move between vacuity and inconsistency. To the extent that moral judgment can be created apart from reference to particular desires, it is too empty to provide concrete direction in moral decision making. To the extent, however, that it incorporates any substance into that which it legislates, it becomes inconsistent as a theoretical position. Kohlberg's position, as in this latter tradition, evidences a weakness along similar lines. To the extent that each of his stages does constitute a recognizably distinct orientation, it is in danger of being the reflection of a particular world view; to avoid giving content to the stages is also, however, to take away the means of empirically testing the concrete instantiation of the stages or to make such testing interpretive. This problem is also revealed in the following ambiguity. One means by which Kohlberg and his associates justify the progressive nature of the stages is by arguing that structural components of earlier stages become content components of later stages.[13] This justification, however, seems to raise certain problems for the form–content distinction itself.

Not only can both the deontological and the naturalistic positions be situated within the modern separation of private and public; they can also be explicated by reference to specific changes occurring in the relation of private and public during the past several centuries. In the eighteenth century, when Kant was writing, the relation of the state to the private sphere of family and desire was relatively remote; the state set only the formal preconditions within which the family could operate. By the latter part of the nineteenth century, the state had begun to take on a more active role in regulating both the family and the economy. Moreover, economic activities had themselves become more "public," moving out of the interior of the household and into interpersonal, "public" space. Many of the needs of the family were now fulfilled through the consumption of factory-produced objects rather than as a consequence of private, household activity. Thus private desire became more the concern of impersonal regulation and production, making understandable the emergence of a moral theory such as utilitarianism, which attempted to organize and calculate private desire.

From the perspective of this type of analysis, Kohlberg's theory would therefore be viewed as in accord with much of modern western moral theory, where movement away from particularity toward abstraction has come to represent a cognitive and attitudinal good. That evaluative principle, although making possible Kohlberg's measurement of people from all cultures, would, according to this position, itself represent a principle most in accord with the values of one.

This type of historical analysis, besides situating Kohlberg's theory, provides us with certain means for responding to arguments Kohlberg puts forth in its defense. One argument, earlier put aside, was Kohlberg's claim of the predictive capacity of his model. This capacity might be explained by the nature of the separation of private and public in modern western society. The family is the source of socialization in all contemporary societies. With the growth of such a separation however, for some children the norms and values of the family become superseded by those of the public sphere. Modern schooling is an important agent in this transformation.[14] As a result, although one may find children moving from the moral particularity characteristic of intimate relations to the moral abstraction characteristic of impersonal, public relations, one will rarely (if ever) find movement in the opposite direction. Similarly, for various historical reasons, a form of social organization characterized by a separation of the private and the public has been and continues to be a dominant mode, replacing those forms of social organization not characterized by such a separation. Thus, one will find cultures developing a public sphere but will not find cultures moving toward the elimination of such a sphere. For these kinds of historical reasons, it is not surprising that the direction exemplified by Kohlberg's model is found in the movement of many people today.[15]

Complicating any arbitration between Kohlberg's theory and my historical critique is that to some extent Kohlberg includes history in his theory. As previously noted, Kohlberg employs a semi-environmentalist position and argues that access to certain types of social environments is conducive to development along his stages. Thus, if western, middle-class, white children tend to progress faster through his stages and reach higher stages in greater numbers than children of other countries or than other groups in western countries, this result would follow, in harmony with his theory, because of their exposure to social environments that encourage such movement. He states,

> My general theory relates differential social experiences in terms of opportunities for social role taking to a differential rate of moral development. Of particular importance for development to later stages of moral reasoning (stages 4 and 5) are opportunities for power, responsibility and participation in the secondary institutions of society (i.e. institutions of government, law and economy, in contrast to the primary institutions of society such as the family, the adolescent peer group, and other small face-to-face groups). Also of importance to rate of development is higher education.[16]

The problem, however, is that although historical context is admitted into his argument, it is only in this limited means of being either conducive or nonconducive to moral development. He does not allow that his notion of progress itself might be a function of a world view emanating from a specific historical context. Thus, Kohlberg views the principle of increased abstraction, which marks movement along the stages, not as *a* good, according to the value system of a particular society, but as *the* good. Moreover, it is this view that inclines his theory to commit the "naturalistic fallacy"—arguing from the fact that people tend to move in a particular direction in moral reasoning to the conclusion that such movement is desirable. Kohlberg recognizes that he needs to philosophically ground the claim that the higher stages are "higher" or more adequate; however, he mitigates this admission by arguing that his model is compatible with a variety of moral theories. Noteworthy, however, is the fact that the diverse moral theories Kohlberg points to as compatible with his model, including those in both the utilitarian and the deontological traditions, are all moral theories of modern, industrial society.[17]

As a final remark on problems with Kohlberg's model, it is important to note a methodological weakness that his theory shares with other cross-cultural models: equivocation. A means by which many theorists project the values of their own culture onto others is to use key words in an ambiguous manner. In Kohlberg's case, his understanding of "abstraction" is ambiguous between an innocuous meaning that his studies do not test for and a more culturally specific meaning, which they do. Useful in elaborating this point is a distinction Susan Buck-Morss makes between simple abstraction, which she claims is endemic to all human existence, and what she calls "abstract formalism." The latter, she states, is typified by a separation of form from content—what is abstracted is formal rather than concrete.[18] This elaboration makes sense of a point she notes about Piaget and his tests: western children perform well on such tests, but others, such as the Kpelle of Liberia, do not, tending instead to understand things by their "function."[19] In other words, it is not that the Kpelle do not abstract but that the criteria on which they do are different from those of children in the west.

The equivocation found in Kohlberg's work between abstraction in its more general sense and abstraction of form from content is replicated in another equivocation in his writings, concerning the meaning of the term "justice." Consider the following: "Justice, the primary regard for the value and equality of all human beings and for reciprocity in human relations, is a basic and universal standard. As social psychologists, the author and his colleagues have gathered considerable evidence to indicate that the concepts of justice inhere in human experience and are not the product of a particular cultural world view."[20] Certainly, if "primary regard for the value and equality of all human beings" and "reciprocity in human relations" are interpreted broadly, then justice, so elaborated, might be found in all human societies. The danger, however, is that justice also has a meaning that is more specific to modern western societies, where it primarily refers to the application of general rules to certain types of interactions of strangers in an impersonal public sphere. In not distinguishing between such broad and more specific meanings, we risk relying on the broad meaning to establish the universality of justice and then shifting to the more specific meaning to establish the superiority of our own society's demonstration of it.

Women's Development

Although from the type of historical perspective earlier described, Kohlberg's theory suffers from a variety of weaknesses, the same, however, can be said of Gilligan's critique. Gilligan, unlike Kohlberg, is much more cautious about generating a cross-cultural position. She specifically states, "No claims are made about the origins of the differences described or their distribution in a wider population, across cultures, or through time."[21] While making such disclaimers, however, Gilligan also speaks of "a woman's voice" and "women's development." The use of such expressions without supplementation by an historical account that would make clear for which women and under what circumstances her descriptions are true leads to a certain implicit false generalization. What tends to be ignored in her analysis are such factors as class, race, and again sheer changes in history as variables. This problem is accentuated by her following of Kohlberg in generating a stage theory that makes "higher" or normative certain types of responses.

To show how these problems are evidenced, it is helpful to describe briefly the model of female development that she offers in response to Kohlberg's:

> In this sequence, an initial focus on caring for the self in order to ensure survival is followed by a transactional phase in which the judgment is criticized as selfish. The criticism signals a new understanding of the connection between self and other which is articulated by the concept of responsibility. The elaboration of this concept of responsibility and its fusion with a maternal morality that seeks to ensure care for the dependent and unequal characterizes the second perspective. At this point, the good is equated with caring for others. However, when only others are legitimized as the recipients of the woman's care, the exclusion of herself gives rise to problems in relationships, creating a disequilibrium that initiates the second transition. . . . The third perspective focuses on the dynamics of relationships and dissipates the tensions between selfishness and responsibility through a new understanding of the interconnection between other and self.[22]

In short, women, according to Gilligan, move from initial selfishness to a position that gives undue consideration to the needs of others and finally to one that integrates the needs of both self and other.

As with Kohlberg's model, one can offer an historical account to explain why the model Gilligan offers might describe the stages many contemporary women traverse in their moral development. An initial period of selfishness understandably attends the moral cognition of many children and adults in highly individualistic modern western society. Within such a society, coextensive with the development of the type of private/public separation previously described, female children have also been encouraged to abandon such selfishness in conjunction with their socialization in becoming "feminine." This development has been particularly true for white, middle-class girls, for whom the ideal of femininity has always been both more imperative as a norm and more possible to attain. Thus, the ideal of femininity has been more directly influential in shaping the behavior of white, middle-class girls than it has been of many black, poor, and nonwestern women. Even, however, for white, middle-class females, the ideal of femininity has become increasingly problematic since the mid-nineteenth century as many females have moved into the public sphere, acting increasingly as political and economic beings. Particularly since the mid-1960s, many such women have had to overcome the conflicts endemic to the conjunction of traditional "feminine" socialization with new expectations for functioning as autonomous individuals. Understandably, therefore, many have had to learn how to integrate a nurturant and an individualistic stance.

This historical analysis is very rough. If this essay were to take a different direction, it could be made more polished. It is sufficient, however, to illustrate how such an account could enable Gilligan to deal with certain questions otherwise left unanswered by her arguments. As previously noted, Gilligan had claimed against Kohlberg that one evidence of his model's gender bias was the fact that females tended to score lower than males on his tests. One way that Kohlberg responded to this objection was to point to studies that showed that at least in some cases, particularly those where such factors as education and opportunities for role taking were controlled, women performed equivalently with men.[23] This finding would of course follow from the previously discussed historical analysis that argued that it was women's traditional exclusion from the public sphere, and not their gender per se, that made them "outsiders" to Kohlberg's model. Given that such a model reflects a particular set of values reflective of certain social arrangements, however, Gilligan could still describe it as biased, independent of the fact that some women now perform equivalently with men.

There does appear, however, a tension between this type of historical analysis and the stage model that Gilligan suggests as an alternative to Kohlberg's.

From the perspective of the historical analysis, the various types of responses she describes might be characterized as adaptations to different historical circumstances rather than as "stages" in moral development. Thus Gilligan's description of the lowest level of female moral response could be seen as an adequate response of those whose lives necessitate such considerations of self—or, as Gilligan describes it, considerations of "survival"—be given first priority. Women who respond at the second level could be seen as embodying what we think of as traditional sex role socialization, again, an adequate response in certain circumstances. Finally, women whose responses are at Gilligan's highest level could be viewed as leading the kinds of lives increasingly typical of western professional women. The point, however, similar to points made against Kohlberg, is that to assume that these responses are progressively more moral is to make normative the circumstances and responses of a particular social group. Like Kohlberg's stage model of moral development, Gilligan's could be viewed as biased against nonwestern, nonwhite, and non–middle-class women, only minus the sexism.

Gilligan argues that we need to recognize two different modes of social experience in contrast to the unitary mode that has traditionally been attended to. Thus, she states, "The failure to see the different reality of women's lives and to hear the differences in their voices stems in part from the assumption that there is a single mode of social experience and interpretation. By positing instead two different modes, we arrive at a more complex rendition of human experience."[24] It may be asked, however, why we need to limit our understanding to the recognition of only two modes. Are two possibilities that much more preferable to Kohlberg's one? One of the important insights that has emerged in feminist politics since the mid-1970s is that there is no singular entity "woman." Recognition of this point does not entail an acceptance of the liberal/individualistic position that general claims are not permissible within public discourse. We can recognize that social theory requires a certain amount of abstraction and thus a certain degree of forgetfulness of the complexity of all of our lives. At this point in the political/cultural history of North America, however, any abstractions that cut the human voice into two, although certainly representing a vast improvement over those abstractions that construed it as one, are much too limited.

CHAPTER TWO

Feminism and Marx: Integrating Kinship with the Economic

As in the seventeenth century, when liberal theory began to reflect the separation of kinship and state taking place in that period, so also in the eighteenth and nineteenth centuries did a new branch of study arise—economic theory, which similarly reflected a comparable separation of the economy from both the state and kinship taking place in these centuries. Whereas nascent versions of an "economy" can be traced back at least to the Middle Ages, it was only by the eighteenth century that this sphere became independent enough to generate its own body of theory, constructed in the writings of such figures as Smith, Ricardo, and Marx.

Distinguishing Karl Marx, not only from Smith and Ricardo but even more strongly from economic theorists who came later, was Marx's recognition that the seemingly autonomous operation of the economy belied its interdependence with other aspects of social life. Marx, more than most economic theorists, had a strong sense of history and in consequence was aware of the origins of contemporary economic relations in older political and familial relations and the continuous interaction of state, family, and economy even in the context of their historical separation. Although Marx, more than most economic theorists, was aware of the interconnection of family, state, and economy, his theory did not consistently abide by this awareness. Most important, the assumption common to much economic theory, that there is cross-culturally an economic component of human existence that can be studied independently of other aspects of human life, exists as a significant strand within his writings and most prominently in what might be called his philosophical anthropology or cross-cultural theory on the nature of human life and social organization. Indeed, Marx, by building a philosophical anthropology on the basis of this assumption, developed and made more explicit that very perspective in much other economic theory that he in other contexts criticized.

This inconsistency makes Marx a crucial figure for feminist theory. As feminist theory has challenged the assumption of the necessary and analytical distinctiveness of the family and state predominant in a liberal world view, so also must it challenge the assumption of a similar distinctiveness of the economic in both a liberal and a Marxist world view. The irony is that in furthering this project, feminist theory has in Marx both a strong ally and a serious opponent. Feminists can employ much of the historical work of Marx and many Marxists in comprehending the separation of family, state, and economy as an historical and not natural phenomenon and the interaction of these spheres even in the context of their separation. In contrast, Marx's philosophical anthropology, by continuing and indeed reinforcing our modern assumptions of the autonomy of the economic, raises serious obstacles for Marxism's understanding of gender. To make this case requires that we examine the content of this anthropology.

Marx and Production

Basic to Marx's views on human life and social organization is his concept of production. From a feminist perspective, however, this concept is fundamentally ambiguous: focusing either on all human activities necessary to the reproduction of the species (including such activities as nursing and child rearing) or exclusively on activities concerned with the making of food and physical objects. This ambiguity in focus is illustrated in the following passage:

> The production of life, both of one's own in labour and of fresh life in procreation now appears as a double relationship: on the one hand as a natural, and on the other as a social relationship. By social we understand the cooperation of several individuals, no matter under what conditions, in what manner and to what end. It follows from this that a certain mode of production, *or industrial stage,* is always combined with a certain mode of cooperation, or social stage, and this mode of cooperation is itself a "productive force." Further, that the multitude of productive forces accessible to men determines the nature of society, hence, that the "history of humanity" must always be studied and treated in relation to the *history of industry and exchange.*[1]

In the first sentence, "production" refers to all of the activities necessary for species survival; by the middle of the passage, its meaning has become restricted to activities that are geared toward the creation of material objects (industrial). Whereas from the meaning of "production" in the first sentence, Marx could include family forms under the "modes of cooperation" he describes, by the middle of the paragraph its meaning has come to include only those "modes of cooperation" found within the "history of industry and exchange." In effect, Marx has eliminated from his theoretical focus all activities basic to human survival that fall outside of a capitalist "economy." Those activities he has eliminated include not only those identified by feminists as "reproductive" (child care, nursing) but also those concerned with social organization (i.e., those regulating kinship relations or in modern societies those we would call "political").[2] Marx's ability to eliminate this range of activities was made possible by his moving from a broad to a narrow meaning of production.

Marx's ambiguous use of "production" can be elaborated by looking at the variety of meanings the word possesses. First, in its broadest sense, it refers to any activity that has consequences. More narrowly, it includes activities that result in objects. Finally, in an even more specific sense, it refers to activities that result in commodities, objects that are bought and sold. If we look at the related words "labor" and "product," we find a similar range of possible meanings: 1) activity requiring any effort and the result of such activity, 2) activity resulting in an object and that object, and 3) activity resulting in a commodity and that commodity.

Marx and many of his followers often do not make clear which of these meanings they are employing when they use these and related words. For example, when Marx claims that labor is the motor of historical change, does he mean all human effort that changes the natural and/or social environment, only effort that results in objects, or effort that results in commodities? Similarly, Marx's concept of the economy often becomes confusing, in part as a consequence of ambiguities in his use of "production." The preface to *A Contribution to the Critique of Political Economy* illustrates this point:

> In the social production of their existence, men inevitably enter into definite relations, which are independent of their will, namely relations of production appropriate to a given stage in the development of their material forces of production. The totality of these relations of production constitutes the economic structure of society, the real foundation, on which arises a legal and political superstructure and to which correspond definite forms of social consciousness. The mode of production of material life conditions the general process of social, political and intellectual life.[3]

In this quote, Marx equates the "economic structure of society" with its "relations of production." Because a reasonable interpretation of "mode of production of material life" is all activities conducive to the creation and recreation of a society's physical existence, the "relations of production" should reasonably include all social interaction having this object as its end. Thus, the family should count as a component of the economy. Even if we interpret the phrase "mode of production of material life" as referring only to activities concerned with the gathering, hunting, or growing of food and the making of objects, the family, in many societies, would still be included as a component of the economy. Neither of these two meanings of economy, however, is the same as its meaning in industrial capitalism, where the economy comes to refer principally to the activities of those engaged in the creation and exchange of commodities. Thus, Marx's concept of economy in the previous quote is ambiguous as a consequence of the ambiguity in his concept of production.

Such ambiguity in the meanings of key words makes possible certain serious problems within the broader theory. In particular, it enables Marx to falsely project features of capitalist society onto all societies and, with most relevance for the purposes of this essay, to cross-culturally project the autonomization and primacy of the economic in capitalist societies. This point is illustrated in Marx's statement that "the changes in the economic foundation lead sooner or later to the transformation of the whole immense superstructure." This statement is intended as a universal claim of social theory; in other words, it is meant to state that in all societies there is a certain relationship between the economy and the superstructure. If we interpret economy to refer to "all activities necessary to meet the conditions of human survival," then the claim is nonproblematic but trivial. More frequently, economy is interpreted by Marx and Marxists to refer to "those activities concerned with the production of food and objects." Here, though the claim ceases to be trivial, it contains problems as a cross-cultural claim. Although all societies have some means of organizing the production of food and objects as well as some means of organizing sexuality and child care, only in capitalist society does the former set of activities become differentiated from the latter under the concept of the economic and take on a certain priority. Thus, by employing the more specific meaning of economic in his cross-cultural claims, Marx projects the separation and the primacy of the economic found in capitalist society onto all human societies.

Let us look more closely at this projection of the primacy of the economic. Marx, by giving primacy to the economic, cannot merely be arguing that the production of food and objects is a necessary condition for the continuation of human life. Such a claim certainly is true, but it also can be said about many other aspects and activities of humans: breathing, communicating with one other through language and other means, engaging in heterosexual activity that results in procreation, creating forms of social organization, raising children, and so forth. Rather Marx appears to be making the stronger and more interesting claim that the ways in which we produce food and objects in turn structure the manner in which other necessary human activities are performed. The force of this claim rests on a feature true only for capitalist society, where the mode in which food and object production is organized to a significant extent does structure other necessary human activities. In capitalist society, the production of food and objects takes on an importance going beyond its importance as a necessary life activity.

In so far as capitalist society organizes the production and distribution of food and objects according to the profit motive, those activities concerned with the making and exchanging of food and goods assume a value and importance relatively independent of their role in satisfying human needs. The ability of such activities to generate a profit gives to them a priority that can be mistakenly associated with their function in satisfying such needs. As Marshall Sahlins has noted, this priority makes credible a kind of reflectionist or economic determinist theory wherein the system of production and exchange appears basic: "Since the objectives and relations of each subsystem are distinct, each has a certain internal logic and a relative autonomy. But since all are subordinated to the requirements of the economy, this gives credibility to the kind of reflectionist theory which perceives in the superstructure the differentiations (notably of class) established in production and exchange."[4] Thus, if in capitalist society such activities as raising children or nursing the sick had been as easily conductive to making a profit, as did become activities concerned with the production of food and objects, we might in turn believe that the manner in which human societies raise children or nurse their sick structures all other life activities.

More significant for the purposes of this essay than even Marx's projection of the primacy of the economic found in capitalist societies into his cross-cultural theory is his projection of the autonomy of the economic into that theory. To illustrate how that projection is a function of certain unique features of his time, it is necessary to examine more closely the historical context in which Marx wrote.

The Historical Context of Marxism

One theorist whose work provides useful tools for understanding the historical context of Marxism is Karl Polanyi. One of the major theses of Polanyi's book *The Great Transformation* is similar to a point stressed here—although it is true that all societies must satisfy the needs of biology to stay alive, it is only true of modern society that the satisfaction of some of these needs in ever-increasing amounts becomes a central motive of action. This transformation Polanyi identifies with the establishment of a market economy whose full development, he argues, did not occur until the nineteenth century. Polanyi acknowledges the existence of markets, both external and local, prior to this century; however, he makes a distinction between what he describes as external, local, and internal trade. External and local trade are complementary to the economies in which they exist. They involve the transfer of goods from a geographic area where they are available to an area where they are not available. The trading that goes on between town and countryside or between areas different in climate represent such types of trading. Internal trade differs from external and local trade in that it is essentially competitive, involving "a very much larger number of exchanges in which similar goods from different sources are offered in competition with one another."[5] Polanyi claims that these different forms of trade have different origins; in particular, internal trade arose neither from external nor local trade, as common sense might suggest, but rather from deliberate intervention by the state.[6] The mercantile system of the fifteenth and sixteenth centuries established its initial conditions, making possible the beginnings of a national market.

Although state intervention was necessary to establish the initial conditions for a national market, the true flourishing of such a market required the absence of at least some of the kinds of state regulation found under mercantilism.[7] A market economy is one in which the movement of the elements of the economy—goods, labor, land, money—is governed by the actions of the market. Under feudalism and the guild system, nonmarket mechanisms controlled two of these elements, land and labor. This nonmarket control over labor and land did not disappear under mercantilism; it merely changed its form. The principles of statute and ordinance became employed over that of custom and tradition.[8] Indeed, as Polanyi claims, it was not until after 1834 in England, with the repeal of the Speenhamland law, which had provided government subsidies for the unemployed and underemployed, that the last of these elements, labor, was freed to become a commodity. Thus, not until the nineteenth century in England could a market economy be said to be fully functioning.

The previous discussion of the emergence of a market economy helps to explain its distinctive features. Of key importance is the dominance of the principle of price as the mechanism for organizing the production and distribution of goods, which means that not until all of the elements necessary to the production and distribution of goods are controlled by price can a market economy be said to be functioning. A market economy demands freeing the elements that comprise the economy from the governance of other social institutions, such as the state and the family. Polanyi does not discuss the decline of the family in governing such elements, but he does stress the separation of the political and the economic as a necessary condition of a market economy:

A self-regulating market demands nothing less than the institutionalized separation of society into an economic and political sphere. Such a dichotomy is, in effect, merely the restatement, from the point of view of society as a whole, of the existence of a self-regulating market. It might be argued that the separateness of the two spheres obtains in every type of society at all times. Such an inference, however, would be based on a fallacy. True, no society can exist without a system of some kind which ensures order in the production and distribution of goods. But that does not imply the existence of separate economic institutions; normally, the economic order is merely a function of the social, in which it is contained. Neither under tribal, nor feudal, nor mercantile conditions was there, as we have shown, a separate economic system in society. Nineteenth century society, in which economic activity was isolated and imputed to a distinctive economic motive was, indeed, a singular departure.[9]

Polanyi goes on to argue that not only does a market economy require the separation of the elements of the economy from other spheres of social life but that this requirement effects the dominance of the principle of the market over other social principles. As two of the elements of the economy, land and labor, are basic features of social life, to subordinate them to market mechanisms is in effect to subordinate society to the market: "But labor and land are not other than the human beings themselves of which every society consists and the natural surrounding in which it exists. To include them in the market mechanism means to subordinate the substance of society itself to the laws of the market."[10]

We might qualify Polanyi's argument by saying that not all labor becomes subordinate to the laws of the market when the economy becomes a market economy; domestic labor does not, at least in any simple sense. Because, however, *some* of the labor essential to human survival does become subordinated to the market, we can still accede to this point of the market's growing dominance. Moreover, we might also agree with Polyani's further claim that the organization of the economic system under a market mechanism means also the dominance of the economic. He argues that this occurs because

> the vital importance of the economic factor to the existence of society precludes any other result. For once the economic system is organized in separate institutions, based on specific motives and conferring a special status, society must be shaped in such a manner as to allow that system to function according to its own laws. This is the meaning of the familiar assertion that a market economy can function only in a market society.[11]

Such an argument can be supplemented by the claim that the alliance of the production of goods with the acquisitive motive results in increased importance of the production of goods over other life activities. To allow acquisitiveness as a motive is to allow it as a dominant one.

Thus, a thesis often thought of as central to Marxism, the separation and dominance of the economic, is in effect a defining condition of a market economy. Moreover, as follows from Polanyi's analysis, it is just this condition that becomes true only in the nineteenth century. One can conclude that Marxism as social theory was a product of its time, insightful as an exposition of what was becoming true and false to the extent that the limited historical applicability of its claims was not recognized.

As Polanyi noted, a defining condition of a market economy is a separation of the economic and the political. Not noted by him but also essential is the separation of the economic from the domestic and familial. Indeed, what is pivotal about industrialization is that the production of goods ceases to be a household activity organized by kinship relations. The creation of goods by members of the household for the purpose of use by the household and organized primarily in accordance with family roles becomes replaced by the creation of goods by members of many different households for the purpose of exchange and organized in accordance with the profit motive. The commodization of the elements of production means not only, as Polanyi notes, a withdrawal of control over these elements on the part of the state but also, as he does not note, a withdrawal of the family. When labor remained at home, its content and organization were primarily a family matter; when it left, only its consequences—wages—remained such.

Thus, from the above analysis, we can comprehend the emergence of the economic as separate from both the family and the state as the outcome of an historical process. This kind of analysis is one that is most in sympathy with the requirements of feminism. It is also one that might be used both to challenge and to explain the tendency among Marx and his followers to employ the category of the economic cross-culturally. The irony, however, is that such an historical analysis could itself be described as "Marxist." Polanyi's work builds on the kinds of historical investigations that Marx himself conducted in studying the emergence of capitalism from earlier social forms. This irony reinforces a point suggested earlier—that although in Marx's concrete historical analysis there is much from which feminism can draw in comprehending the changing relation of family, state, and economy, it is in Marx's cross-cultural claims that the theory becomes most unhelpful to feminism. To elaborate on this point—to show that it is precisely Marx's ahistoricity that accounts for the theory's weaknesses in analyzing gender—I now focus specifically on the consequences of these problems for Marxism's analysis of gender.

Marx on Women, Gender Relations, and the Family

In comprehending Marxism on gender, it is important to note that Marx's concept of class relies on the narrow translation of "production" and "economic"—as incorporating only those activities concerned with the making of food and objects. Thus, the criterion that Marx employs to demarcate class position, "relation to the means of production," is understood as relation to the means of producing food and objects. For Marx, the first class division arose over the struggle for appropriation of the first social surplus, meaning the first social surplus of food and objects. A consequence of such a definition of class is to eliminate from consideration historical conflicts over other socially necessary activities, such as child bearing and rearing. A second consequence is to eliminate from consideration changes in the organization of such activities as components of historical change. The theory thus eliminates activities that historically have been at least one important component in gender relations. But here we can ask of the theory certain questions: why should we eliminate or count as less important in our theory of history changes in reproduction or child-rearing practices than changes involved in food- or object-producing activities? First does it even make sense to attempt to separate the changes involved before the time when these activities were themselves differentiated (i.e., before the time when the "economy" became differentiated from the "family")? Furthermore, is not the assumption of the greater importance of changes in production itself a product of a society that gives priority to food and object creation over other life activities?

Many feminist theorists have noted the consequences for Marx of leaving reproductive activities out of his theory of history. Mary O'Brien, for example, argues that one effect is to separate historical continuity from biological continuity, which one might note is particularly ironic for a "materialist."

> Thus Marx talks continuously of the need for men to "reproduce" themselves, and by this he almost always means reproduction of the self on a daily basis by the continual and necessary restoking of the organism with fuel for its biological needs. Man makes himself materially, and this is of course true. Man, however, is also "made" reproductively by the parturitive labour of women, but Marx ultimately combines these two processes. This has the effect of negating biological continuity which is mediated by women's reproductive labour, and replacing this with productive continuity in which men, in making themselves, also make history.[12]

Similarly, though from a different perspective, Marx's lack of consideration of reproductive activities enables him to ignore, to the extent that he does, the component of socialization in human history. In other words, the failures in Marx's theory that result from his attraction to a narrow interpretation of materialism might have been alleviated had he paid more attention to the activity of child rearing.

As O'Brien points out, there is a tendency for Marx to negate the sociability and historicity of reproductive activities and to see such activities as natural and thus ahistorical.[13] Alternatively, he occasionally treats changes in the organization of such activities as historical effects of changes in productive relations. Thus, she notes that in *The Communist Manifesto,* Marx treats the family as a superstructural effect of the economy.[14] This view also is evidenced in a letter to P. V. Annenkov of 28 December 1846, in which Marx states, "Assume particular stages of development of production, commerce and consumption and you will have a corresponding social constitution, a corresponding organization of the family, of orders and classes, in a word, a corresponding civil society."[15] Here again, such tendencies can be explained by reference to Marx's acceptance of the ideology of the family in an industrial society. When "productive" activities leave the household and in turn come to constitute the world of change and dynamism, then activities of "reproduction" come to be viewed as either the brute, physiological and nonhistorical aspects of human existence or the byproducts of changes in the economy.

One problem that results from seeing reproductive activities as universally the consequence of productive activities is that we are prevented from comprehending the integration of production and reproduction in precapitalist societies. Consequently, we fail to see how women and men in such societies occupy very distinctive relations to those activities concerned with the making of food and objects in connection with rules regulating marriage and sexuality. Moreover, this distinctive relationship to productive activities cannot be described solely in terms of a "division of labor." Although there appears to be some consistent gender division of labor throughout history in relation to the making of food and objects, women also have had less control over the means and results of such activities than men, again in connection to the rules that govern marriage and sexuality in kinship-organized societies.

Understanding the integration of production and reproduction in precapitalist societies will not be achieved merely by supplementing the former concept with the latter. To adequately understand how this integration works in these forms of society, and its similarities *and differences* with later forms, requires focusing on what is historically specific about such societies—the dominance of kinship as an organizing principle of society.

This last point brings us finally to the issue of Marxism's ability to analyze gender in capitalist society. Much of my criticism of Marx has rested on the claim that he falsely generalized features of capitalist society onto societies where such features do not hold; this failure accounts for the theory's weaknesses in analyzing gender. The implication of this argument would seem to be that the theory is adequate as an account of capitalism and of gender relations within capitalist society; however, this conclusion neglects that capitalist society contains within itself many precapitalist aspects that are highly relevant to gender. For example, in capitalist society, the economy becomes more autonomous of other realms than is the case in earlier societies; but, in so far as Marxism views the economic as autonomous, it loses sight of the ways in which even capitalist economies grew out of and continue to be affected by noneconomic aspects of human existence. Indeed, Marxism, by attributing autonomy to the economic, comes close to a liberal position of denying the influence of factors such as gender, religion, and politics on the market. Of course, in specific contexts and in certain disagreements with liberals and conservatives, Marxists often argue for the determinacy of such noneconomic factors. Again, however, Marxism as historical analysis appears incompatible with Marxism as cross-cultural theory.

Thus, Marxists need consistently to think of the progressive domination of the state and later the market over kinship as an historical process.[16] This type of approach could enable Marxism to correct two failures that are linked in the theory: its failure in analyzing gender and its failure to be adequately cognizant of the historical context of its claims. By recognizing that the progressive domination of the market has been an historical process, it might avoid the latter failure. By recognizing both the centrality of kinship in structuring early societies and the centuries-long interaction of kinship with such other institutions as the state and the market, it could provide itself with a means for analyzing gender. It is ironic that Marxists have occasionally described radical feminism as ahistorical. Whereas radical feminism pointed to the universality of the family, Marxists argued that this institution is always the changing effect of economic developments. It may, however, be a function of Marxism's failure to pay sufficient attention to the fundamentality of kinship and its changing relationship to other social institutions and practices that has caused the theory to become falsely ahistorical itself.

Marxism and Feminism

From the previous analysis of the failures of Marxism in explaining gender, we can resolve certain disputes among Marxist feminists. As noted, Marxist feminists have recognized that Marx's category of production excludes an account of many traditional female activities. In response, some have argued that we need to augment this category with the category of reproduction. This response is the position of O'Brien: "What does have to be done is a modification of Marx's sociohistorical model, which must now account for two opposing substructures, that of production and that of reproduction. This in fact improves the model."[17] Other Marxist feminists offer similar or somewhat revised models. Ann Ferguson and Nancy Folbre prefer to label the augmented category "sex-affective production" rather than "reproduction." They note that the term "reproduction" is used by Marx to describe the "economic process over time." To employ this term to refer to activities such as child bearing and rearing might result in some confusion. Moreover, they argue, by including these traditionally female-identified tasks under the category of "production," we are reminded of the social usefulness of such tasks.[18] Such proposals have been described by Iris Young as constituting variants of what she labels "dual systems theory." Young also recognizes the narrowness of Marx's category of production: "Such traditional women's tasks as bearing and rearing children, caring for the sick, cleaning, cooking, etc., fall under the category of labor as much as the making of objects in a factory. Using the category of production or labor to designate only the making of concrete material objects in a modern factory has been one of the unnecessary tragedies of Marxian theory."[19]

Young, however, does not approve of focusing on activities that have fallen outside of this category to make Marxism more explanatory of gender. One weakness in such a solution is that it fails to account for gender relations that occur within production.[20] In other words, Young is making the point stated earlier in this essay: that gender has been a significant variable even in activities concerned with the making of food and objects. Thus, any analysis of gender must do more than enlarge the traditional category.

The basic problem of dual systems theory, according to Young, is that it does not seriously enough challenge the framework of Marxism.[21] That this framework is gender blind must indicate an important deficiency whose remedy cannot merely be supplementation. Moreover, dual systems theory, by making the issue of women's oppression separate and distinct from what is addressed in Marxism, reinforces the idea that women's oppression is merely supplemental to the major concerns of Marxism.

The analysis put forth in the preceding paragraphs enables us both to understand the attractiveness of dual systems theory and to meet Young's challenge. Dual systems theorists are correct in recognizing that an important source of Marxism's inability to analyze gender is the narrowness of its category of production. Where they go wrong, however, is in not seeing this problem as a function of Marxism's adoption of the narrow categories of its time. Within industrial society, many of the activities that the category excludes have become viewed as outside of production. This exclusion is reflected in Marx's categories.

This assessment of the failure of Marx's category provides us with a remedy different from that proposed by dual systems theorists. Although we might agree with such theorists that the addition of the category of reproduction to the category of production might be necessary for understanding gender relations within industrial society, neither category is necessarily useful for analyzing earlier societies. Indeed, because there is no reason to believe that the kinds of social divisions expressed by these categories played a significant role in structuring gender relations within such societies, there would be no reason to employ them, which is not to suggest, of course, that gender did not play a significant role in earlier societies. It is rather that the categories through which we need to grasp it must be understood as historically changing, reflecting the changing emergence, dominance, and decline of different institutions. Therefore, in earlier societies, it appears that the key institution in structuring gender, as well as activities that we would label political or economic, is kinship. Social theory must focus on the differential power relations expressed within this institution to explain relations between men and women as well as among men and women as groups. For later periods, we need to focus on the transformation of kinship into family and on the emergence of the economy and the state as separated spheres. For the modern period we need to focus on the very historical separation of spheres that led liberals to problematically naturalize the separation of the family and the state and Marxists to problematically universalize the separation of production and reproduction.

Conclusion

In sum, the Marxist tendency to employ categories rooted in capitalist social relations and its failure in comprehending gender are deeply related. In so far as Marxists interpret production as necessarily distinct from reproduction, then aspects of capitalist society are falsely universalized and gender relations in both precapitalist and capitalist societies are obscured. In precapitalist societies, child-rearing practices, sexual relations, and what we call productive activities are organized conjointly through the medium of kinship. Thus, in these societies, issues of gender and issues of class are inseparable. Moreover, within capitalist society, this integration of gender and class continues in so far as the progressively separating sphere of the economic bears traces of its origins in its continued functioning and also in so far as the separation of the economic from the family and household remains incomplete. Understanding gender, both in its precapitalist and capitalist manifestations, requires an awareness of the historical nature of the separation of the economic rather than its presupposition in the categories employed.

The complication is that Marxism both does and does not maintain such an awareness. Certainly, both Marx and most of his followers are, on one level, aware of the autonomization of the economic as an historical process. This awareness is, however, conjoined with a theoretical framework that presupposes the separation of the economic as a cross-cultural phenomenon. Of note is that it is theorists associated with critical theory who have distinguished

Marxism as historical analysis from Marxism as cross-cultural theory and who have tended to support the former over the latter. Georg Lukács, in *History and Class Consciousness*, first raised the question of the cross-cultural applicability of Marx's concept of class, and Jürgen Habermas, in *Knowledge and Human Interests*, distinguished Marx's empirical analyses and his philosophical self-understanding.[22]

Not noted, however, by these theorists or by others who have raised similar questions about Marxism as cross-cultural theory is the power of gender to serve as a concrete and fundamental example of the problem. As argued, it is in the very ambiguities of Marx's concept of production, that the theory's failures in understanding gender and its tendency to falsely universalize capitalist social relations come together. The feminist critique of Marxism goes beyond what is often perceived as a relatively superficial call to incorporate gender to become a powerful voice in the analysis of its basic weaknesses and a necessary means in the task of its reconstruction.

CHAPTER THREE

Feminist Theory: The Private and the Public

The primary propose of this essay is methodological—to clarify confusions in feminist theory connected with the use of the categories "private" and "public." These categories have rightly played an important role within feminist theory. Many feminist theorists have correctly intuited that these categories point to societal divisions that have been central to the structuring of gender in at least modern western societies. Some theorists have even argued that a more general separation, expressed in the opposition between "domestic" and "public," has been universally important in organizing gender. Even so, I sense among feminist theorists a suspicion of such categories conjoined with a suspicion toward employing dualistic frameworks altogether. Rosalind Petchesky illustrates this tendency:

> [A] further analytical insight [was] that "production" and "reproduction," work and the family, far from being separate territories like the moon and the sun or the kitchen and the shop, are really intimately related modes that reverberate upon one another and frequently occur in the same social, physical and even psychic spaces. This point bears emphasizing, since many of us are still stuck in the model of "separate spheres" (dividing off "woman's place," "reproduction," "private life," "the home," etc. from the world of men, production, "public life," the office, etc.). We are now learning that this model of separate spheres distorts reality, that it is every bit as much an ideological construct as are the notions of "male" and "female" themselves. Not

only do reproduction and kinship, or the family have their own historically determined products, material techniques, modes of organization, and power relationships, but reproduction and kinship are themselves integrally related to social relations of production and the state; they reshape those relations all the time.[1]

Iris Young's article on dual systems theory elaborates this position.[2] Young notes that Marxist feminists, in their attempt to make Marxism more explanatory of gender, have often merely added onto the Marxist categories an additional set, creating models composed of two systems. Many have tended to think in terms of "production" and "reproduction" and "capitalism" and "patriarchy." The specific oppression of women is then accounted for by appealing to the interaction of these basically separated spheres of social relationships. Young persuasively points out the many problems with this type of approach. She notes that the "production/reproduction" model or those similar to it tend to universalize the division of labor peculiar to capitalist society. Only in capitalism has "production" become separated from "reproduction" or have some of those activities associated with the making of food and objects been separated from such domestic activities as child bearing and rearing. To make this separation the basis for one's theoretical model is thus to project onto much of history a separation unique to modern society. Moreover, Young argues that dual systems theory suffers from other major problems: it obscures the integration that exists between the separated spheres; it fails to account adequately for the nature of women's oppression outside of the home; and at the most fundamental level, it leaves unchallenged the assumption that women's oppression is a separable and thus peripheral element in social life.[3]

Michelle Zimbalist Rosaldo has also criticized early work by both herself and others that stressed a "domestic/public" opposition as helpful in explaining the social organization of gender.[4] Rosaldo has argued that this opposition tended to explain gender in psychological/functional terms. She now claims that such formulations obscure cross-cultural diversity in the structuring and evaluation of gender.

All of these arguments are extremely helpful and must be taken seriously. I do, however, see a possible confusion in the conclusion that might be drawn. From such arguments, we might be led to abandon oppositions, such as "private" and "public," that, properly interpreted, provide an important clue for understanding gender. The problem with some of the dualisms Petchesky and Young pointed to, in particular the opposition of "production" and "reproduction," follows not from their duality, but from the fact that, improperly understood, such distinctions obscure history. As Young correctly notes, the use of the opposition "production/reproduction" inaccurately projects backward onto all human history a division of labor specific to capitalism. Similarly, many of the ways in which the opposition "domestic/public" has been formulated tend also to universalize falsely a late capitalist division of labor. In the same way, certain understandings of the opposition "private" and "public," tend to treat it as a homogeneous separation rather than one to be interpreted differently from century to century and from country to country.

In short, I would stress that the errors in the models Petchesky, Young, and Rosaldo attacked was their ahistoricity. If we interpret such oppositions as that between "domestic" and "public" or "private" and "public" historically—as separations rooted in history and not in some biological or otherwise stipulated cross-cultural division of labor—we might then acquire tools to help us understand important components of our own past history of gender. Moreover, by historicizing these separations, we may be able to see what is wrong with much existing social theory, which tends falsely to universalize aspects of these separations.

Marxism, for example, tends to universalize the modern separation between family and economy. Thus Marx and many Marxists have tended on occasion to assert that changes in the family can be understood as effects of changes in the economy.[5] The difficulty with such a position is that it assumes that one can cross-culturally separate claims about the family from claims about the economy. Yet not until the establishment of a market economy in the modern period did activities concerned with the production and distribution of food and objects become organized, on any significant scale, separate from activities considered the province of the family. Indeed, part of what we mean by the term "market economy" is that activities of production and distribution become freed from the institutions of family, church, and state, and become organized mainly by the laws of the market. Of course, this separation, even in our own times, has not been complete. Even within contemporary society, in which fast-food chains absorb ever more of the final stages of food production, this activity is still largely carried out within the home. The point, however, is that we adequately understand neither the existing divisions nor their limitations if we do not view them in historical terms.

By ontologizing the separation of family and economy, we also lose sight of the kinds of connections that have existed between the separated spheres, connections that have occurred in the very process of their separation. Thus, as many feminists have pointed out, even when many women have left the home for wage-earning activities in the twentieth century, the social relations of their paid jobs often replicate the social relations of the homes they have left. This transference of gender roles from the home to the work world has been described by some feminists as the rise of "public patriarchy" and may indicate certain weaknesses in the traditional Marxist cure for ending women's oppression: "Get thee to the workplace!" In any case, this phenomenon illustrates one weakness of a theoretical framework that fails to understand the separation of family and economy as an historical process rather than as an ontological given.

If Marxism has been guilty of obscuring our understanding of gender by universalizing the separation of the family and the economy, liberalism has been equally guilty of providing a comparable obstacle, that of universalizing the separation between the family and the state. Again, it appears that the task for feminist theory is to disprove the universalization of this separation while also elaborating its historical development.

What is meant by the claim that liberalism universalizes the separation of family and state? Theorists associated with the liberal tradition assume that there are two different kinds of human needs best satisfied by two different institutions. On the one hand are the needs for intimacy, affection, sexuality, and the various types of aid and support that other humans can provide. The family is the institution best designed for satisfying such needs. Within liberalism's history, the exact specification of these needs has varied, corresponding to real changes in the institution of the family. For example, the need for intimacy and affection on the part of all family members began to be stressed only during the eighteenth century. Also historically variable is the extent to which sexual needs are attributed to women. But no matter what the specification and allocation of needs is, what is consistent is the claim that there exist some needs, naturally present in whomever they are allocated to, that can best be met through the family.

In conjunction with the claim that the family exists to satisfy certain natural human needs is a further claim that the family alone is insufficient to regulate social life adequately. Early liberal "state of nature" theorists, such as Locke, although admitting families within the state of nature, did not believe them capable of preventing or solving the problems endemic to that condition. Locke and others have argued that some type of political institution, such as the state, is also necessary. The most fundamental purpose of the state is to prevent or resolve conflict arising among individuals who are not members of the same family. According to this theory, if the human population were small enough and constituted by only one family or by a few families widely scattered (a situation Locke attributed to the beginning days of human history), states would not be necessary. Given, however, both a human population composed of more than one family and the problems Locke and others attribute to a stateless society, the need for a state arises.

It is important to stress that, for liberal theory, although the state "organizes" relations between members of different families in a manner somewhat analogous to the way families "organize" their individual members, states are *not* families writ large. Not only is there a difference in size between the two institutions, but they also differ widely in purpose and in terms of the nature of the relationships that constitute both. Within liberal theory, there has been much diversity in the description of the extent and nature of the differences between families and states. Such diversity is evident, for example, in the seventeenth-century parliamentary responses to the royalists' identification of monarchal and paternal authority. The seventeenth-century parliamentarians at times sought to discredit the identification; at other times, they used the identification to justify parliamentarianism.[6] In Locke's writings, one finds arguments supporting both the similarities and the differences in familial and political relations. For example, Locke argues against Sir Robert Filmer for the contractarian nature of political relationships in part through a claim about the contractarian nature of the marriage relationship. He also points to certain differences between the two, such as the rights over life and death, which states, but not families, have over their members. In general, however, all liberal theorists assume certain dissimilarities in the governance of families and political institutions based on a belief in certain qualitative differences in the nature of the two institutions. Although these differences are not always made explicit, a not untypical list would include reference to such features as their respective sizes and purposes, the composition of their membership, and the respective relations of their members to property.

The point feminist theory needs to make against this position is not that families and states are similar. The slogan radical feminism introduced, "The personal is political," may aid us in seeing certain similarities between personal and political relationships and between families and states, but we cannot ignore the real differences between both the personal and the political and the family and the state. In opposition to liberal theory, however, feminist theory must show the historical nature of these differences. Liberal theory has been correct in describing the social divisions that have existed, and sometimes its arguments on the normative implications of these divisions have been sound. What has remained untested, however, is the thesis of the inevitability of such divisions.

It is for a number of reasons particularly appropriate for feminist theory to begin making such a challenge. Earlier I argued that Marxism creates obstacles to understanding the history of gender by universalizing our contemporary separation of the familial and the economic. I would also accuse liberalism of creating similar obstacles by tending to naturalize the family and by universalizing its separation from the state. As a consequence, it has little to tell us about why the social relations of the family are as they are or why the political sphere has excluded women to the extent that it has. Answers to such questions can be obtained only by viewing the family, the state, and their interconnections in historical terms.

This point can be demonstrated by examining certain work by feminist scholars and others on the history of the family. One example is an analysis of the relationship between the family and the state developed by Marilyn Arthur.

Although Arthur's focus is primarily on the evolution of the Greek city-state, she perceives certain parallels between that evolution and the development of the modern state in western Europe. In both cases, a basically aristocratic or feudal society organized around kinship gave way to a society dominated by a more egalitarian state. She describes the changes occurring in preclassical Greece as follows:

> Aristocratic or feudal society is usually dominated by a landholding nobility defined by birth whose social relationships preserve many of the features of tribal society. . . . In the midst of this society a class of commercial entrepreneurs arises. They derive from all social and economic groups: wealthy landowners interested in trade, younger or illegitimate sons of the nobility involved in maritime ventures, craftsmen and other specialists and wealthy, independent peasants. In archaic Greece the rise of this class was associated with the discovery of iron, whose ready availability made possible small-scale cultivation of land and thus transformed the method of production. The artisans worked the new materials, the merchants traded in it, and agriculture was intensified through its use. This new middle class was thus still strongly tied to the land (the economic base of society was agriculture throughout all of antiquity) but it was a larger and more diverse group than the landowning aristocracy. At this point in history the small household emerged as the productive unit of society, and any head of a household (who was simultaneously a landowner) automatically became a citizen or member of the state. Conversely, the state itself, the *polis* was defined as the sum of all individual households.[7]

One can carry a parallel between preclassical Greece and modern Europe only so far; too many obvious factors differentiate the two periods. On a very general level, however, there is an important similarity: in both periods, a democratic state emerges in connection with a relatively nuclearized household-familial unit. This connection makes sense conceptually if we consider the extension of political power in the modern period and in the preclassical period. Political power, in both cases, rather than resting in a tribal chief or a head of kin, becomes more widely shared among the diverse constituents of a new middle class whose justification for political representation lay in a position as head of household. Thus, the growth of more widespread political representation and the development of a more nuclearized household-familial unit appear as correlate phenomena. This thesis on the interconnection of a more democratic state and a more nuclearized family unit finds support in the work of others. Hannah Arendt, for example, long ago pointed out that the foundation of the polis was preceded by the destruction of all organized units resting on kinship, such as the *phratria* and the *phyle*.[8] In reference to the modern period, Lawrence Stone has argued that kinship, lordship, and clientage, the forms of social organization that structured medieval aristocratic life, were antithetical to the functioning of the modern state:

> The modern state is a natural enemy to the values of the clan, of kinship, and of good lordship and clientage links among the upper classes, for at this social and political level they are a direct threat to the state's own claim to prior loyalty. Aristocratic kinship and clientage lead to faction and rebellion, such as the Wars of the Roses or the Fronde, to the use of kin loyalty and client empires by entrenched local potentates to create independent centres of power and to make the working of the jury system of justice impossible by the subordination of objective judgment to ties of blood or local loyalty.[9]

Stone claims that one of the tools used by the emerging state in its battle for power with existing feudal lords was to transfer the idea of "good lordship" from these lords to the individual male head of household. The subordination of the household members of their head was in turn described as analogous to and supportive of the subordination of subjects to the sovereign. Thus, Stone notes that the principle of patriarchy was transformed by the state from a threat to its existence into a formidable buttress for it.[10]

Both Arthur and Stone derive implications from their analyses for changes in gender roles. Arthur, for example, after noting the status of woman as object of exchange in the period before the one with which she is concerned, argues that the transformations that resulted in the rise of the household's importance as a political unit in ancient Greece added a new dimension to this status. As the integrity of each individual household came to possess political significance, so also did the biological activities of women, who could potentially violate that integrity. Adultery, for example, when practiced by women, became seen as a crime against society and not merely as a personal transgression.[11] The corollary to the legal sanctions against adultery by women was the idealization given to the citizen wife who produced legitimate heirs. This idealization has caused some to argue that the overall status of women in classical Athens was not all that bad.[12] Arthur's position is that the idealization given to the citizen wife does not mitigate the fundamental misogynistic attitude of classical Athens. The proper Athenian housewife may have been praised when she acted as she ought, but beyond the praise stood the fear that she might not:

> This praise of women in the marriage relationship does not invalidate the idea that the fundamental attitude of the Greeks toward women remained misogynistic. As social beings, women in the polis entered into a partnership with men that fostered civilization, and only in this relationship did women gain favor. As we have seen, the misogyny of the Greeks originally sprang from the association of women with the world of instincts and passions,

which was hostile to civilized life. Unlike man, the woman of the polis was regarded as a hybrid creature, a domesticated animal who could be adapted to the needs of society but whose fundamental instincts were antagonistic to it.[13]

In so far as the polis depended on the autonomy and inviolability of the individual household and thus the legitimacy of each man's heirs, it is understandable that women's sexuality would be highly feared. Women, whose sexuality had the power to disrupt the political order, were idealized for acting correctly while being hated and feared for their power to do wrong. In such a context, it follows that women's activities generally would be closely watched. This deduction is supported by other accounts on the situation of women in classical Athens, such as that of Sarah Pomeroy, whose work documents the degree to which the lives of women in classical Athens were dominated by restriction and seclusion to the household interior.[14]

Stone similarly argues that the nuclearization of the family unit in the early modern period had certain distinct implications for gender roles. Women's declining ties to an extended kinship system meant a loss of a countervailing power to their husbands' authority. An increased power of the male head of household was also brought about during this period as a consequence of other related phenomena. The Lutheran Reformation increased the spiritual authority of the father and the husband while reducing the countervailing authority of the priest and the Church.

Although Arthur's and Stone's analyses seem to suggest that the rise of a state organized around nuclearized household units is on the whole bad for women, I do not want to commit to that claim. The status of women is always an extremely complicated phenomenon, and though the broad generalizations that I have delineated may be helpful for providing a first step in understanding gender relations, they provide only a first step. To continue, we must pay more attention to the specificities of the particular period in question. Such specificities must include reference to the fact that if, as in classical Greece, the production unit was a household, it was a very different kind of household from that of modern Europe. The idealization of marriage as a type of partnership, for example, which began to emerge in the modern period, importantly differentiates the status of women in modern Europe from the classical era, as does also the emergence of the concept of the individual with natural rights. Thus, the purpose of the previous use of Arthur's and Stone's analyses was not to derive specific conclusions on the status of women in the modern period, but rather to suggest the type of procedures we need to employ even to begin the process of reaching such conclusions. The point is that unless we view the family and the state in historical relation to each other, the status of women must remain for us, as it does in much of liberal theory, an unsolvable mystery. In other words, within liberal theory, the social relations of the family are assumed as universal and a function of such facts, to quote Locke, that men are "stronger" and "abler." In the seventeenth century, while liberalism was breaking new ground in extending political representation to male heads of households, it had little to say about why women were not also to be included in the political sphere. Even by the twentieth century, when women's rights to political participation were becoming recognized, liberalism has provided little insight into its previous position. The failure of understanding in all cases can be attributed to an inability to see the family in conjunction with the state as a social institution, with the two sharing interrelated histories.

Thus, the conclusion I want to draw from those analyses is primarily methodological: that an important task for feminist theory is to show the historical origins and evolution of those divisions others have assumed to be inevitable. Phrasing the project in this way enables us to clarify certain confusions. Petchesky, in her earlier quoted remarks, stated that the separation between the public and the private, between the family and work, is ideological. The intention behind this claim is similar to what was intended by the slogan, "The personal is political." In both cases it was recognized that divisions such as between the private and the public or the personal and the political do obscure our understanding of the dynamics of gender. The ironic point that I have been emphasizing is that to prove such claims, we need to show how the private did become separated from the public or the personal from the political. In other words, to break the ideological hold that such divisions maintain over our lives, we need to show the historical origins and changing nature of these divisions. Only by doing so can we make sense of the effects these divisions have had on women's and men's lives, of the ways in which the divisions themselves have only been partial, and of the arbitrary nature of the divisions themselves.

Interpreting "Gender"

"Gender" is a strange word in feminism. Although many of us assume that it has a clear and commonly understood meaning, it is actually used in at least two very different and somewhat contradictory ways. On the one hand, "gender" was developed and is still often used in contrast to "sex" to depict that which is socially constructed as opposed to that which is biologically given. Here, "gender" is typically thought to refer to personality and behavior in distinction from the body; "gender" and "sex" are understood as distinct. On the other hand, "gender" has increasingly become used to refer to any social construction having to do with the male/female distinction, including those constructions that separate "female" bodies from "male" bodies. This latter usage emerged when many people came to realize that society shapes not only personality and behavior but also the ways in which the body appears. But if the body is itself always seen through social interpretation, then "sex" is not separate from "gender," but is that which is subsumable under it. Joan Scott provides an eloquent description of this second understanding of "gender" where the subsumption of "sex" under "gender" is made clear: "It follows then that gender is the social organization of sexual difference. But this does not mean that gender reflects or implements fixed and natural physical differences between women and men; rather gender is the knowledge that establishes meanings for bodily differences. . . . We cannot see sexual differences except as a function of our knowledge about the body and that knowledge is not 'pure,' cannot be isolated from its implication in a broad range of discursive contexts."1

I argue that although this second understanding of gender has become more dominant within feminist discourse, the legacy of the first survives. The result is that "sex" subtly lingers in feminist theory as that which stands outside culture and history in framing the male/female distinction. To see how, we need to elaborate more fully the origins of the term "gender" itself.

"Gender" has its roots in the coming together of two ideas important within modern western thought: that of the material basis of self-identity and of the social constitution of human character. By the time of the emergence of the second wave of feminism in the late 1960s, one legacy of the first idea was the conception, dominant in most industrialized societies, that the male/female distinction was caused by and expressed, in most essential respects, "the facts of biology." This conception was reflected in the fact that the word most commonly used to depict this distinction, "sex," had strong biological associations. Early second-wave feminists correctly saw this concept as conceptually underpinning "sexism" in general. Because of its implicit claim that differences between women and men are rooted in biology, the concept of "sex" lent itself to the idea of the immutability of such differences and of the hopelessness of attempts for change. Feminists of the late 1960s drew on the idea of the social constitution of the human character to undermine the power of this concept. Within English-speaking countries, its power was undermined by extending the meaning of the term "gender." Before the late 1960s, the term "gender" had been used primarily to refer to the difference between feminine and masculine forms within language. As such, it conveyed strong associations about the role of society in distinguishing "male"- and "female"-coded phenomena. Second-wave feminists extended the meaning of the term to refer also to many of the differences between women and men exhibited in personality and behavior.

But most interesting is that "gender," at that time, was, by and large, not seen as a replacement for "sex"; it was viewed, rather, as a means to undermine the encompassing pretensions of "sex." Most feminists during the late 1960s and early 1970s accepted the premise that there existed real biological phenomena differentiating women and men that in all societies are used in similar ways to generate a male/female distinction. The new idea was only that many of the differences associated with women and men were neither of this type nor the direct effects of such. Thus "gender" was introduced as a concept to supplement "sex," not to replace it. Moreover, "gender" was not only viewed as not replacing "sex" but "sex" seemed essential in elaborating the very meaning of "gender." An example can be found in one of the most influential discussions of "gender" in early second-wave literature. In her important article, "The Traffic in Women," Gayle Rubin introduced the phrase "the sex/gender system" and defined it as "the set of arrangements upon which a society transforms biological sexuality into products of human activity, and in which these transformed sexual needs are satisfied.² Here, the biological was assumed as the basis on which cultural meanings are constructed. Thus, at the very moment the influence of the biological is being undermined, it is also being invoked.

Rubin's position in this essay is not idiosyncratic. It reflects an important feature of much twentieth-century thinking about "socialization," including the feminist application of such thinking to the male/female distinction. Many who accept the idea that character is socially formed, and thus reject the idea that it emanates from biology, do not necessarily reject the idea that biology is the site of character formation. In other words, they still view the physiological self as the "given" on which specific characteristics are "superimposed"; it provides the location for establishing where specific social influences are to go. The feminist acceptance of such views meant that "sex" still retained an important role: it provided the site on which "gender" was thought to be constructed.

Such a conception of the relationship between biology and socialization makes possible what can be described as a type of "coat rack" view of self-identity. Here the body is viewed as a type of rack on which differing cultural artifacts, specifically those of personality and behavior, are thrown. Such a model made it possible for feminists to theorize about the relationship between biology and personality in a way that kept some of the advantages of biological determinism while avoiding some of its disadvantages. If one thinks of the body as a "rack" on which certain features of personality and behavior are "thrown," then one can think of the relationship between the givens of the "rack" itself and what gets thrown on it as both weaker than determinative but stronger than accidental. One does not *have to* throw coats and scarves on a coat rack; one can, for example, throw sweaters or even very different kinds of objects if one changes the material nature of the rack sufficiently. If, however, one always finds coat racks with coats and scarves, little explanation is required; after all, they are coat racks.

I label this view of the relationship among the body, personality, and behavior "biological foundationalism" to indicate its difference and similarity with biological determinism. In common with biological determinism, my label postulates a more than accidental relationship between certain aspects of personality and behavior with biology. But, distinct from biological determinism, it allows for the possibility that the givens of biology can coexist without such aspects. Such an understanding of the relationship among biology, behavior, and personality thus enabled feminists to maintain a claim often associated with biological determinism, that the constancies of nature are responsible for certain social constancies, without having to accept one of the crucial disadvantages of such a position from a feminist perspective, that such social constancies cannot be transformed.

Another significant advantage of this view of the relationship among biology, personality, and behavior is that it enabled feminists to assume both commonalities and differences among women. If one thinks of the body as the common rack on which different societies impose different norms of personality and behavior, then one can explain both how some of those norms might be the same in different societies and how some of those norms might be different. Again, though it is not surprising that one tends to find coats and scarves on a coat-rack, such apparel might very well come in different sizes and shapes.

I have gone to some lengths to elaborate biological foundationalism because I see this position, and the "coat rack" view of identity in general, as standing in the way of truly understanding differences among women, differences among men, and differences regarding who gets counted as either. Through the belief that "sex identity" represents that which is common across cultures, we have frequently falsely generalized that which is specific to modern western culture or to certain groups within it. Moreover, it has been difficult to identify such faulty generalization as such because of the alliance of all forms of biological foundationalism with social constructionism. Feminists have long come to see how claims about the biological causes of personality and behavior falsely generalize socially specific features of human personality and behavior onto all human societies. But biological foundationalism is not equivalent to biological determinism for, unlike the latter, it includes some element of social constructionism. Even the earliest feminist position, which construed "sex" as independent of "gender," in using the term "gender" at all allows for some social input into the construction of character. Any position that recognizes at least some of what is associated with the male/female distinction as a social response tends to theorize a certain amount of differences among women. Although a biological foundationalist, unlike a biological determinist, position does allow for the recognition of differences among women, it does so in limited and problematic ways.

Most basically, it leads us to think of differences between women as coexisting, rather than intersecting, with differences of race, class, and so forth. Because of the assumption that commonalities of sex lend themselves to commonalities in gender, there is the tendency to think of gender as representing what women have in common and features of race or class representing how women differ. In other words, we are left thinking that all women "in patriarchal societies" will end up acting like coats and scarves though we may differ somewhat in size and shape. We are thus led to develop what Elizabeth Spelman describes as an additive, or "pop bead," analysis of identity in which all women share the gender "bead" but differ in relation to the other "beads" that are added. But, as she notes, such analyses typically describe the gender bead in terms of its most privileged manifestations. They also tend to depict the differences marking nonprivileged women only in negative terms. Spelman describes some of these problems in regard to analyses of the relation of sexism and racism:

> In sum, according to an additive analysis of sexism and racism, all women are oppressed by sexism; some women are further oppressed by racism. Such an analysis distorts Black women's experiences of oppression by failing to note important differences between the contexts in which Black women and white women experience sexism. The additive analysis also suggests that a woman's racial identity can be "subtracted" from her combined sexual and racial identity.[3]

In other words, a dualistic approach obscures the possibility that what we are describing as commonalities may themselves be interlaced with differences. Who we are *as women* does not differ just in relation to accidental qualities; it also differs at a deeper level. There are no common features emanating from biology.

In short, feminism needs to abandon biological foundationalism along with biological determinism. As I argue, the human population differs within itself not only in terms of social expectations about how we think, feel, and act; there are also differences in the ways in which we understand the body. Consequently, we need to understand social variations in the male/female distinction as related to differences that go "all the way down"—those differences tied not just to the limited phenomena many of us associate with "gender" (i.e., to cultural stereotypes of personality and behavior) but as also tied to culturally various understandings of the body. This understanding does not mean that the body disappears from feminist theory. Rather, it becomes a variable, rather than a constant, no longer able to ground claims about the male/female distinction across large sweeps of human history but still there as always potentially an important element in how the male/female distinction plays out in any society.

I am not disclaiming the idea that all societies possess some form of a male/female distinction. All available evidence seems to indicate that they do. Nor am I rejecting the possibility that all societies relate this distinction in some way or another to the body. It is rather that differences in the meaning and importance of the body exist. These kinds of differences in turn affect the meaning of the male/female distinction. The consequence is that there appears no one set of criteria constituting "sex identity" from which one can extrapolate anything about the joys and oppressions of "being a woman." To think that there are leads us astray.

Historical Context

The tendency to think of sex identity as given, basic, and common cross-culturally is very powerful. To weaken its hold on us requires some sense of its historical context. To the extent that we can see sex identity as historically rooted, as the product of a belief system specific to modern western societies, is the extent to which we might come to appreciate the deep diversity in the forms through which the male/female distinction has and can come to be understood.

Let me begin this task by going back in European history to the early modern period. It was in the period from the seventeenth through the nineteenth centuries that there developed, particularly among "men of science," the tendency to think about people as matter in motion—physical beings, who are ultimately distinguishable from others by reference to their occupied spatial and temporal coordinates. This idea translated into a tendency to think about human in increasingly "thing-like" terms, both as similar to the objects around us—because we are composed of the same substance, "matter"—and as separate from such objects and from one other—because of the distinctive spatial and temporal coordinates that each self occupies.[4]

It is not only that the language of space and time became increasingly central as a means for providing identity to the self. The growing dominance of a materialist metaphysics also meant an increasing tendency to understand the "nature" of specific phenomena in terms of the specific configurations of the matter they embodied. The import of this tendency for emerging views of self-identity was a growing understanding of the "nature" of human selves in terms of the specific configurations of the matter they too embodied. Thus, the material or physical features of the body increasingly took on the role of providing testimony to the nature of the self it housed.

A word of qualification must be made about how such a claim should be understood in the context of seventeenth- and eighteenth-century thinking. In the late twentieth century, to think about the body taking on an increasing role in providing testimony to the nature of the self it houses is to assume an increasing belief in biological determinism. It must, however, be emphasized that during the seventeenth and eighteenth centuries a growing sense of the self as "natural" or "material" conjoined two emphases that only in later centuries came to be viewed by many as antithetical: a heightened consciousness of the body as a source of knowledge about the self and a sense of the self as shaped by the influences the self receives from the external world. Both emphases are present in the writings of many seventeenth- and eighteenth-century writers, but they were not seen, as they frequently came to be later, as necessarily antithetical. A heightened consciousness of the self as bodily can be illustrated by the kinds of issues seventeenth- and eighteenth-century theorists increasingly thought relevant. Thus, for example, while an early seventeenth-century patriarchalist such as Sir Robert Filmer might have used the Bible to justify women's subordination to men, the later natural law theorist John Locke cited differences in male and female bodies to accomplish a related goal.[5] But "nature" for natural law theorists such as Locke did not just mean the body in distinction from other kinds of phenomena. It could also refer to the external influences provided by vision or education. Thus, though Locke might point to differences in women's and men's bodies to make a point, he could also in his writings on education view the minds of girls and boys as malleable in relation to the specific external influences to which they were subject. In short, "materialism" at this point in history combined the seeds of what later became two very different and opposing traditions. On the one hand, out of seventeenth- and eighteenth-century materialism emerged a tradition that looked to the physical characteristics of the individual as a source of knowledge about the individual. On the other hand, seventeenth- and eighteenth-century materialists talked about processes that later came to be described as "socialization"—as that which shaped identity in opposition to the body. During late–seventeenth- and eighteenth-century discourses, however, these ways of thinking about the self were often conjoined within an overall naturalistic perspective. Ludmilla Jordanova makes a related point:

> It had become clear by the end of the eighteenth century that living things and their environment were continually interacting and changing each other in the process. . . . The customs and habits of day-to-day life such as diet, exercise and occupation, as well as more general social forces such as mode of government, were taken to have profound effects on all aspects of people's lives. . . The foundation to this was a naturalistic conceptual framework for understanding the physiological, mental and social aspects of human beings in a coordinated way. This framework underlay the relationship between nature, culture and gender in the period.[6]

As Jordanova notes, this tendency to view the bodily and the cultural as interrelated is expressed in the use of such eighteenth-century "bridging" concepts as temperament, habit, constitution, and sensibility.[7]

That during the seventeenth and eighteenth centuries a growing focus on the materiality of the self did not translate simply into what many today understand as biological determinism does not negate the point that the body was increasingly emerging as a source of knowledge about the self in contrast to older theological views. One way in which this focus on the body began to shift understandings of self-identity was that, particularly during the eighteenth century, the body increasingly began to be employed as a resource for attesting to the differentiated nature of humans. One context where this is striking is in the emergence of the idea of "race." As many commentators have pointed out, "race" was only first employed as a means of categorizing humans in the late seventeenth century, and it was only in the eighteenth century with such publications as the influential *Natural System* by Carolus Linnaeus (1735) and Friedrich Blumenbach's *Generis Humani Varietate Native Liber* (*On the Natural Variety of Mankind,* 1776) that there began to be made what were taken to be authoritative racial divisions of humans.[8] This emergence does not mean that physical differences between, for example, Africans and Europeans were not noted by Europeans before the eighteenth century. They certainly were noted and were used to justify slavery. But, as Winthrop Jordan points out, physical differences were only one of the differences noted and used by Europeans to justify slavery.[9] That Africans, from a European perspective, engaged in strange social practices and were "heathens" (i.e., were not Christians) also provided justification in the European mind for the practice of taking Africans as slaves. In short, to note a physical difference, or even to attribute moral and political significance to it, is not the same as using it to "explain" basic divisions among the human population as the concept of "race" increasingly did beginning in the late eighteenth century.

The Sexed Body

The preceding example of "race" illustrates how the growing dominance of a materialist metaphysics did not mean the construction of new social distinctions *ex nihilo,* as it meant the elaboration and "explanation" of previously existing distinctions in new ways. Thus, in the case of "sex," the growth of a materialistic metaphysics did not create a male/female distinction. Such a distinction obviously existed in western Europe before the emergence of such a metaphysics. Moreover, an attention to physical differences played a role in the meaning of this distinction. The growth of a materialistic metaphysics, however, also entailed changes—changes in the importance of physical characteristics and in their role. Most basically, it transformed the meaning of physical characteristics from being a sign or a marker of this distinction to being that which generated or caused it. Moreover, at the time such a metaphysics was increasingly taking hold, other social changes were also occurring—such as an intensified separation of a domestic and public sphere. These changes meant that physical characteristics came to be seen not only as causing the male/female distinction but also as causing it as a very binary distinction.

Thomas Laqueur, in his study of medical literature on the body from the Greeks through the eighteenth century, identifies a significant change in this literature in the eighteenth century. Specifically, he identifies a view present from the Greeks until the eighteenth century, that while clearly diverse in many respects is similar in one important respect: it operates with what he describes as a "one sex" view of the body. This view contrasts with the "two sex" view, which began to emerge during the eighteenth century. Whereas in the earlier view, the female body was seen as a lesser version of the male body "along a vertical axis of infinite gradations," in the later view, the female body became "an altogether different creature along a horizontal axis whose middle ground was largely empty."[10]

That in the earlier view physical differences between the sexes were viewed as differences of degree rather than of kind manifests itself in a variety of ways. Whereas we, for example, view female sexual organs as different organs from those of men, in the earlier view, these organs were viewed as less developed versions of male organs. Thus, in the old view, the female vagina and cervix did not constitute something distinct from the male penis; rather, together, they constituted a less developed version of it. Similarly, in the old view, the process of menstruation did not describe a process distinctive to women's lives. Rather, menstruation was seen as just one more instance of the tendency of human bodies to bleed, the orifice from which the blood emerged being perceived as not very significant. Thus, it was thought that if a woman vomited blood, she would stop menstruating.[11] Bleeding itself was viewed as one way that bodies in general got rid of an excess of nutriments. Because men were thought to be cooler beings than women, they were thought to be less likely to possess such a surplus and hence less likely to possess a need to bleed.[12] Similarly, Laqueur points to Galen's argument that women must produce semen, because otherwise, Galen asks, there would be no reason for them to possess testicles, which they clearly did.[13] In short, the organs, processes, and fluids we think of as distinctive to male and female bodies were rather thought of as convertible within a "generic corporeal economy of fluids and organs."[14]

This "generic corporeal economy of fluids and organs" began to give way to a new "two sex" view. Laqueur describes aspects of the process: "Organs that had shared a name—ovaries and testicles—were now linguistically distinguished. Organs that had not been distinguished by a name of their own—the vagina, for example–were given one. Structures that had been thought common to man and woman—the skeleton and the nervous system—were differentiated so as to correspond to the cultural male and female."[15]

That even a structure such as the skeleton would now be seen as different in women and men is illustrated in the work of Londa Scheibinger. As Schiebinger notes, in 1796, the German anatomist Samuel Thomas von Soemmerring produced what was one of the first illustrations of a female skeleton. This date, she notes, is quite remarkable because many anatomists had been drawing the human anatomy since the sixteenth century.[16] This illustration, however, was representative of a larger movement of the late eighteenth century where "discovering, describing and defining sex differences in every bone, muscle, nerve, and vein of the human body became a research priority in anatomic science."[17]

Another manifestation of this new "two sex" view was the delegitimation of the concept of "hermaphroditism." As Michel Foucault points out, in the eighteenth century, the hermaphrodite of previous centuries became the "pseudo-hermaphrodite" whose "true" sexual identity required only sufficiently expert diagnosis.

> Biological theories of sexuality, juridical conceptions of the individual, forms of administrative control in modern nations, led little by little to rejecting the idea of a mixture of the two sexes in a single body, and consequently to limiting the free choice of indeterminate individuals. Henceforth, everybody was to have one and only one sex. Everybody was to have his or her primary, profound, determined and determining sexual identity; as for the elements of the other sex that might appear, they could only be accidental, superficial, or even quite simply illusory. From the medical point of view, this meant that when confronted with a hermaphrodite, the doctor was no longer concerned with recognizing the presence of the two sexes, juxtaposed or intermingled, or with knowing which of the two prevailed over the other, but rather with deciphering the true sex that was hidden beneath ambiguous appearances.[18]

But beyond the tendency to view the physical differences separating women and men in increasingly binary terms was also the new tendency to see such physical differences as the cause of the male/female distinction itself. As Laqueur points out, it is not as though, in the older view, there did not exist a distinction or that biology played no role in it. However, the distinction was seen not so much as "caused" by biology as being the logical expression of a certain cosmological order governed by difference, hierarchy, and interrelation. Within this world view, biological differences between women and men were perceived more as "markers" of the male/female distinction than as its basis or "cause." Laqueur points to the Aristotelian position as illustrative of the older view:

> Aristotle did not need the facts of sexual difference to support the claim that woman was a lesser being than man; it followed from the *a priori* truth that the material cause is inferior to the efficient cause. Of course males and females were in daily life identified by their corporeal characteristics, but the assertion that in generation the male was the efficient and the female the material cause was, in principle, not physically demonstrable; it was itself a restatement of what it *meant* to be male or female. The specific nature of the ovaries or the uterus was thus only incidental to defining sexual difference. By the eighteenth century, this was no longer the case. The womb, which had been a sort of negative phallus, became the uterus—an organ whose fibers,

nerves, and vasculature provided a naturalistic explanation and justification for the social status of women.[19]

In other words, when the Bible or Aristotle was the source of authority about how the relationship between women and men was to be understood, any asserted differences between women and men were justified primarily through reference to these texts. The body was not very important as a source. When, however, the texts of Aristotle and the Bible lost their authority, nature became the means for grounding any perceived distinction between women and men. In so far as the body was perceived as the representative of nature, it took on the role of nature's "voice," meaning that to the extent that there was perceived a need for the male/female distinction to be constituted as a strongly binary one, the body had to "speak" this distinction as a binary one. The consequence was a "two sex" view of the body.

In sum, during the eighteenth century, there occurred a replacement of an understanding of women as lesser versions of men along an axis of infinite gradations to one in which the relationship between women and men was perceived in more binary terms and where the body was thought of as the source of such binarism. The consequence is our idea of "sex identity"—a sharply differentiated male and female self rooted in a deeply differentiated body.

"Sex" and "Gender"

This concept of "sex identity" was dominant in most industrialized countries at the time of the emergence of second-wave feminism. But there were also existing ideas that feminists could draw on to begin to challenge it. Previously, I discussed the growing importance of a materialistic metaphysics in early modern western societies. Not mentioned was that the growth of such a metaphysics was never uncontested; many cultural and intellectual movements throughout western modernity have strived to prove the distinctiveness of human existence in relation to the rest of the physical world.[20] Some of these movements, particularly those grounded in religion, have continued to stress a religious, rather than a physiological, grounding of the male/female distinction. Moreover, even from within a materialist metaphysics, there emerged, before the growth of second-wave feminism, perspectives that challenged completely physiological understandings of "sex identity." Earlier I noted how many seventeenth- and eighteenth-century materialists put together two ideas that later often came to be seen as antithetical: the idea of the physiological basis of human "nature" and of the social construction of human character. In the nineteenth century, one theorist who combined both—who maintained a strong materialism while also elaborating with great theoretical sophistication the idea of the social constitution of human character—was Karl

Marx. He, along with many other nineteenth- and twentieth-century thinkers, contributed to a way of thinking about human character that acknowledged the deep importance of society in constituting character. Second-wave feminists could draw on this way of thinking to begin to challenge a pure physiological understanding of "sex identity." But, as I earlier claimed, although the challenge to this latter understanding of sex identity has been extensive in second-wave writings, it has also been incomplete. Still maintained is the idea that there exists some physiological "givens" that in all cultures are similarly used to distinguish women and men and that at least partially account for certain commonalities in the norms of personality and behavior affecting women and men in many societies. This position, which I have labeled "biological foundationalism," has enabled many feminists to reject explicitly biological determinism while holding onto one of its features—the presumption of commonalities across cultures.

What I am calling "biological foundationalism," rather than being understood as a single position, is best understood as representing a range of positions bounded on one side by a strict biological determinism and on the other side by a complete social constructionism. One advantage of viewing "biological foundationalism" as representing a range of positions is that it counters a common tendency to think of "social constructionist" positions as all alike in the role that biology plays in them. Second-wave feminists have frequently assumed that as long as one acknowledges *any* distance from biological determinism, one thereby avoids all of the problems associated with this position. But the issue is more relative: second-wave positions have exhibited more or less distance from biological determinism and have exhibited greater or fewer numbers of the problems associated with that position—specifically its tendency to generate faulty generalizations that represent projections from the theorist's own cultural context—in accord with the degree to which they have exhibited such distance.

That one might be "more or less" of a social constructionist follows from the point that any phenomenon can be thought to contribute "more or less" to a given outcome. Normally, we speak of biological determinism when a particular phenomenon is thought to be completely the consequence of biological factors. Thus, to be a social constructionist is merely to argue that society has some input into a given outcome. It is, however, easy to see that from within such a perspective there might exist a range of positions on how important such input is. In the work of many second-wave theorists, social constructionism exists as almost a token position. Although it allows for the presumption of a certain amount of difference among women, its minimal role entails that such difference is restricted either to the margins of human history or to depicting "secondary" qualities of "womanhood"—those that do not affect the basic definition of what it means to be a woman. To show how social constructionism can function in such a token way, let me now turn to the writings of two thinkers who are explicitly social constructionist yet who both use the body to create generalizations about women in ways not significantly different from biological determinism.

The first writer is Robin Morgan.[21] In Morgan's introduction to *Sisterhood Is Global,* she is explicit about the many ways that women's lives vary across culture, race, nationality, and so forth; however, she also believes that certain commonalities exist among women. As she makes clear, such commonalities are for her not *determined* by biology but are rather "the result of a common condition which, despite variations in degree, is experienced by all human beings who are born female."[22] Although she never explicitly defines this common condition, she comes closest to doing so in the following passage:

> To many feminist theorists, the patriarchal control of women's bodies as the means of reproduction is the crux of the dilemma. . . . The tragedy within the tragedy is that because we are regarded primarily as reproductive beings rather than full human beings, we are viewed in a (male-defined) sexual context, with the consequent epidemic of rape, sexual harassment, forced prostitution, and sexual traffic in women, with transacted marriage, institutionalized family structures, and the denial of individual women's own sexual expression.[23]

Passages such as this one suggest that there is something about women's bodies, specifically their reproductive capacities, that though not necessarily resulting in or determining a particular social outcome, nevertheless, sets the stage for or makes possible a certain range of male reactions across cultures that are common enough to lead to a certain commonality in women's experience as victims of such reactions. Again, this commonality in female bodies does not *determine* this range of reactions in the sense that in *all* cultural contexts such a commonality would generate a reaction of this type, but nevertheless, this commonality does lead to this kind of reaction across many contexts. The difference between this type of a position and biological determinism is very slight. As I noted, biological determinism is commonly thought to apply only to contexts in which a phenomenon is not affected by *any* variations in cultural context. Because Morgan is allowing that *some* variations in cultural context could affect the reaction, she is not here being a strict biological determinist. But, because she believes that this commonality in female bodies leads to a common reaction across a wide range of cultural contexts, there is, in reality, only a small difference that separates her position from strict biological determinism. When we see that, within a theory, biology can have "more or less" of a determining influence, so can we also see that one can be "more or less" of a social constructionist.

Another writer who explicity rejects biological determinism but whose position also ends up functionally close to it is Janice Raymond. In her book *A Passion for Friends,* Raymond explicity rejects the view that biology is the cause of women's uniqueness: "Women have no biological edge on the more humane qualities of human existence, nor does women's uniqueness proceed from any biological differences from men. Rather, just as any cultural context distinguishes one group from another, women's 'otherness' proceeds from women's culture."[24]

This position is also present in Raymond's earlier book, *The Transsexual Empire*.[25] What is very interesting about this book, however, is that much of its argument, like Morgan's, rests on the assumption of an extremely invariant relationship between biology and character, though again, an invariance that is not of the usual biological determinist kind. In this work, Raymond is extremely critical of transsexuality in general, what she labels "the male-to-constructed-female" in particular, and most especially those "male-to-constructed-females" who call themselves "lesbian feminists." Although many of Raymond's criticisms stem from the convincing position that modern medicine provides a very problematic ground for transcending gender, other parts of her criticism emerge from certain assumptions about an invariant relationship between biology and character. Specifically, Raymond doubts the veracity of claims on the part of any biological male to have "a female within him": "The androgynous man and the transsexually constructed lesbian-feminist deceive women in much the same way, for they lead women into believing that they are truly one of us—this time not only one in behavior but one in spirit and conviction."[26] For Raymond, *all* women differ in certain important respects from *all* men. This difference is not because the biologies of either directly determine a certain character. Rather she believes that the possession of a particular kind of genitals (i.e., those labeled "female") generates certain kinds of reactions that are different in kind from the reactions generated by the possession of "male" genitals. The commonality among these reactions and their differences from those generated by male genitals are sufficient to ensure that no one born with male genitals can claim enough in common with those born with female genitals to warrant the label "female." Thus, she claims, "We know that we are woman who are born with female chromosomes and anatomy, and that whether or not we were socialized to be so-called normal women, patriarchy has treated and will treat us like women. Transsexuals have not had this same history. No man can have the history of being born and located in this culture as a woman. He can have the history of *wishing* to be a woman and of *acting* like a woman, but this gender experience is that of a transsexual, not of a woman.[27]

Raymond qualifies her claims in this passage to those living within patriarchal societies, but she is assuming enough of a homogeneity of reaction across such societies such that biology, for all intents and purposes, becomes a "determinant" of character within such societies. To be sure, biology does not here *directly* generate character. But, as it invariably leads to certain common reactions that have a specific effect on character, it becomes *in effect* a cause of character. In common with Morgan, Raymond is not claiming that biology generates specific consequences independent of culture. For both, however, variability within and among a wide range of societies becomes so muted that culture becomes a vanishing variable. The invocation of culture does, of course, allow these theorists to postulate differences existing side by side with the commonalities and it also leaves open the possibility of a distant society where biology might not have such effects. But in neither case does it interfere with the power of biological givens to generate important commonalities among women across a wide span of human history.

In the preceding discussion, I have focused on the writings of Morgan and Raymond for the purpose of illustration. The type of biological foundationalism exemplified in their writings is not unique to these two writers but represents a major tendency in second-wave theory, particularly in radical feminism. This tendency among radical feminists is not surprising. Since the early 1970s, radical feminists have been in the vanguard of those who have stressed the similarities among women and their differences from men. But it is difficult to justify such claims without invoking biology in some way. During the 1970s, many radical feminists explicity endorsed biological determinism.[28] Biological determinism became, however, increasingly distasteful among feminists for a variety of reasons. Not only did it possess an unpleasant association with antifeminism, but it also seemed to disallow differences among women and—in the absence of feminist biological warfare—seemed to negate any hope for change. The task became that of creating theory that allowed for differences among women, made at least theoretically possible the idea of a future without sexism, and also justified cross-cultural claims about women. Some version of a strong form of biological foundationalism became the answer for many radical feminists.

Radical feminist writings are a rich source of strong forms of biological foundationalism. Even theories that pay more attention to cultural history and diversity than do those of many radical feminists, however, often rely on some use of biological foundationalism to make critical moves. I claimed that since the early 1970s, radical feminists have been in the vanguard of those who have wished to stress the commonalities among women and their differences from men. But, beginning in the 1970s and early 1980s, much second-wave feminism began to move in such a direction, changing from what Young has called a "humanistic" stance to a more "gynocentric" one.[29] The enormous attention given at this time to books such as Carol Gilligan's *In a Different Voice* and Nancy Chodorow's *The Reproduction of Mothering* can be said to follow from the usefulness of the former in elaborating differences between women and men and of the latter in accounting for it.[30] Although both of these works strikingly exemplify a "difference" perspective, neither fits easily into the category of "radical feminism." In both of these volumes, however, as well as in others of this period that also emphasize difference, such as in the writings of such French feminists as Luce Irigiray, there is an interesting overlap with perspectives embodied in much radical feminist analysis. Specifically, in such works, a strong correlation is claimed between people with certain biological characteristics and people with certain character traits. To be sure, in a work such as Chodorow's *The Reproduction of Mothering,* such claims are built on a rich and complex story about *culture*—about how the possession of certain kinds of genitals gets one placed in a particular psychosocial dynamic only in specific types of circumstances and only in so far as those genitals possess certain kinds of meanings. Nevertheless, I would still describe a work such as *The Reproduction of Mothering* as biologically foundationalist because its complex and sophisticated story of child development, as a story supposedly applicable about a wide range of cultures, rests on the assumption that the possession of certain kinds of genitals does possess a common enough meaning across this range of cultures to make possible the postulation of such a fundamentally homogeneous set of stories about child development. To assume that the cultural construction of the body functions as an unchanging variable across sweeps of human history and combines with other relatively static aspects of culture to create certain commonalities in personality formation across such history suffices to indicate some fairly significant version of biological foundationalism.

A problem running throughout the preceding theories that many commentators have cited is that "a feminism of difference" tends to be "a feminism of uniformity." To say that "women are different from men in such and such ways" is to say that women *are* "such and such." But, inevitably, characterizations of women's "nature" or "essence"—even if this "nature" or "essence" is described as socially constructed—tend to reflect the perspective of those making the characterizations. And because those who have the power to make such characterizations in contemporary European-based societies are often white, heterosexual, and from the professional class, such characterizations tend to reflect the biases of these groups. It was thus not surprising that the gynocentric move of the 1970s soon gave way to outcries from women of color, lesbians, and those of working-class backgrounds that the stories being told did not reflect their experiences. Thus, Chodorow was soon critiqued for elaborating a basically heterosexual story and she, Gilligan, and radical feminists such as Mary Daly have been accused of speaking primarily from a white, western, middle-class perspective.[31]

My argument is that in all of those cases in which feminist theory makes generalizations across large sweeps of history, what is, and must be assumed are common perspectives throughout such history about the meaning and import of female and male bodies. Many writers have pointed out how, in these types of theories, the specific content of the claim tends to reflect the culture of the theorist making the generalization. But also being borrowed from the theorist's cultural context and making the generalization possible is a specific understanding of the meaning of bodies and of their relationship to culture: that bodies are always construed in specific ways and, in consequence, as setting in motion a particular story of character development or societal reaction. The methodological move here is not different from that employed by biological determinists: the assumed "givenness" and commonality of nature across culture is being drawn on to give credibility to the generality of the specific claim. In short, it is not only that certain specific ideas about women and men—that women are relational, nurturing, and caring whereas men are aggressive and combative—are being falsely generalized, but also being falsely generalized, and indeed making these further generalizations about character possible, are certain specific assumptions about the body and its relationship to character—that there are commonalities in the distinctive givens of the body that generate commonalities in the classification of human across cultures and in the reactions by others to those so classified. The problems associated with "a feminism of difference" are both reflected in and made possible by biological foundationalism.

A rejoinder might be made: what my argument is failing to allow for is that in many, if not most, historical contexts people *have* interpreted the body in relatively similar ways, and this common interpretation has led to certain cross-cultural commonalities in the treatment of or experiences of women. True, it might be the case that some feminist scholarship falsely assumed the generalizability of some *specific* character traits found in contemporary middle-class western life—that women are more nurturant than men. It has not generally been problematic to assume, however, for contemporary western societies as well as for most others, that the possession of one of two possible kinds of bodies does lead to the labeling of some people as women and others as men, and this labeling bears *some* common characteristics with *some* common effects.

This response is powerful, but, I would claim, derives its power from a subtle misreading about how gender operates cross-culturally. Most every society known to western scholarship does appear to have some kind of a male/female distinction. Moreover, most appear to relate this distinction to some kind of bodily distinction between women and men. From such observations it is very tempting to move to the above claims; however, I would argue that such a move is faulty. The reason is that "some kind of male/female distinction" and "some kind of bodily distinction" include a wide range of possible subtle differences in the meaning of the male/female distinction and of how the bodily distinction works in relationship to it. Because these differences may be subtle, they are not necessarily the kinds of things that contemporary, western feminists will first see when they look at premodern European cultures or cultures not dominated by the influence of modern Europe. Subtle differences around such issues may, however, contain important consequences in the very deep sense of what it means to be a man or a woman. For example, certain Native American societies that have understood identity more in relation to spiritual forces than has been true of modern western, European-based societies have also allowed for some of those with male genitals to understand themselves and be understood by others as half man/half woman in ways not possible in modern western, European-based societies. Within these latter societies, the body has been interpreted as such an important signifier of identity that someone with female genitals has also not been thought to ever legitimately occupy the role of "husband"; whereas in many African societies this limitation is not the case. In short, though all of these societies certainly possess some kind of a male/female distinction and also relate this distinction in some important way to the body, subtle differences in how the body itself is viewed may contain some very basic implications in what it means to be male or female and, consequently, important differences in the degree and ways in which sexism operates. In short, such subtle differences in the ways in which the body is read may relate to differences in what it means to be a man or a woman that "go all the way down."[32]

This point may be established not only by looking at the relation between contemporary western, European-based societies and certain "exotic" others. Even within contemporary western, European-based societies, we can detect important tensions and conflicts in the meaning of the body and how the body relates to male and female identity. Although certainly these are societies that over the last several centuries have operated with a strongly binary male/female distinction and have based this distinction on an attributed, binary biology, they have also been societies that, in varying degrees, have articulated notions of the self that deny differences among women and men, and this denial is not just a consequence of feminism. In part, denial is manifest in the degree to which the belief that "women and men are fundamentally the same" is also a part of the hegemonic belief system of the societies in which many of us operate and has been available for feminists to draw on as an attack on differences. Indeed, it is at least partly as a consequence of a general cultural tendency in some European-based societies to somewhat disassociate biology and character that feminism itself was made possible. One of the weaknesses of a difference-based feminism is that it cannot account for the phenomenon of such societies having produced feminists—beings whose genitals, by virtue of the account, should have made us completely feminine but whose actual political skills and/or presence in such previously male-dominated institutions as the academy must indicate a certain dosage of masculine socialization. Moreover, it seems inadequate to conceptualize such a dosage as merely an "add on" to certain "basic" commonalities. In short, it is because of a certain prior dis-association of biology and socialization that, at a very basic level, many of us are who we are.

In short, a feminism of difference, and the biological foundationalism on which it rests, contain, in contemporary European-based societies, elements of both truth and falsity. Because these are societies that, to a significant degree, perceive female and male genitals as binary and also link character to such genitals, people born with "male" genitals are likely to be different in many important respects from people born with "female" genitals. A feminism of difference and the biological foundationalism on which it rests are, however, also false not only because of the failure of both positions to recognize the historicity of their own insights but also, and related, because neither allows for the ways in which, even within contemporary European-based societies, the belief system their insights reflect possess a multitude of cracks and fissures. Thus, a feminism of difference can provide no insight into those of us whose psyches are the manifestation of such cracks. Take, for example, those who are born with "male" genitals yet think of themselves as female. Raymond, in *The Transsexual Empire,* claims that "male-to-constructed-females" are motivated by the desire to seize control, at least symbolically, of women's power to reproduce.[33] She also claims that "female-to-constructed-males" are motivated by the desire to seize the general power given to men; that is, they are "male-identified" to the extreme.[34] Assuming for the sake of discussion that such accounts are valid, they still leave unanswered such questions about why *some* women are so male-identified or why only some men and not others want to seize symbolic control of women's power to reproduce or do it in *this* way. Any appeals to "false consciousness," like their earlier Marxist counterparts, merely place the lack of an answer at a deeper level, because again, no account is made of why some and not others succumb to "false consciousness."[35] Thus, even to the extent that the culture itself links gender to biology, a feminist analysis that follows this approach is unable to account for those who deviate.

Because a feminism of difference is both true and false within the societies in which many of us operate, the process of endorsing or rejecting it has certain strange elements. It is similar to looking at pictures in psychology textbooks where one moment the picture looks like the head of a rabbit and the next moment it looks like the head of a duck. Within each "view," features stand out that had previously been hidden, and the momentary interpretation feels like the only possible one. Much of the power of books such as Chodorow's *The Reproduction of Mothering* and Gilligan's *In a Different Voice* lay in the fact that they generated radically new ways of viewing social relations. The problem, however, is that these new ways of configuring reality, though truly powerful, also missed so much. Like a lens that illuminates only certain aspects of what we see by shadowing others, these visions kept from sight the many contexts in which we as women and men deviate from the generalizations these analyses generated either because the cultural contexts of our childhoods were not ones in which these generalizations were encompassing or because the specific psychic dynamics of our individual childhoods undermined any simple internalization of these generalizations. Thus, it became impossible for women to acknowledge both the ways in which the generalizations generated from the analyses poorly captured their/our own notions of masculinity and femininity and also, even when they did, how their/our own psyches might embody masculine traits. Any acknowledgment of this latter deviation seemed to make one's membership in the feminist community particularly suspect.

This last point illuminates what is often forgotten in debates about the truth of such generalizations: because evidence can be accumulated both for their truth and their falsity, their endorsement or rejection is not a consequence of a dispassionate weighing of the "evidence." Rather, it is our disparate needs, both individual and collective, that push those of us who are women to see ourselves more or less like other women and different from men. At a collective level, the need for some to see themselves as very much like each other and different from men made a lot of things possible at a certain moment in history. Most important, it made it possible to uncover sexism in its depth and pervasiveness and to build communities of women organized around its eradication. It also contained some major weaknesses, however, most notably its tendency to eradicate differences among women. The question facing feminism today is whether we can generate new visions of gender that retain what has been positive in "a feminism of difference" while eliminating what has been negative.

How Then Do We Interpret "Woman"?

Within contemporary European-based societies there is a strong tendency to think in either/or ways regarding generalities: either there are commonalities that tie us all together *or* we are all just individuals. A large part of the appeal of theories that supported "a feminism of difference" was that they generated strong ammunition against that common societal tendency to dismiss the import of gender, to claim that feminism is not necessary because "we are all just individuals." "A feminism of difference" uncovered many important social patterns of gender, patterns that enabled many women to understand their circumstances in social rather than idiosyncratic terms.

My argument against "a feminism of difference" does not mean that we should stop searching for such patterns. It is rather that we understand them in different and more complex terms than we have tended to do, particularly that we become more attentive to the historicity of the patterns we uncover. As we search for that which is socially shared, we need to be simultaneously searching for the places where such patterns break down. My argument thus points to the replacement of claims about women as such or even women "in patriarchal societies" with claims about women in particular contexts.[36]

The idea that we can make claims about women that span large historical stretches has been facilitated by the idea that there is something common to the category of "woman" across such historical stretches: that all share, at some basic level, certain features of biology. Thus, what I have called "biological foundationalism" gives content to the claim that there exist some common criteria defining what it means to be a woman. For political purposes, such criteria are thought to enable us to differentiate enemy from ally and to provide the basis for feminism's political program. There will be many people who view my attack on biological foundationalism as an attack on feminism itself: if we do not possess some common criteria providing meaning to the word "woman," how can we generate a politics around this word? Does not feminist politics require that the word "woman" have some determinate meaning?

To counter this idea that feminist politics requires that "woman" possess some determinate meaning, I borrow some ideas about language from Ludwig Wittgenstein. In arguing against a philosophy of language that claimed that meaning in general entailed such determinacy, Wittgenstein pointed to the word "game." He argued that it is impossible to come up with any one feature that is common to everything that is called a "game."

> For if you look at them [the proceedings that we call "games"] you will not see something that is common to *all*, but similarities, relationships, and a whole series of them at that. . . . Look for example at board-games, with their multifarious relationships. Now pass to card-games; here you find many correspondences with the first group but many common features drop out, and others appear. When we pass next to ball-games, much that is common is retained, but much is lost. . . . And the result of this examination is: we see a complicated network of similarities overlapping and criss-crossing: sometimes overall similarities, sometimes similarities of detail.[37]

Thus, the meaning of "game" is revealed not through the determination of some specific characteristic, or set of such, but through the elaboration of a complex network of characteristics, with different elements of this network being present in different cases. Wittgenstein used the phrase "family relationships" to describe such a network because members of a family may resemble one another without necessarily sharing any one specific feature in common. Another metaphor that suggests the same point is that of a tapestry unified by overlapping threads of color but where no one particular color is found throughout the whole.[38]

I want to suggest that we think of the meaning of "woman" in the same way that Wittgenstein suggested we think about the meaning of "game," as a word whose meaning is not found through the elucidation of some specific characteristic but is found through the elaboration of a complex network of characteristics. This suggestion certainly allows for the fact that there might be some characteristics—such as possessing a vagina and being over a certain age—that play a dominant role within such a network over long periods of time. It also allows for the fact that the word may be used in contexts in which such characteristics are not present—for example, in English-speaking countries before the adoption of the concept of "vagina" or in contemporary English-speaking societies to refer to those who do not have vaginas but who still feel themselves to be women (i.e., to transsexuals before a medical operation). Moreover, if our frame of reference is not only the English term "woman" but also all of those words into which "woman" is translatable, then such a mode of thinking about the meaning of "woman" becomes even more helpful.

It is helpful mostly because of its nonarrogant stance toward meaning. As I mentioned, such a way of thinking about the meaning of "woman" and of its non-English cognates does not reject the idea that over stretches of history there will be patterns. To give up on the idea that "woman" has one clearly specifiable meaning does not entail that it has no meaning. Rather, this way of thinking about meaning works on the assumption that such patterns are *found* within history and must be documented as such. We cannot presuppose that meaning that is dominant in contemporary, industrialized western societies must be true everywhere or across stretches with indeterminate boundaries. Thus, such a stance does not reject the idea that the "two sex" body has played an important role is structuring the male/female distinction and thus the meaning of "woman" over a certain portion of human history. It does, however, demand that we be clear about what exact portion that is and even within it, the contexts in which it does not apply. Moreover, because such a stance recognizes that the meaning of "woman" has changed over time, it also recognizes that those presently advocating nontraditional understandings of it, such as transsexuals, cannot be dismissed merely on the grounds that their interpretations contradict standard patterns. Raymond claims that no one born without a vagina can claim to have had comparable experiences to those born with one. How can she know this? How can she know, for example, that some people's parents were not operating with a greater slippage between biology and character than is true for many in contemporary industrialized societies and thus really did provide to their children with "male" genitals experiences comparable with those born with vaginas? History is made by some having experiences that really are different from those that have predominated in the past.

Thus, I am advocating that we think about the meaning of "woman" as illustrating a map of intersecting similarities and differences. In such a map, the body does not disappear; rather it becomes an historically specific variable whose meaning and import are recognized as potentially different in varying historical contexts. Such a suggestion, in assuming that meaning is found rather than presupposed, also assumes that the search itself is not a research/political project that an individual scholar will be able to accomplish alone in her study. Rather, it implies an understanding of such a project as necessarily a collective effort undertaken by many in dialogue.

Moreover, as both the previous reference to transsexuals and my earlier discussion of commonality among women and differences with men should indicate, it is a mistake to think of such a search as an "objective" task undertaken by scholars motivated only by the disinterested pursuit of truth. What we see and feel as commonalities and differences will at least partially depend on our diverse psychic needs and political goals. To articulate the meaning of a word where any ambiguity exists and where diverse consequences follow from diverse articulations is a political act. Thus, the articulation of the meaning of many concepts in our language, such as "mother," "education," "science," and "democracy," though often described as merely descriptive acts, are, in actuality, stipulative. With a word as emotionally charged as "woman," where so much hangs on how its meaning is articulated, any claim about its meaning must be viewed as a political intervention.

But if elaborating the meaning of "woman" represents an ongoing task and an ongoing political struggle, does this not undermine the project of feminist politics? If those who call themselves feminists cannot even decide on who "women" are, how can political demands be enacted in the name of women? Does not feminism require the very presupposition of unity around meaning that I am saying we cannot possess?

To respond to these concerns, let me suggest a slightly different way of understanding feminist politics than has often been taken for granted. Normally when we think of "coalition politics," we think of groups with clearly defined interests coming together on a temporary basis for purposes of mutual enhancement. On such a view, coalition politics is something that feminists enter into with "others." But, we could think about coalition politics as something not merely external to feminist politics but as also internal to it. This approach would mean that we think about feminist politics as the coming together of those who want to work around the needs of "women" where such a concept is not understood as necessarily singular in meaning or commonly agreed on. The "coalition" politics of such a movement would be formulated in the same way as "coalition politics" in general are formulated, as composed of lists of demands that address the diverse needs of the groups constituting the coalition, as composed of demands articulated at a certain abstract level to include diversity, or as composed of specific demands around which diverse groups temporarily unite. Indeed, such strategies are those that feminists have increasingly adopted in the past twenty-five years. Thus, white feminists started talking about reproductive rights instead of abortion on demand when it became clear that many women of color saw access to prenatal care or freedom from involuntary sterilization as at least as relevant to their lives, if not more so, than access to abortion. In other words, feminist politics of the past twenty-five years has already been exhibiting internal coalitional strategies. Why cannot our theorization of "woman" reflect such a politics?

This type of politics does not demand that "woman" possess a singular meaning. Moreover, even when feminist politics does claim to speak on behalf of some single understanding of "woman," can it not explicitly acknowledge such an understanding as political and thus provisional, as open to whatever challenges others might put forth? In other words, can we not be clear that any claims we make on behalf of "women" or "women's interests" are stipulative rather than descriptive, as much based on an understanding of what we want women to be as on any collective survey on how those who call themselves women perceive themselves? Acknowledging the political character of such claims means, of course, abandoning the hope that it is easy to determine whose definition of "women" or "women's interests" one will want to adopt. But that determination has never been easy. Feminists, speaking in the name of "women," have often ignored the claims of right-wing women as they have also taken on ideals about "women's interests" from the male left. That white feminists in the United States have increasingly felt it necessary to take seriously the demands of women of color and not the demands of white, conservative women is not because the former possess vaginas that the latter do not but because the ideals of many of the former more closely conform to many of their own ideals than do those of the conservative women. Maybe it is time that we explicitly acknowledge that our claims about "women" are not based on some given reality but emerge from our own places within history and culture; they are political acts that reflect the contexts out of which we emerge and the futures we would like to see.

CHAPTER FIVE

The Myth of the Traditional Family

The categories we have for sorting our world affect how we think about our present situation and possible alternatives. Unfortunately, the categories we have for organizing families—particularly the language that sorts them into "traditional" and "alternative" ones—make too many of us needlessly ashamed of the way we live. This dichotomy of possibilities leads many of us to think that the way we arrange our sexual, affective, and domestic arrangements is somewhat unusual and other than what it should be. Not only gays and lesbians but also heterosexuals who live alone; unmarried heterosexuals who live together; married couples with husbands at home caring for children or wives who work outside of the home; and children who live in single-parent, stepfamily, or alternating households are either "in the closet" or somewhat embarassed about how they live.[1]

This shame is needless for the language of the categories is duplicitous. The "traditional" family is not all that traditional, its most basic features emerging out of certain transformations in social life that occurred in western Europe and North America during the eighteenth and nineteenth centuries. Although by the late nineteenth century, such transformations had resulted in an ideal of family life in rough conformity with the version familiar today, it was only in the immediate post–World War II period that a specific form of this ideal became a mass phenomenon, particularly in the United States. The economic prosperity of the United States during the postwar period, an enormous housing boom resulting from the overcrowding and lack of housing construction of the 1930s and 1940s, and an increasing view of the family as *not* including grandparents, aunts, uncles, and cousins contributed to very large numbers of people constructing lives in conformity with a relatively new and very specific ideal of family life. But, as the 1950s' model family was made possible by certain historically specific factors, so too did other historical factors—such as the growing participation of married women in the paid labor force, rising divorce rates, and the creation of homosexual communities—lead to the emergence of new family types. Such family types are no more "alternative" to what had preceded them than had been the 1950s' type to its historical predecessors.

The "traditional" family possesses no more claims to "naturality" or historical universality than do "alternative" families. In addition, what constitutes "traditionality" itself keeps changing. The "traditional" family of the 1950s is not the same as the one of the 1990s. These historical observations lead to the recognition that the distinction between the "traditional" and the "alternative" family functions not descriptively but normatively, legitimizing certain family types over others on the basis of dubious historical assumptions.

The question then arises as to the basis for the privileging function of this distinction, independent of its historical claims. Two arguments apply. First, the specific type of privileging we today give to the "traditional" family—in either its 1950s' or its 1990s' form—has morally dubious origins, being strongly associated with the post–World War II period's racism as well as tendencies to marginalize poverty and to classify as un-American modes of life that did not conform to middle-class life. Certainly, not only the post–World War II period has privileged certain family types over others. But the specific form that the privileging assumed in this period must be related to certain specific features of the period, many of which are morally problematic.

Second, abandoning the distinction between "traditional" and "alternative" does not, as some critics have suggested, leave us with an "anything goes" attitude toward family types. We can still evaluate family types or specific features of family types on the basis of their consequences on people's lives and in relation to the contexts of their functioning. Whether a type of family provides economic and emotional sustenance to its members, with special attention to children, given the resources at its disposal and the demands it must face, should constitute the primary criterion by which it is evaluated. The distinction between "traditional" and "alternative" families gets in the way of making such considered evaluations.

The "Traditional" Family

When present-day English speakers use the word "family," they can mean one of two things by it. They can refer to the relatively small unit composed of people related by marriage, blood, or adoption who live together, or they may mean all of the people with whom one is related. Grandmothers, even very great ones, as well as distant cousins, aunts, and so forth, get counted here. This latter meaning of "family" makes "family" synonymous with "kin."

The institution of "kinship" is a phenomenon of many, if not all, societies. In a wide variety of societies, at birth babies are placed in a system of relationships constituted through some set of rules having to do with marriage and/or maternity and paternity. Societies differ widely in defining kinship, attributing, for instance, more or less importance to biology as a factor in its determination. In some societies, for example, biological children conceived "out of wedlock" do not count as "really" related. Societies also differ in how important kinship is in determining, for example, where one lives, with whom one lives, or one's access to material resources. Nevertheless, in a wide assortment of societies, some aspects of one's life circumstances are affected by one's stipulated place in some type of kinship system.[2]

Thus, in so far as "family" is equated with "kinship," a good case can be made for thinking of "family" as ranging over most, if not all, human societies. When conservatives claim that "the family" is under attack, however, their concern is not with the preservation of "family" in this sense. Rather, the "family" to which they are typically referring is the unit of parents with children who live together. This concern is typically justified with the argument that what is being destroyed is "universal." In other words, there is a slippage in the use of language so that the universality of one type of institution becomes claimed about another only because the two institutions share the same name—" family."

To be sure, many people recognize the family form of only parents with children as somewhat recent; however, they tend to think of this institution—typically referred to as the "nuclear family"—as an only slightly modified version of the "extended family." Indeed, the "extended family" is frequently thought of as a nuclear family with only some extra relatives attached; and, because it is widely believed that this extended family is in fact universal, its underlying similarity with the nuclear family makes it appear appropriate to think of the "nuclear family" as basically universal, even if somewhat shrunken in size in recent times.

This common-sense view of family history is, however, mythical. Although there is a good deal of debate within the field of family history about how far back the nuclear family extends and what type of family form immediately preceded it, no one credits any family form as universal. Too much anthropological literature exists that documents the variability of kinship systems, living arrangements, and the ways in which these combine across cultures. Indeed, when conservatives claim that we need to hang on to the "traditional family," I am often tempted to retort that a true enactment of such would have us all organized into tribes or into the actual living arrangements of very early humans.

Certainly, the rejoinder might be made that even if the nuclear or extended family does not encompass *all* of human history, this basic family type extends far enough back to provide adequate grounds for calling it "traditional." To ascertain the validity of this claim, we need to determine what family history tells us about the origins of what many of us consider "family."

Family history, a relatively new subfield of the discipline of history, has evidenced a great deal of controversy in its short life. Part of the problem is that this branch of history, like other branches, yields different types of stories depending on the questions asked and the methods used for answering them. One of the studies that became prominent early in the development of this subfield was carried out by Peter Laslett and his colleagues at Cambridge University.[3] The Cambridge group wanted to debunk the thesis of extended family structures in pre-industrial Europe. Through the examination of various records, they demonstrated that the average size of coresident groups in the west dating back at least as far as the seventeenth century and extending to the early twentieth century was approximately 4.75 people per household. These figures were believed to show that the nuclear family unit extended much farther back in western history and was a more stable family type than many had previously thought.

The work of the Cambridge group was soon, however, called into question. Part of the problem was the utility of using average size to demonstrate anything. As Wally Seccombe points out, a focus on a mean, or average, size discounts the possibility that some households may have been very large and others very small.

> By fixating on mean household size, the Cambridge paradigm disregards the elementary fact that more people live in large households than in small ones. Given this asymmetry, the average size of households is a deceptive index; the more illuminating measure is the proportion of the population living in households of a certain size. In fact (as Laslett himself acknowledged), when the average size of households was 4.75 persons, *53 per cent of the population lived in households of six or more people.*[4]

Seccombe's point is elaborated in the work of the historian Jean-Louis Flandrin. In examining one of the villages cited by Laslett in *The World We Have Lost,* Flandrin noted that Laslett's data ignored issues of class. The village of Goodnestone next-Wingham in Kent did indeed possess in 1676 a small median household size, one of 4.47. This figure was, however, the result of compiling the size of the households of the lower social classes, which were very small, with the size of the households of the yeoman and gentry, which were much larger. Although the smaller households comprised the majority, approximately two-thirds of the population lived in the much larger households of the yeomen and gentry.[5]

It is not only that a focus on mean size ignores the question of variation in size in relation to class; it also ignores the question of how household members viewed each other, whatever their number. Were all members of a household counted as family? Did family go beyond the household? In short, was family coextensive with household? To answer these kinds of questions, one needs answers to the question of how the word "family" itself has been defined over time. Flandrin has done much of the influential work in this branch of European family history. In *Families in Former Times,* Flandrin argues that in western Europe before the nineteenth century, the word "family" did not mean relatives who lived together—whether extended or nuclear. Rather, focusing on the period of the seventeenth and eighteenth centuries, he claims that the word "family" had two meanings, neither of which was this one. Its meanings included an extended kinship network that did not co-reside, similar to one of our contemporary meanings. But the meaning is not quite identical. In earlier periods, this meaning of family tended to be applied only to extended kinship networks of some wealth, though wealth of a certain sort. It tended to be more widely used of the bourgeoisie than of the aristoracy, the latter more typically referring to themselves as of a given "house."

A second meaning of "family" also was prevalent during this period. This meaning referred to those who lived together, those related through kinship as well as those who were not. This meaning is reflected in the opening section of Samuel Pepy's diary, where he stated, "I lived in Axe Yard, having my wife, and servant Jane, and no more in family than us three."[6] This meaning of "family" tended in fact to be the prominent meaning of this period, being listed first or principally in many English and French seventeenth- and eighteenth-century dictionaries, though becoming less important in France during the eighteenth century.[7] Michael Mitterauer and Reinhard Sieder point to a similar meaning of the word "familia" as used in the romance languages throughout the Middle Ages and into early modern times. The ancient Latin word, "familia" meant "house" including all those residing therein, children as well as servants. What was crucial in this meaning, as well as in such terms as "pater" and "mater," were not issues of genealogy but authority:

> Likewise, *pater* and *mater* are notions that express not genealogical connection but dependence on authority. . . . The position of *pater familias* has, in fact, nothing to do with natural fatherhood. It derives, rather, from a specific position of authority. The *pater* was originally the master of the household, the *des-potes* (*domus-potis*), the person who had authority over wife, children, slaves and other persons belonging to the household, who collectively composed the *familia.*[8]

What was the context, therefore, for the emergence of that meaning of "family" that made it synonymous with neither extended kinship nor household membership but referred to that collection of close kinship members who resided together? The context seems a wide variety of factors taking place in western Europe and North America beginning in the sixteenth century but that began to coalesce in a certain form during the eighteenth and nineteenth centuries. Skimming over the surface of a great deal of detailed work that has been done on the history of the modern western European family, one can identify certain very broad trends. For one, among those of property, there occurred very early in the modern period a diminishment in the importance of the ties of the extended kinship network and a greater sense that one's fortune was tied to one's more closely related kin. Lawrence Stone, in depicting what he calls "The Restricted Patriarchal Nuclear Family" of England of the period 1550–1700, emphasizes the increasing tightness of the bonds between parents and children in this period over earlier times.[9] As Natalie Zemon Davis notes, this change signified an increasing sense of the nuclear family unit as a type of planning unit oriented to the future welfare of its members.[10]

But, beginning in the early modern period, it was not only that the ties that bound close kin to a more extended kinship network became increasingly diminished for people of property. There also emerged, particularly in the eighteenth century, a change in what constituted the character and meaning of household life. Before about the middle of this century, households of property appeared to be strongly organized around relations of authority, where the status of servants was not very different from that of wives, younger siblings, or children. During the eighteenth century, such relations of authority seemed to give way to relations of greater equality and affection among kin-related members and to more contractual relations between servants and heads of household.

This transformation is documented in many histories of the modern family, but a particularly vivid account of it is provided by Randolph Trumbach in his depiction of aristocratic household life in England during the eighteenth century. Trumbach describes the period as one of tension between an older and newer form of household organization, which he labels respectively "patriarchy" and "domesticity." Noting the coexistence during this period of both forms, for example, in the distinction often made by aristocrats between their "great family" and their "little family," he also depicts the growing supercession of the domestic form over the patriarchal one. Trumbach focuses on the manifestations of this supercession both in relations among family members and between the family and servants. Within the family, it meant a new sense of husband and wife as partners. Between parents and children, it meant an understanding of the mother, *rather* than the father, as the guardian of the children's welfare. Servants became less like children and more like employees as their moral, religious, and sexual behavior became viewed more as their own re-sponsibility rather than the responsibility of the head of household. Servants also increasingly became thought of as potentially harmful to the affective and moral connections between parents and children. A striking example of this last trend was the intense campaign directed at aristocratic women to give up their wet nurses.[11]

Thus, what we mean by the "traditional family" is an institution that began to emerge for the upper classes during the eighteenth century. It is typified by a strong sense of the separation of the unit of parents and children from both a more extended kinship network and from such non–kin-related people as servants. It is marked by a norm of partnership between husband and wife and by the special role of the mother in shaping the character of her children.[12] In brief, it represents an institution less organized around relationships of authority and more geared toward relationships of affection as the household became a unit less focused on production and more on sexuality, affection, and consumption.

One might, however, claim that the kinds of households Trumbach is de-scribing represent a very particular kind of household, the very exceptional ones of great property. What about the households of the more common folk? To what extent did these households before the eighteenth century resemble those we associate today with "traditional" family life? Certainly in terms of numbers there is a greater resemblance between the older peasant household and the contemporary nuclear one than is the case with the wealthy, as the households of the lower classes were much more "nuclear" in size than were the households of those of wealth.[13] However, qualifications can be made against thinking of the older peasant form as resembling the contemporary "nuclear family" even in terms of numbers. Edward Shorter argues that in many parts of western Europe the typical pattern was that of the stem family where one set of grandparents were in residence with the conjugal family.[14] And Seccombe argues that even in contexts in which a basic conjugal family type seemed to prevail, closer examination reveals what he describes as a "weak family stem type" where grandparents were either living very close by or merely absent at a particular stage in the family cycle.[15] Moreover, even the "conju-gal" unit often deviated from our ideal model of "nuclear family" with mar-riages ending early because of death, children leaving home at early ages, and many households, even of modest means, having "servants" (i.e., individuals taken in to assist with the tasks of farming).[16]

As one turns from the question of household composition and looks at other types of issues, the lack of a parallel between the older and more contempo-rary form becomes even more pronounced. With more common folk, it was not that the older form was more "patriarchal" than "domestic." Among the lower classes, relations among family members appeared more egalitarian than among those of property even in the earlier period.[17] But that pre–eighteenth-century peasant households were governed less by principles of patriarchal authority than were the households of the aristocracy does not mean that they resembled the later domestic model. Rather, the transformation—taking place more predominantly in the nineteenth rather than in the eighteenth century—seems to have been one from a household whose members were more allied to their respective peers in the village than they were to one another to a household in which conjugal ties took precedence over external ones. In other words, if domesticity arose in the upper classes in the eighteenth century in opposition to a certain model of patriarchal authority, in the lower classes it arose in the nineteenth century in opposition to a distinctive model of village life.

In pre-industrial Europe, the village exerted considerable control over individual life. Households were often clustered together with an open field system prevailing and much agricultural work done collectively.[18] This structure meant much community control not only over work life but also over issues such as migration, morality, sexuality, and the formation of the marital couple.[19] Such control was explicitly exerted through "the chivari," a loud, public gathering where those who deviated from the norms of the village were subject to humiliation. The targets were men who impregnated single women; cuckholded husbands; men and women who married someone much younger or older than themselves; or those who failed to perform some customary obligation, such as opening their wedding dance to the public.[20]

The traditional European village did not exert its ties over the household just in matters of control. Also, those within the household were more likely to spend any leisure time they had with their peers outside of the household than they were with one another. This tendency was particularly true of men, whose leisure activity was almost exclusively composed of socializing with other men of the village. A strict and explicit sexual division of labor and a notion of the wife's subordination to her husband together worked against the sense of a "companionate marriage" so dominant today.

According to Shorter, the rise of a nonlocal, free-market economy destroyed this way of life.

> The free market was like an acid bath for the traditional village and small town. In the name of agricultural individualism, common lands were apportioned out, jointly farmed and collectively administered fields were broken up into individual plots and common herds disaggregated into family livestock. In the name of private enterprise the guilds were shattered, so that individual producers might compete against one another rather than collectively administering their monopoly.[21]

The consequence was a strenghtening of the ties that bound the conjugal unit of husbands, wives, and children for both the new middle classes as well as the emerging working classes. Shorter argues that the middle classes tended to adopt a new notion of domesticity both earlier and more extensively than did the working classes. In France, for example, whereas by the late eighteenth century a new notion of domesticity had arisen among the bourgeois urban middle classes, it was not until the mid-nineteenth century that a similar family model could be found among the working classes. Even by this time, members of the working classes tended to replicate more extensively many of the older patterns, for example, in the ways that they spent their leisure time. Whereas those of the middle class tended to socialize more as couples, seeing their leisure time as an extension rather than a break with domesticity, members of the working classes retained strong ties with their peer groups, as exemplified in "the buddies at the bar syndrome."[22]

Indeed, it appears that by the late nineteenth, and early twentieth century, working-class households both did and did not exemplify the new ideal of domesticity developed by the aristocracy and bourgeoisie in the second half of the eighteenth century. Certainly, with the decline of the strength of village constraints, there had developed for the poor the notion that marriage was something chosen by the couple rather than organized by external authorities. There was a similar idea of the conjugal couple with children as an autonomous unit in a hostile world. But there were also many aspects of the new norm of domesticity that were unattainable for the poor. Households require a certain amount of economic resources for even minimal maintenance. For the poor, achieving such resources often required the creation of living arrangements not quite in keeping with the new form. Thus, in working-class households, there was often the presence of "boarders" or families sharing lodging.[23]

If one turns to the U.S. context, the content of much of the social reform movements of the late nineteenth and early twentieth centuries appears aimed at strenghtening the new ideal. In the late nineteenth century, campaigns directed toward making poor and immigrant families conform to the new ideal of domesticity were often spearheaded by private charity organizations; however, the actions of such groups often led to the actual breakup of poor families whose behavior did not conform to the norms the ideal demanded. Reformers during the progressive era not only turned from private organizations to the federal government to promulgate the ideal but also worked for legislation that would keep more families intact.[24] The goals were clear: households where husbands worked, wives stayed home, children went to school, and no one other than these individuals lived in the home. Child labor legislation, protective labor legislation for women, the creation of Mother's Pensions, and federally supervised arbitration aimed at ensuring male heads of households "a family wage" all were geared to furthering these ends. Stephanie Coontz elaborates on how a very specific notion of family life pervaded the reform movements of the time:

> Convinced that "home, above all things means privacy," reformers advocated state action not only to regulate slum lords but also to end the "promiscuous" socializing of the lower classes in urban tenements and streets. They grew hysterical about the dangers of boarders and lodging, once respectable middle-class practices, and referred to the "street habit" as if it were a dangerous addiction, much like crack cocaine. To root out this addiction, Progressives promulgated new zoning laws and building codes prohibiting working-class families from sharing quarters. . . . As late as the 1970's, food stamps were automatically denied to any poor family or individual who did the sensible thing and shared cooking facilities with others.[25]

The notion of "proper" family life that spearheaded much of the social legislation of the progressive era did not die during the 1930s and 1940s. The Great Depression and World War II did, however, place strong limits on the degree to which it could be lived out by large numbers of people. It was not until after World War II that the ideal became a real possibility for the masses. Most basically, the great economic boom of the 1950s made for an increase in real wages. It also made possible substantial amounts of government spending on a G.I. bill, on sewer and highway construction, and on extensive subsidization of home mortgages. These factors, combined with the savings that many Americans had been able to generate during the war years, contributed to massive housing construction and the creation of suburbia. During the depression and World War II, many Americans had lived with relatives or strangers in crowded housing conditions; the idea of a "home of one's own" containing only one's spouse and children came to seem highly desirable to many.[26]

As Coontz points out, the 1950s family was experienced by most people of the time as something new. Many of the films and television plays of the period dealt with people trying to negotiate ties to a larger kin network with ties to the nuclear family. Invariably, the "happy" ending meant that ties to the nuclear family won. She notes how many commentators urged young couples to "adopt a 'modern' stance and strike out on their own."[27]

What was new was not only that wide segments of the population were coming to believe in the desirability of living only with spouse and children; also new were many of the expectations people held about such a family. Although the Victorian ideal of domesticity included wife and mother at home, it portrayed her household activities in very different ways than did the ideal of the 1950s. A notion of woman as moral guardian of the hearth who left her more practical tasks to servants gave way to an ideal of woman who was morally and psychologically fulfilled through housework and child bearing. The family became seen as the site of leisure and consumption where, ideally, leisure activities were carried out together.[28]

In general, the new ideal was highly delineated, where the proper outcome of a wide assortment of life's decisions were clearly spelled out, including, for example, decisions about the appropriate timing of marriage and the appropriate timing and number of children.[29] It was also an ideal that was sought after and attained by a large proportion of the population, the section of the population that was coming to think of itself as "middle class." Indeed, changes in the U.S. class structure and the emergence of a large middle class in this period can be significantly related to the emergence of the idea that the ideal family of the 1950s constituted the "traditional" family.

The economic boom of the 1950s was a strange phenomenon. On the one hand, a significant percentage of the population prospered. Kenneth Jackson has claimed that the post–World War II United States represented the first society in the history of the world where the distribution of wealth did not reflect the shape of a pyramid or tree.[30] On the other hand, the economic expansion of the 1950s left out a large number of people; unemployment rates, for example, remained significantly high.[31] This divided prosperity meant that while the boom changed the economic circumstances of most, it also left unaffected the lives of many. As Robert Lekachman noted, "Thus, most Americans have never had it so good; possibly 15 to 20 percent of Americans have had it as bad as ever."[32]

Two factors contributed to one's group placement: 1) whether one was in the right place at the right time with the right skills, and 2) racism. Both factors led to a growing correlation between being African American and being poor.[33] The economic expansion of the 1950s was not industrial. Rather, the period witnessed a decline in industrial jobs as the service and professional sector of the economy expanded.[34] The families of many European American immigrants had already been in urban settings long enough to have acquired the types of education and skills that were necessary to flourish in this new type of economy. The families of many African Americans whose emigration to northern cities occured primarily later in the century did not have these advantages. This factor, combined with the strong racism that prevailed in the United States during the 1950s, meant that many African Americans were excluded from the expansion of the period.

During the 1950s, African American family types were not as different from those of European Americans as later became the case. Differences in types of family formation between African and European Americans only gradually began to emerge after 1940, intensifying after the 1970s in conjunction with the economic downturn beginning then and the growing exclusion of African American men from the work force.[35] But, during the 1950s, African Americans, as well as poor European Americans, were more likely than those who were becoming prosperous to possess features of family life that were associated with economic hardship: "extra" relatives in a household, a greater likelihood that a household would be female headed, and the presence of boarders.

These differences meant that family type could serve, along with other factors, as indicator of whether one had made it into the new middle class. The nuclear family with the wife at home became as much a symbol of middle class life as a house in the suburbs. To be sure, family type had served as a class indicator before in U.S. history. It had long been the case that the ability to keep a wife outside of the work force signaled a man's class status. The difference, however, was that in the 1950s a certain type of family life was becoming a mass possibility as entrance into the new middle class was becoming available to large numbers of people.

The mass nature of the new economic prosperity meant that many people in the United States could think of their country as possessing "one great middle class." Because many of those who were not considered part of this class were African Americans and increasingly lived in areas physically isolated from middle-class European Americans, the poor could become marginalized in the consciousness of those who had "made it." As Michael Harrington brilliantly noted, by the early 1960s the poor in the United States had become invisible, constituting what he called "the other America." Being poor, being African American, not living within the "Ozzie and Harriet"–type family came to mean for many people not really being American. The racism that had long existed in the United States, combined with the homogeneity of class that was coming to dominate much of the consciousness of the period, created a new belief in the universality and/or superiority of a certain narrow conception of family life.

"Alternative" Families

Even as a certain ideal of family was coming to define "the American way of life," however, such trends as a rising divorce rate, increasing participation of married women in the paid labor force, and the growth of female-headed households were making this way of life increasingly atypical. In all cases, such trends preceded the 1950s. That by the 1950s these trends were confined to relatively small percentages of the population and within the general population tended to be more true of those who were poor or from negatively viewed ethnic and racial groups, made it possible for the ideal to come to appear during the period as both indomitable and as natural. It has been only recently, as such trends have continued to accelerate, that it has become easier to see the fragility of the 1950s' ideal.

A version of the 1950s' ideal is still thought of as natural. The irony, however, is that what is today understood as the "traditional" family is not the same as the 1950s version. Certain features of the older ideal, which earlier had been viewed as both essential to the ideal and as expressing what was natural about it, are now seen as having been less crucial all along.

A striking example are changing perceptions about married women in the paid labor force. Married women have entered the paid labor force in ever greater percentages during the twentieth century. In 1890 in the United States, only 4.6 percent of married women were in the paid labor force. By 1950, the figure had climbed to 23.8 percent. By 1970, it was 40.8 percent, and by 1985, 54.2% percent.[36]

That by 1950 the percentage of married women in the paid labor force was only 23.8 percent meant that working wives could still be seen as anomalous. Moreover, a high proportion of that percentage was made up of women who were otherwise stigmatized racially and/or economically. Consequently, it is not surprising that in 1950 the idea of the husband as breadwinner and wife as stay-at-home mother and housekeeper was considered natural and as what partly constituted the nuclear family as "traditional." Indeed, in the 1950s, working wives were often portrayed in terms similar to how gay households are portrayed today, as unnatural and as a threat to society. A 1954 article in *Esquire* magazine labeled working wives a "menace"; an author of *Life* magazine called married women's employment a "disaster."[37]

Today, not only do a very high percentage of married women work in the paid labor force, but so do a large number of married women with small children. Consequently, very few people think of married women working as unnatural. Similarly, as long as both partners are heterosexual, the families of working wives are considered traditional. The criteria defining a "traditional" family have changed.

Families constituted by second marriages are also interesting in the light that they shed on changing criteria of "traditionality." As with married women's participation in the paid labor force, divorce rates have steadily increased during the twentieth century. As Kingsley Davis noted, "Despite fluctuations associated with wars and depression, the increase in the U.S. divorce rate was remarkably consistent from the 1860's (the first years for which information is readily available) until the 1980's. In 1983 the rate was 18 times what it had been in 1860, and 2.4 times what it had been in 1940."[38]

One result of the growing incidence of divorce is that families in which one or both of the adult partners have been previously married are increasingly being allowed to count as "traditional families" to the degree that they appear at a given moment similar to the old-style family. As I previously noted, the 1950s' "traditional" family was associated with strict rules about the timing of marriages and the timing and number of children. The increase of the divorce rate has undermined those rules. People have reconciled older notions of a traditional family with the rising divorce rate by discounting the importance of prior marital history or means by which children have been acquired. Without such discounting, too few contemporary families would be "traditional" and the label itself would become dangerously irrelevant.

Gays and lesbians have made use of this tendency to discount some of the old rules by describing the households they create as families.[39] They point to the similarities between their households and those of heterosexuals, with adults making long-term financial and emotional commitments to each other comparable to heterosexuals. They note that their households also sometimes include children who relate to adults in the same kinds of ways as do children in heterosexual households. An emphasis on such similarities makes it easier to isolate only one factor, the same gender of the adult partners, as differentiating gay and lesbian households from heterosexual ones.

An obstacle that gays and lesbians face is that the same gender of adult partners makes gay and lesbian households appear different from heterosexual ones in visual terms. And, although there has been a general tendency for people to discount prior history and to focus on contemporary arrangements, they have tended to do so to the degree to which current arrangements "look like" the older model. Many of the changes that have taken place since the 1950s, such as the rising divorce rate, rising rates of heterosexuals living together outside of marriage, or rising rates of children born outside of marriage, are not changes that appear on the surface in interactions with strangers. Because family forms created within these new contexts tend often to "look like" the 1950s' model, it is easier for many to assimilate them into that model and thus think of them as "traditional."

The converse of this point is that family forms that are not traditional but that "look so" on the surface reinforce ideas about the pervasiveness of the "traditional" family. Many people today who appear related in traditional ways are, on closer examination, related in very untraditional ways: gay men and heterosexual women who socialize together, older men and women who live together but are not married, married couples with children having a complex premarital history, and so forth. In the eyes of strangers, such relationships are perceived as "traditional" and reinforce a sense of the pervasiveness of the "traditional" family.

These ways in which "traditionally" is superimposed intersect with cultural ideologies of race, class, and age. Thus a well-dressed, young, white woman alone with a baby will not be perceived as an "unwed mother," whereas an African American woman from a range of classes may very well be. An older heterosexual couple of any race or class will be perceived as married, whereas class and race may influence whether a younger heterosexual couple is so perceived. The ways in which "traditionality" is imposed are heavily influenced by ideologies of race, class, and age. In general, however, the belief in the "traditional" family has been sustained, even in the context of widespread changes, because of the surface invisibility of many of the changes, which allows people to impose "traditionality" even where it does not exist. This factor, combined with a general cultural tendency to allow "traditionality" to apply to families with known histories of divorce or of nonstandard ways of acquiring children, particularly to the extent that such families otherwise "look like" the 1950s' model, has helped to maintain the idea of "traditionality" even in the context of widespread change.

To be sure, the tendency to discount history and to focus on present arrangements, particularly on present surface arrangements, is not without its backlash. In judicial decisions by conservative judges, there appears an increasing impetus to assert the primacy of biology in deciding child custody cases. There is a growing amount of "anti-divorce" talk in recent conservative discourse. Thus, to say that families that appear similar to the 1950s' model are increasingly being accepted as "traditional," whatever their prior history, is not to say that everyone is happy with such a change.

Evaluating Families

Sometimes those who criticize the idea of the "traditional" family are regarded as allowing an "anything goes" attitude toward family forms. To attack the distinction between "traditional" and "alternative" families is seen as permitting no evaluative distinction between families at all. This reasoning does not follow. We can evaluate family forms even when discarding this distinction. To be sure, when we attack the idea of the naturality or historical universality of the "traditional" family and describe all family types as historically specific adaptations to particular contexts, there is implied a certain tolerance for all types of family forms. Indeed, such tolerance is in many cases warranted; when new family types emerge on a wide basis, there are probably good reasons for their emergence. But such a statement does not entail that tolerance is always warranted or warranted to include all specifics. In some contexts, one might want to intervene in the circumstances that make the creation of the new family type reasonable; in others, one might want to effect more localized changes to influence specific elements of the type in question. In all cases, however, what seems most appropriate is to examine the specific consequences of family types on people's lives rather than to base our judgments on historically dubious references to "traditionality."

A focus on two contemporary family types illustrate this argument: the family type described by Carol Stack in her important work *All Our Kin* and the "traditional" family of the 1990s' (i.e., a two-parent with children household, with both parents working). By evaluating these two forms, we can see how both the contemporary "traditional" family and a family type few would find "traditional" both possess positive and negative features independent of their affinity with "traditionality."

Stack spent several years becoming close with members of a poor black community in a midwestern city in the late 1960s. From her observations of the way in which this community operated, she described a family type very different from what is considered the "traditional" nuclear family. Her claim was that this family type was both a reaction to and a necessary adaptation to the poverty and economic instability members of this community faced.[40]

Individuals in this community depend on a wide network of relationships, constituted by both "real" and "assumed" kinship ties to meet economic needs. Among members of a personal kindred there is continuous and extensive exchanging—of money, furniture, clothes, services, children, food stamps, and so forth. The norms of the community demand that when an individual requests something from another member of her or his personal kindred, such as a sofa, the request is granted when it is possible to do so. The recipient is then in debt to the giver for goods and services of an equivalent value repayable at a later time. Individual households have elastic boundaries; Stack says that they "expand or contract with the loss of a job, a death in the family, the beginning or end of a sexual relationship, or the end of a friendship."[41] Ties over three generations often are strong and extend over a lifetime. Households frequently are female-headed with men, such as boyfriends, brothers, and husbands, circulating over time.

The advantage of this family structure is that it provides a social insurance system for those with barely enough economic resources to survive. This type of structure gives people flexibility in meeting economic demands. One may not have the rent money at the end of the month, but one may be able to come up with the money later or be able to give someone a television set one acquired in a more flush period. Given that many of the jobs that people in this community are able to get are temporary or seasonal, providing for someone else when one has a job means that one will not be completely without resources when one does not. One's chances of finding housing if one's house is condemned are enlarged if households are understood as having flexible boundaries. Without money for child care services, it is important to have people available to look after one's child when one cannot.

There are costs to be paid for these benefits. Within such a system, it is impossible to accumulate the kind of resources necessary to move into middle-class life. Stack tells the story of a couple, Calvin and Magnolia Waters, who inherited $1,500 when an uncle who had recently sold an old farm in Mississipi died. Their first thought was to use the money as a down payment on a home; however, the welfare office immediately cut off benefits to Magolia's children on hearing of the inheritance. Within the next few weeks, when family emergencies arose, such as an ill sister being threatened with eviction, a former boyfriend of Magnolia's dying and needing a burial, children and grandchildren needing coats, hats, and shoes, it was to Magnolia and Calvin that people turned. Within a month and a half, the money was gone.[42] This family structure also discourages marriages or overriding commitments to a romantic partner. Other members of one's personal kindred tend to view such commitments as threats to one's ability or willingness to share resources. Given the job instability of many black men, women, not surprisingly, will tend to see their personal kinship network as a more reliable source of support than that potentially available from any one man. But instability in heterosexual relationships also means that children frequently experience instability in relationships with father figures. At the end of a romantic relationship, although some men do continue relationships with children, both with those they have created as well as those they have helped to raise and grandfathers and uncles often provide long-term meaningful relationships, children frequently do not have the type of long-term relationships with father figures that is taken as normative in middle-class households.

In short, we see a family type with both advantages and disadvantages for its members, but the same can be said of the 1990s' "traditional" family. As earlier noted, because of declining real wages during the past forty-year period, both adults participate in the paid labor force in most middle-class families. Contrary to some conservative discourse, this participation is not because such families seek "luxuries" but because it is necessary to maintain a middle-class existence. Thus, without both adults working, few middle-class households could think about purchasing a home, sending children to college, making sure children have orthodontic work, and so forth. When there are only two adults in a household and both work at full-time jobs outside of the home, tremendous time pressures are placed on the adults in combining such work with the tasks of running a household and raising children. As most studies indicate, this pressure falls disproportionately on women.[43] Moreover, because many of our current institutions, such as schools, are geared to there being an adult at home to take care of children during the summers, after school, and when children become sick, time conflicts between child rearing and paid labor demands are intensified.

The small size of the 1990s' "traditional" family also places heavy emotional and psychological burdens on its members. For children, it means that if one or both parents are emotionally or physically abusive, there is little recourse to other adults to mitigate the abuse. For the adult members, heavy expectations are placed on the other partner to satisfy needs for companionship and love. When work often takes people in different directions from their spouses, fulfilling those needs for companionship can become difficult. The conflict between twentieth-century expectations that marriage be based on companionship and passion and the real-life factors that mitigate against either lasting over time certainly accounts for a significant portion of the rising divorce rate throughout the century. When divorce does occur, the small economic base of the nuclear family often means that one or both of the households subsequently created will lose access to many of the accoutrements of middle-class life. Finally, this family type is restricted to those adults who desire companionship and passion with someone of the "opposite" sex. The 1990s' "traditional" family still requires heterosexuality of its adult members.

All of these disadvantages not mean that this family type has no advantages for some. Although its small size places heavy psychological burdens on its members to provide companionship and love for each other, when they do, this family type can be very satisfying. The small size works toward an intimacy among members. Because this family type is associated with the institution of marriage and the expectation that the obligations of all members to one another are life-long, it also can bring with it very long-term connections. Moreover, the economic insulation of this family type from the demands of extended family or community means that it sometimes can stockpile resources for such purchases as buying a house or sending children to college.

Thus, neither of these family types is without benefits and liabilities. The family type that Stack describes possesses certain weaknesses, but it also seems a highly rational response to economic deprivation and instability. It seems pointless to attempt to eliminate it without ending the economic deprivation and instability that make it a reasonable response. To be sure, certain of its features might be changeable even in the context of the continuation of the economic status quo. Government policy could be geared, for example, toward encouraging long-term ties between children and fathers within the basic framework of this family type. Similarly, there are local initiatives that government could make to diminish some of the weaknesses of the 1990s' "traditional" family. For example, providing resources for schools for infirmaries to temporarily house sick children could reduce some of the conflict between child rearing and participation in the paid labor force. In short, in both cases we need to be attentive to the specific features as well as the factors that appear to cause them, which make each family type both advantagous and disadvantagous to the people they serve. The distinction between "traditional" and "alternative" has little to contribute to such attentiveness.

Conclusion

As I have argued, the distinction between the "traditional" and the "alternative" family is dubious, historically and morally. Historically, it attributes a sense of false universality to a family type that is of relatively recent creation and is continuously in change. This false historical attribution is then used to give legitimacy to certain family types and not others independent of the specific consequences of each on the lives of the people they serve. Thus, on both historical and moral grounds, the distinction is problematic.

But the distinction is also politically problematic. Although there is a growing tolerance toward some new family forms, the 1950s' model of family life still structures many of our institutions and attitudes. But most people today live out large portions of their lives in family types that clash with that model—for example, the adult partners are gay or lesbian, one of the adult partners has children living in a different household with whom she or he is trying to maintain a loving relationship, or the fact of both partners working makes summer or after-school hours a real source of problems. The distinction between "traditional" and "alternative" families encourages those who experience such clashes to think of them as the relatively isolated affects of living a slightly "deviant" life. We need to acknowledge fully that in relation to many contemporary conceptions of "traditionality," most of us are "deviants." Having done that, we can begin to mobilize the political power necessary to make our present institutions conform more adequately to our needs. But acknowledging that most of us are "deviants" means recognizing that the distinction between "traditional' " and "alternative" families no longer has meaning.

Part II

Postmodernism and the Problem of Connection

Social Criticism Without Philosophy: An Encounter Between Feminism and Postmodernism

with Nancy Fraser

eminism and postmodernism have emerged as two of the most important political-cultural currents of the last decade. So far, however, they have kept an uneasy distance from one another. Indeed, so great has been their mutual wariness that there have been remarkably few extended discussions of the relations between them.[1]

Initial reticences aside, there are good reasons for exploring the relations between feminism and postmodernism. Both have offered deep and far-reaching criticisms of the institution of philosophy. Both have elaborated critical perspectives on the relationship of philosophy to the larger culture. Most central to the concerns of this essay, both have sought to develop new paradigms of social criticism that do not rely on traditional philosophical underpinnings. Other differences notwithstanding, one could say that during the last decade feminists and postmodernists have worked independently on a common nexus of problems: they have tried to rethink the relationship between philosophy and social criticism to develop paradigms of criticism without philosophy.

On the other hand, the two tendencies have proceeded from opposite directions. Postmodernists have focused primarily on the philosophy side of the problem. They have begun by elaborating antifoundational metaphilosophical perspectives and from there have drawn conclusions about the shape and the character of social criticism. For feminists, however, the question of philosophy has always been subordinate to an interest in social criticism. Consequently, they have begun by developing critical political perspectives and from there have drawn conclusions about the status of philosophy. As a result of this difference in emphasis and direction, the two tendencies have ended up with complementary strengths and weaknesses. Postmodernists offer sophisticated and persuasive criticisms of foundationalism and essentialism, but their conceptions of social criticism tend to be anemic. Feminists offer robust conceptions of social criticism, but they tend at times to lapse into foundationalism and essentialism.

Thus, each of the two perspectives suggests some important criticisms of the other. A postmodernist reflection on feminist theory reveals disabling vestiges of essentialism, whereas a feminist reflection on postmodernism reveals androcentrism and political naivete.

It follows that an encounter between feminism and postmodernism will initially be a trading of criticisms; but there is no reason to suppose that this is where matters must end. In fact, each of these tendencies has much to learn from the other; each is in possession of valuable resources that can help to remedy the deficiencies of the other. Thus, the ultimate stake of an encounter between feminism and postmodernism is the prospect of a perspective that integrates their respective strengths while eliminating their respective weaknesses. It is the prospect of a postmodernist feminism.

In what follows, we aim to contribute to the development of such a perspective by staging the initial, critical phase of the encounter. In the first section, we examine the ways in which one exemplary postmodernist, Jean-François Lyotard, has sought to derive new paradigms of social criticism from a critique of the institution of philosophy. We argue that the conception of social criticism so derived is too restricted to permit an adequate critical grasp of gender dominance and subordination. We identify some internal tensions in Lyotard's arguments, and we suggest some alternative formulations that could allow for more robust forms of criticism without sacrificing the commitment to antifoundationalism. In the second section, we examine some representative genres of feminist social criticism. We argue that in many cases feminist critics continue tacitly to rely on the sorts of philosophical underpinnings that their own commitments, like those of the postmodernists, ought in principle to rule out. We identify some points at which such underpinnings could be abandoned without any sacrifice of social-critical force. Finally, in a brief conclusion, we consider the prospects for a postmodernist feminism. We discuss some requirements that constrain the development of such a perspective, and we identify some pertinent conceptual resources and critical strategies.

Postmodernism

Postmodernists seek, *inter alia,* to develop conceptions of social criticism that do not rely on traditional philosophical underpinnings. The typical starting point for their efforts is a reflection on the condition of philosophy today. Writers such as Richard Rorty and Lyotard begin by arguing that Philosophy with a capital P is no longer a viable or credible enterprise. They go on to claim that philosophy and, by extension, theory in general can no longer function to *ground* politics and social criticism. With the demise of foundationalism comes the demise of the view that casts philosophy in the role of *founding* discourse vis-à-vis social criticism. That "modern" conception must give way to a new "postmodern" one in which criticism floats free of any universalist theoretical ground. No longer anchored philosophically, the very shape or character of social criticism changes; it becomes more pragmatic, ad hoc, contextual, and local. With this change comes a corresponding change in the social role and political function of intellectuals.

Thus, in the postmodern reflection on the relationship between philosophy and social criticism, the term "philosophy" undergoes an explicit devaluation; it is cut down to size if not eliminated altogether. Yet, even as this devaluation is argued explicitly, the term "philosophy" retains an implicit structural privilege. It is the changed condition of philosophy that determines the changed character of social criticism and of engaged intellectual practice. In the new postmodern equation, then, philosophy is the independent variable whereas social criticism and political practice are dependent variables. The view of theory that emerges is not determined by considering the needs of contemporary criticism and engagement. It is determined, rather, by considering the contemporary status of philosophy. This way of proceeding has important consequences, not all of which are positive. Among the results is a certain underestimation and premature foreclosing of possibilities for social criticism and engaged intellectual practice. This limitation of postmodern thought will be apparent when we consider its results in the light of the needs of contemporary feminist theory and practice.

Let us consider as an example the postmodernism of Lyotard because it is genuinely exemplary of the larger tendency. Lyotard is one of the few social thinkers widely considered postmodern who actually uses the term; indeed, it was he who introduced it into current discussions of philosophy, politics, society, and social theory. His book *The Postmodern Condition* has become the *locus classicus* for contemporary debates, and it reflects in an especially acute form the characteristic concerns and tensions of the movement.[2]

For Lyotard, postmodernism designates a general condition of contemporary western civilization. The postmodern condition is one in which "grand narratives of legitimation" are no longer credible. By "grand narratives," he means overarching philosophies of history, such as the Enlightenment story of the gradual but steady progress of reason and freedom, Hegel's dialectic of Spirit coming to know itself, and, most important, Marx's drama of the forward march of human productive capacities via class conflict culminating in proletarian revolution. For Lyotard, these metanarratives instantiate a specifically modern approach to the problem of legitimation. Each situates first-order discursive practices of inquiry and politics within a broader totalizing metadiscourse that legitimates them. The metadiscourse narrates a story about the whole of human history that purports to guarantee that the pragmatics of the modern sciences and of modern political processes—the norms and the rules that govern these practices, determining what counts as a warranted move within them—are themselves legitimate. The story guarantees that some sciences and some politics have the *right* pragmatics and so are the *right* practices.

We should not be misled by Lyotard's focus on narrative philosophies of history. In his conception of legitimating metanarrative, the stress properly belongs on the *meta* and not on the *narrative,* for what most interests Lyotard about the Enlightenment, Hegelian, and Marxist stories is what they share with other nonnarrative forms of philosophy. Like ahistorical epistemologies and moral theories, they aim to show that specific first-order discursive practices are well formed and capable of yielding true and just results. "True" and "just" here mean something more than results reached by adhering scrupulously to the constitutive rules of some given scientific and political games. They mean, rather, results that correspond to Truth and Justice as they really are in themselves independent of contingent, historical social practices. Thus, in Lyotard's view, a metanarrative is *meta* in a very strong sense. It purports to be a privileged discourse capable of situating, characterizing, and evaluating all other discourses but not itself to be infected by the historicity and contingency that render first-order discourses potentially distorted and in need of legitimation.

In *The Postmodern Condition,* Lyotard argues that metanarratives, whether philosophies of history or nonnarrative foundational philosophies, are merely modern and dépassé. We can no longer believe, he claims, in the availability of a privileged metadiscourse capable of capturing once and for all the truth of every first-order discourse. The claim to *meta* status does not stand up. A so-called metadiscourse is in fact simply one more discourse among others. It follows for Lyotard that legitimation, both epistemic and political, can no longer reside in philosophical metanarratives. Where, then, he asks, does legitimation reside in the postmodern era?

Much of *The Postmodern Condition* is devoted to sketching an answer to this question. The answer, in brief, is that in the postmodern era legitimation becomes plural, local, and immanent. In this era, there will necessarily be many discourses of legitimation dispersed among the plurality of first-order discursive practices. For example, scientists no longer look to prescriptive philosophies of science to warrant their procedures of inquiry. Rather, they themselves problematize, modify, and warrant the constitutive norms of their own practice even as they engage in it. Instead of hovering above, legitimation descends to the level of practice and becomes immanent in it. There are no special tribunals set apart from the sites where inquiry is practiced. Rather, practitioners assume responsibility for legitimizing their own practice.

Lyotard intimates that something similar is or should be happening with respect to political legitimation. We cannot have and do not need a single, overarching theory of justice. What is required, rather, is a "justice of multiplicities."[3] What Lyotard means by this phrase is not wholly clear. On one level, he can be read as offering a normative vision in which the good society consists in a decentralized plurality of democratic, self-managing groups and institutions whose members problematize the norms of their practice and take responsibility for modifying them as situations require. But, paradoxically, on another level, he can be read as ruling out the sort of larger-scale, normative political theorizing that from a modern perspective at least, would be required to legitimate such a vision. In any case, his justice of multiplicities conception precludes one familiar, and arguably essential, genre of political theory: identification and critique of macrostructures of inequality and injustice that cut across the boundaries separating relatively discrete practices and institutions. There is no place in Lyotard's universe for critique of pervasive axes of stratification, for critique of broad-based relations of dominance and subordination along lines such as gender, race, and class.

Lyotard's suspicion of the large extends to historical narrative and social theory as well. Here, his chief target is Marxism, the one metanarrative in France with enough lingering credibility to be worth arguing against. The problem with Marxism, in his view, is twofold. On the one hand, the Marxist story is too big because it spans virtually the whole of human history. On the other hand, the Marxist story is too theoretical because it relies on a *theory* of social practice and social relations that claims to *explain* historical change. At one level, Lyotard simply rejects the specifics of this theory. He claims that the Marxist conception of practice as production occludes the diversity and plurality of human practices and that the Marxist conception of capitalist society as a totality traversed by one major division and contradiction occludes the diversity and plurality of contemporary societal differences and oppositions. Lyotard does not, however, conclude that such deficiencies can and should be remedied by a better social theory. Rather, he rejects the project of social theory *tout court*.

Once again, Lyotard's position is ambiguous because his rejection of social theory depends on its own theoretical perspective of sorts. He offers a postmodern conception of sociality and social identity, a conception of what he calls "the social bond." What holds a society together, he claims, is not a common consciousness or institutional substructure. Rather, the social bond is a weave of criss-crossing threads of discursive practices, of which no single one runs continuously throughout the whole. Individuals are the nodes or posts at which such practices intersect and so they participate in many practices simultaneously. It follows that social identities are complex and heterogeneous. They cannot be mapped onto one another nor onto the social totality. Indeed, strictly speaking, there is no social totality and *a fortiori* no possibility of a totalizing social theory.

Thus, Lyotard insists that the field of the social is heterogeneous and non-totalizable. As a result, he rules out the sort of critical social theory that employs general categories, such as gender, race, and class. From his perspective, such categories are too reductive of the complexity of social identities to be useful. There is apparently nothing to be gained, in his view, by situating an account of the fluidity and diversity of discursive practices in the context of a critical analysis of large-scale institutions and social structures.

Thus, Lyotard's postmodern conception of criticism without philosophy rules out several recognizable genres of social criticism. From the premise that criticism cannot be grounded by a foundationalist philosophical metanarrative, he infers the illegitimacy of large historical stories, normative theories of justice, and social-theoretical accounts of macrostructures that institutionalize inequality. What, then, *does* postmodern social criticism look like?

Lyotard tries to fashion some new genres of social criticism from the discursive resources that remain. Chief among these is smallish, localized narrative. He seeks to vindicate such narrative against both modern, totalizing metanarrative and the scientism that is hostile to all narrative. One genre of postmodern social criticism, then, consists in relatively discrete, local stories about the emergence, transformation, and disappearance of various discursive practices treated in isolation from one another. Such stories might resemble those told by Michel Foucault, although without the attempts to discern larger synchronic patterns and connections that Foucault sometimes made.[4] Like Michael Walzer, Lyotard evidently assumes that practitioners would narrate such stories when seeking to persuade one another to modify the pragmatics or constitutive norms of their practice.[5]

This genre of social criticism is not the whole postmodern story, however, for it casts critique as strictly local, ad hoc, and ameliorative, thus supposing a political diagnosis according to which there are no large-scale systemic problems that resist local, ad hoc, ameliorative initiatives. Yet, Lyotard recognizes that postmodern society does contain at least one unfavorable structural tendency that requires a more coordinated response. This tendency is to universalize instrumental reason, to subject all discursive practices indiscriminately to the single criterion of efficiency, or "performativity." In Lyotard's view, this tendency threatens the autonomy and integrity of science and politics because these practices are not properly subordinated to performative standards. It would pervert and distort them, thereby destroying the diversity of discursive forms.

Thus, even as he argues explicitly against it, Lyotard posits the need for a genre of social criticism that transcends local mininarrative. Despite his strictures against large, totalizing stories, he narrates a fairly tall tale about a large-scale social trend. Moreover, the logic of this story, and of the genre of criticism to which it belongs, calls for judgments that are not strictly practice-immanent. Lyotard's story presupposes the legitimacy and integrity of the scientific and political practices allegedly threatened by performativity. It supposes that one can distinguish changes or developments that are *internal* to these practices from externally induced distortions. But this drives Lyotard to make normative judgments about the value and character of the threatened practices. These judgments are not strictly immanent in the practices judged. Rather, they are metapractical.

Thus, Lyotard's view of postmodern social criticism is neither entirely self-consistent nor entirely persuasive. He goes too quickly from the premise that Philosophy cannot ground social criticism to the conclusion that criticism itself must be local ad hoc, and nontheoretical. As a result, he throws out the baby of large historical narrative with the bath water of philosophical meta-narrative and the baby of social-theoretical analysis of large-scale inequalities with the bath water of reductive Marxist class theory. Moreover, these allegedly illegitimate babies do not in fact remain excluded. They return like the repressed within the very genres of postmodern social criticism with which Lyotard intends to replace them.

We began this discussion by noting that postmodernists orient their reflections on the character of postmodern social criticism by the falling star of foundationalist philosophy. They posit that, with philosophy no longer able credibly to ground social criticism, criticism itself must be local, ad hoc, and nontheoretical. Thus, from the critique of foundationalism, they infer the illegitimacy of several genres of social criticism. For Lyotard, the illegitimate genres include large-scale historical narrative and social-theoretical analyses of pervasive relations of dominance and subordination.[6]

Suppose, however, that one were to choose another starting point for reflecting on postfoundational social criticism. Suppose that one began not with the condition of Philosophy but with the nature of the social object that one wanted to criticize. Suppose, further, that one defined that object as the subordination of women to and by men. Then, we submit, it would be apparent that many of the genres rejected by postmodernists are necessary for social criticism, as a phenomenon as pervasive and multifaceted as male dominance simply cannot be adequately grasped with the meager critical resources to which they would limit us. On the contrary, effective criticism of this phenomenon requires an array of different methods and genres. It requires at minimum large narratives about changes in social organization and ideology, empirical and social-theoretical analyses of macrostructures and institutions, interactionist analyses of the micropolitics of everyday life, critical-hermeneutical and institutional analyses of cultural production, historically and culturally specific sociologies of gender, and so forth. The list could go on.

Clearly, not all of these approaches are local and nontheoretical, but all are nonetheless essential to feminist social criticism. Moreover, all can in principle be conceived in ways that do not take us back to foundationalism, even though, as we argue in the next section, many feminists have not wholly succeeded in avoiding that trap.

Feminism

Feminists, like postmodernists, have sought to develop new paradigms of social criticism that do not rely on traditional philosophical underpinnings. They have criticized modern foundationalist epistemologies and moral and political theories, exposing the contingent, partial, and historically situated character of what has passed in the mainstream for necessary, universal, and ahistorical truths. They have called into question the dominant philosophical project of seeking objectivity in the guise of a "god's eye view" that transcends any situation or perspective.[7]

If, however, postmodernists have been drawn to such views by a concern with the status of philosophy, feminists have been led to them by the demands of political practice. This practical interest has saved feminist theory from many of the mistakes of postmodernism: women whose theorizing was to serve the struggle against sexism were not about to abandon powerful political tools merely as a result of intramural debates in professional philosophy.

Yet, even as the imperatives of political practice have saved feminist theory from one set of difficulties, they have tended at times to incline it toward another. Practical imperatives have led some feminists to adopt modes of theorizing that resemble the sorts of philosophical metanarrative rightly criticized by postmodernists. To be sure, the feminist theories that we have in mind here are not pure metanarratives; they are not ahistorical normative theories about the transcultural nature of rationality or justice. Rather, they are very large social theories—theories of history, society, culture, and psychology that claim, for example, to identify causes and constitutive features of sexism that operate cross-culturally. Thus, these social theories purport to be empirical rather than philosophical; but, as we show, they are actually quasi-metanarratives. They tacitly presuppose some commonly held but unwarranted and essentialist assumptions about the nature of humans and the conditions for social life. In addition, they assume methods and concepts that are uninflected by temporality or historicity and that therefore function *de facto* as permanent, neutral matrices for inquiry. Such theories then, share some of the essentialist and ahistorical features of metanarratives: they are insufficiently attentive to historical and cultural diversity, and they falsely universalize features of the theorist's own era, society, culture, class, sexual orientation, and ethnic or racial group.

On the other hand, the practical exigencies inclining feminists to produce quasi-metanarratives have by no means held undisputed sway. Rather, they have had to coexist, often uneasily, with counterexigencies that have worked to opposite effect—for example, political pressures to acknowledge differences among women. In general, then, the recent history of feminist social theory reflects a tug of war between forces that have encouraged and forces that have discouraged metanarrative-like modes of theorizing. We illustrate this dynamic by looking at a few important turning points in this history.

When in the 1960s women in the New Left began to extend prior talk about women's rights into the more encompassing discussion of women's liberation, they encountered the fear and hostility of their male comrades and the use of Marxist political theory as a support for these reactions. Many men of the New Left argued that gender issues were secondary because they were subsumable under more basic modes of oppression—namely, class and race.

In response to this practical-political problem, radical feminists such as Shulamith Firestone resorted to an ingenious tactical maneuver: Firestone invoked biological differences between women and men to explain sexism. This strategy enabled her to turn the tables on her Marxist comrades by claiming that gender conflict was the most basic form of human conflict and the source of all other forms, including class conflict.[8] Firestone drew on the pervasive tendency within modern culture to locate the roots of gender differences in biology. Her coup was to use biologism to establish the primacy of the struggle against male domination rather than to justify acquiescence to it.

The trick, of course, is problematic from a postmodernist perspective in that appeals to biology to explain social phenomena are essentialist and monocausal. They are essentialist in so far as they project onto all women and men qualities that develop under historically specific social conditions. They are monocausal to the extent that they look to one set of characteristics, such as women's physiology or men's hormones, to explain women's oppression in all cultures. These problems are only compounded when appeals to biology are used in conjunction with the dubious claim that women's oppression is the cause of all other forms of oppression.

Moreover, as Marxists and feminist anthropologists began insisting in the early 1970s, appeals to biology do not allow us to understand the enormous diversity of forms that both gender and sexism assume in different cultures. In fact, it was not long before most feminist social theorists came to appreciate that accounting for the diversity of the forms of sexism was as important as accounting for its depth and autonomy. Gayle Rubin aptly described this dual requirement as the need to formulate theory that could account for the oppression of women in its "endless variety and monotonous similarity."9 How were feminists to develop a social theory adequate to both demands?

One approach that seemed promising was suggested by Michelle Zimbalist Rosaldo and other contributors in the influential 1974 anthropology collection, *Woman, Culture, and Society.* They argued that common to all known societies was some type of separation between a domestic sphere and a public sphere, the former associated with women and the latter with men. Because in most societies to date women have spent a good part of their lives bearing and raising children, their lives have been more bound to the domestic sphere. Men, in contrast, have had both the time and the mobility to engage in out-of-the-home activities that generate political structures. Thus, as Rosaldo argued, although in many societies women possess some or even a great deal of power, women's power is always viewed as illegitimate, disruptive, and without authority.10

This approach seemed to allow for both diversity and ubiquity in the manifestations of sexism. A very general identification of women with the domestic and of men with the extradomestic could accommodate a great deal of cultural variation in both social structures and gender roles. At the same time, it could make comprehensible the apparent ubiquity of the assumption of women's inferiority above and beyond such variation. This hypothesis was also compatible with the idea that the extent of women's oppression differed in different societies. It could explain such differences by correlating the extent of gender inequality in a society with the extent and rigidity of the separation between its domestic and public spheres. In short, the domestic/public theorists seemed to have generated an explanation capable of satisfying a variety of conflicting demands.

This explanation, however, turned out to be problematic in ways reminiscent of Firestone's account. Although the theory focused on differences between men's and women's spheres of activity rather than on differences between men's and women's biology, it was essentialist and monocausal nonetheless. It posited the existence of a domestic sphere in all societies and thereby assumed that women's activities were basically similar in content and significance across cultures. (An analogous assumption about men's activities lay behind the postulation of a universal public sphere.) In effect, the theory falsely generalized to all societies an historically specific conjunction of properties: women's responsibility for early child rearing, women's tendency to spend more time in the geographic space of the home, women's lesser participation in the affairs of the community, a cultural ascription of triviality to domestic work, and a cultural ascription of inferiority to women. The theory thus failed to appreciate that, although each individual property may be true of many societies, the conjunction is not true of most.[11]

One source of difficulty in these early feminist social theories was the presumption of an overly grandiose and totalizing conception of theory. Theory was understood as the search for the one key factor that would explain sexism cross-culturally and illuminate all of social life. In this sense, to theorize was by definition to produce a quasi-metanarrative.

Since the late 1970s, feminist social theorists have largely ceased speaking of biological determinants or a cross-cultural domestic/public separation. Many, moreover, have given up the assumption of monocausality. Nevertheless, some feminist social theorists have continued implicitly to suppose a quasi-metanarrative conception of theory. They have continued to theorize in terms of a putatively unitary, primary, culturally universal type of activity associated with women, generally an activity conceived as domestic and located in the family.

One influential example is the analysis of mothering developed by Nancy Chodorow. Intending to explain the internal, psychological dynamics that have led many women willingly to reproduce social divisions associated with female inferiority, Chodorow posited a cross-cultural activity, mothering, as the relevant object of investigation. Her questions thus became, "How is mothering as a female-associated activity reproduced over time?" and "How does mothering produce a new generation of women with the psychological inclination to mother and a new generation of men not so inclined?" The answer she offered to these questions was in terms of gender identity: female mothering produces women whose deep sense of self is relational and men whose deep sense of self is not.[12]

Chodorow's theory has struck many feminists as a persuasive account of some apparently observable psychic differences between men and women, yet the theory has clear metanarrative overtones. It posits the existence of a single activity, mothering, that, although differing in specifics in different societies, nevertheless constitutes enough of a natural kind to warrant one label. It stipulates that this basically unitary activity gives rise to two distinct sorts of deep selves, one relatively common across cultures to women and the other relatively common across cultures to men. It claims that the difference thus generated between feminine and masculine gender identity causes a variety of supposedly cross-cultural social phenomena, including the continuation of female mothering, male contempt for women, and problems in heterosexual relationships.

From a postmodern perspective, all of these assumptions are problematic because they are essentialist. But the second one, concerning gender identity, warrants special scrutiny because of its political implications. Consider that Chodorow's use of the notion of gender identity presupposes three major premises. One is the psychoanalytic premise that everyone has a deep sense of self that is constituted in early childhood through one's interactions with one's primary parent and that remains relatively constant thereafter. Another is the premise that this deep self differs significantly between men and women but is roughly similar among women, on the one hand, and among men, on the other hand, both across cultures and within cultures across lines of class, race, and ethnicity. The third premise is that this deep self colors everything that one does; there are no actions, however trivial, that do not bear traces of one's masculine or feminine gender identity.

One can appreciate the political exigencies that made this conjunction of premises attractive. It gave scholarly substance to the idea of the pervasiveness of sexism. If masculinity and femininity constitute our basic and ever-present sense of self, then it is not surprising that the manifestations of sexism are systemic. Moreover, many feminists had already sensed that the concept of sex-role socialization, an idea Chodorow explicitly criticized, ignored the depth and intractability of male dominance. By implying that measures such as changing images in school textbooks or allowing boys to play with dolls would be sufficient to bring about equality between the sexes, this concept seemed to trivialize and coopt the message of feminism. Finally, Chodorow's depth-psychological approach gave a scholarly sanction to the idea of sisterhood. It seemed to legitimate the claim that the ties that bind women are deep and substantively based.

We have no wish to quarrel with the claim of the depth and pervasiveness of sexism nor with the idea of sisterhood, but we do challenge Chodorow's way of legitimating them. The idea of a cross-cultural, deep sense of self specified differently for women and men becomes problematic when given specific content. Chodorow states that women everywhere differ from men in their greater concern with "relational interaction," but what does she mean by this term? Certainly not any and every kind of human interaction because men have often been more concerned than women with some kinds of interactions, such as those pertaining to the aggrandizement of power and wealth. Of course, it is true that many women in modern western societies have been expected to exhibit strong concern with those types of interactions associated with intimacy, friendship, and love, interactions that dominate one meaning of the late–twentieth-century concept of relationship. Surely, however, this meaning presupposes a notion of private life specific to modern western societies of the last two centuries. Is it possible that Chodorow's theory rests on an equivocation on the term "relationship"[13]

Equally troubling are the aporias that this theory generates for political practice. Although gender identity gives substance to the idea of sisterhood, it does so at the cost of repressing differences among sisters. Although the theory allows for some differences among women of different classes, races, sexual orientations, and ethnic groups, it construes these differences as subsidiary to more basic similarities. But it is precisely as a consequence of the request to understand such differences as secondary that many women have denied an allegiance to feminism.

We have considered at length Chodorow's claims because of the great influence that her work has enjoyed, but she is not the only recent feminist social theorist who has constructed a quasi-metanarrative around a putatively cross-cultural, female-associated activity. On the contrary, theorists such as Ann Ferguson, Nancy Folbre, Nancy Hartsock, and Catharine MacKinnon have built similar theories around notions of sex-affective production, reproduction, and sexuality, respectively.[14] Each claims to have identified a basic kind of human practice found in all societies that has cross-cultural explanatory power. In each case, the practice in question is associated with a biological or quasi-biological need and is construed as functionally necessary to the reproduction of society. It is not the sort of thing, then, whose historical origins need be investigated.

The difficulty here is that categories such as sexuality, mothering, reproduction, and sex-affective production group together phenomena that are not necessarily conjoined in all societies while they separate from one another phenomena that are not necessarily separated. It is, in fact, doubtful whether these categories have any determinate cross-cultural content. Thus, for a theorist to use such categories to construct a universalistic social theory is to risk projecting the socially dominant conjunctions and dispersions of her own society onto others, thereby distorting important features of both. Social theorists would do better first to construct genealogies of the *categories* of sexuality, reproduction, and mothering before assuming their universal significance.

Since around 1980, many feminist scholars have abandoned the project of grand social theory. They have stopped looking for *the* causes of sexism and have turned to more concrete inquiry with more limited aims. One reason for this shift has been the growing legitimacy of feminist scholarship. The institutionalization of women's studies in the United States has meant a dramatic increase in the size of the community of feminist inquirers, a much greater division of scholarly labor, and a large and growing fund of concrete information. As a result, feminist scholars have come to regard their enterprise more collectively, more like a puzzle whose various pieces are being filled in by many different people than like a construction to be completed by a single, grand, theoretical stroke. In short, feminist scholarship has attained its maturity.

Even in this phase, however, traces of youthful quasi-metanarratives remain. Some theorists who have ceased looking for the causes of sexism still rely on essentialist categories, such as gender identity. Dependence on these categories is especially true of those scholars who have sought to develop gyno-centric alternatives to mainstream androcentric perspectives but who have not fully abandoned the universalist pretensions of the latter.

Consider, as an example, the work of Carol Gilligan. Unlike most of the theorists we have considered so far, Gilligan has not sought to explain the origins or nature of cross-cultural sexism. Rather, she set herself the more limited task of exposing and redressing androcentric bias in the model of moral development of psychologist Lawrence Kohlberg. Thus she argued that it is illegitimate to evaluate the moral development of women and girls by reference to a standard drawn exclusively from the experience of men and boys. She proposed to examine women's moral discourse on its own terms to uncover its immanent standards of adequacy.[15]

Gilligan's work has been appropriately regarded as important and innovative. It challenged mainstream psychology's persistent occlusion of women's lives and experiences and its insistent but false claims of universality. Yet, in so far as Gilligan's challenge involved the construction of an alternative feminine model of moral development, her position was ambiguous. On the one hand, by providing a counterexample to Kohlberg's model, she cast doubt on the possibility of any single, universalist developmental schema. On the other hand, by constructing a female countermodel, she invited the same charge of false generalization that she had herself raised against Kohlberg, although now from other perspectives, such as class, sexual orientation, race, and ethnicity. Gilligan's disclaimers notwithstanding,[16] to the extent that she described women's moral development in terms of *a* different voice; to the extent that she did not specify which women, under which specific historical circumstances have spoken with the voice in question; and to the extent that she grounded her analysis in the explicitly cross-cultural framework of Nancy Chodorow, her model remained essentialist. It perpetuated in a newer, more localized fashion traces of previous more grandiose quasi-metanarratives.

Thus, vestiges of essentialism have continued to plague feminist scholarship, despite the decline of grand theorizing. In many cases, including Gilligan's, the influence of this mode of theorizing represents the continuing subterranean effects of the very mainstream modes of thought and inquiry from which feminists have wanted to break.

The practice of feminist politics in the 1980s has, however, generated a new set of pressures that have worked against metanarratives. In recent years, poor and working-class women, women of color, and lesbians have finally won a wider hearing for their objections to feminist theories that fail to illuminate their lives and address their problems. They have exposed the earlier quasi-metanarratives, with their assumptions of universal female dependence and confinement to the domestic sphere, as false extrapolations from the experience of the white, middle-class, heterosexual women who dominated the beginnings of second-wave feminism. For example, writers such as bell hooks, Gloria Joseph, Audre Lord, Maria Lugones, and Elizabeth Spelman have unmasked the implicit reference to white Anglo women in many classic feminist texts. Likewise, Adrienne Rich and Marilyn Frye have exposed the heterosexist bias of much mainstream feminist theory.[17] Thus, as the class, sexual, racial, and ethnic awareness of the movement has altered, so has the preferred conception of theory. It has become clear that quasi-metanarratives hamper rather than promote sisterhood because they elide differences among women and among the forms of sexism to which different women are differentially subject. Likewise, it is increasingly apparent that such theories hinder alliances with other progressive movements because they tend to occlude axes of domination other than gender. In sum, there is growing interest among feminists in modes of theorizing that are attentive to differences and to cultural and historical specificity.

In general, then, feminist scholarship of the 1980s evinces some conflicting tendencies. On the one hand, as scholarship has become more localized, issue oriented, and explicitly fallibilistic, interest in grand social theories has waned. On the other hand, essentialist vestiges persist in the continued use of ahistorical categories such as gender identity without reflection as to how, when, and why such categories originated and were modified over time. This tension is symptomatically expressed in the current fascination, on the part of U.S. feminists, with French psychoanalytic feminisms: the latter propositionally decry essentialism even as they performatively enact it.[18] More generally, feminist scholarship has remained insufficiently attentive to the *theoretical* prerequisites of dealing with diversity, despite widespread commitment to accepting it politically.

By criticizing lingering essentialism in contemporary feminist theory, we hope to encourage such theory to become more consistently postmodern. This is not, however, to recommend merely any form of postmodernism. On the contrary, as we have shown, the version developed by Jean-François Lyotard offers a weak and inadequate conception of social criticism without philosophy. It rules out genres of criticism, such as large historical narrative and historically situated social theory, which feminists rightly regard as indispensable. But it does not follow from Lyotard's shortcomings that criticism without philosophy is in principle incompatible with criticism with social force. Rather, as we argue next, a robust postmodern-feminist paradigm of social criticism without philosophy is possible.

Toward a Postmodern Feminism

How can we combine a postmodernist incredulity toward metanarratives with the social-critical power of feminism? How can we conceive a version of criticism without philosophy that is robust enough to handle the tough job of analyzing sexism in all its endless variety and monotonous similarity?

A first step is to recognize, contra Lyotard, that postmodern critique need forswear neither large historical narratives nor analyses of societal macrostructures. This point is important for feminists because sexism has a long history and is deeply and pervasively embedded in contemporary societies. Thus, postmodern feminists need not abandon the large theoretical tools needed to address large political problems. There is nothing self-contradictory in the idea of a postmodern theory.

If postmodern-feminist critique must remain theoretical, however, not just any kind of theory will do. Rather, theory would be explicitly historical, attuned to the cultural specificity of different societies and periods and to that of different groups within societies and periods. Thus, the categories of postmodern-feminist theory would be inflected by temporality, with historically specific institutional categories such as the modern, restricted, male-headed, nuclear family taking precedence over ahistorical, functionalist categories like reproduction and mothering. Where categories of the latter sort were not eschewed altogether, they would be genealogized—in other words, framed by a historical narrative and rendered temporally and culturally specific.

Moreover, postmodern-feminist theory would be nonuniversalist. When its focus became cross-cultural or transepochal, its mode of attention would be comparativist rather than universalizing, attuned to changes and contrasts instead of to covering laws. Finally, postmodern-feminist theory would dispense with the idea of a subject of history. It would replace unitary notions of woman and feminine gender identity with plural and complexly constructed conceptions of social identity, treating gender as one relevant strand among others, attending also to class, race, ethnicity, age, and sexual orientation.

In general, postmodern-feminist theory would be pragmatic and fallibilistic. It would tailor its methods and categories to the specific task at hand, using multiple categories when appropriate and forswearing the metaphysical comfort of a single feminist method or feminist epistemology. In short, this theory would look more like a tapestry composed of threads of many different hues than one woven in a single color.

The most important advantage of this sort of theory would be its usefulness for contemporary feminist political practice. Such practice is increasingly a matter of alliances rather than one of unity around a universally shared interest or identity. It recognizes that the diversity of women's needs and experiences means that no single solution, on issues such as child care, Social Security, and housing, can be adequate for all. Thus, the underlying premise of this practice is that, although some women share some common interests and face some common enemies, such commonalities are by no means universal; rather, they are interlaced with differences and even conflicts. This practice, then, is made up of a patchwork of overlapping alliances, not one circumscribable by an essential definition. One might best speak of it in the plural as the practice of feminisms. In a sense, this practice is in advance of much contemporary feminist theory. It is already implicitly postmodern. It would find its most appropriate and useful theoretical expression in a postmodern-feminist form of critical inquiry. Such inquiry would be the theoretical counterpart of a broader, richer, more complex, and multilayered feminist solidarity, the sort of solidarity that is essential for overcoming the oppression of women in its "endless variety and monotonous similarity."

CHAPTER SEVEN

Bringing It All Back Home: Reason in the Twilight of Foundationalism

Two models of reason dominate the contemporary philosophical landscape. An older model, challenged in many respects, still exerts influence. In this model, reason is understood as adherence to a set of principles—of logic, of objectivity, of scientific method, and of discursive justification—which, when followed, produce the best understanding of nature and ourselves of which we are capable or the best social order we can construct. Although "foundationalism . . ."—in other words, belief in the possibility of ultimate grounding claims or rules—has become highly unpopular, remnants of it linger in the idea of principles of judgment or discourse whose justification is believed to transcend reference to a limited context. Such principles, even if they do not provide us with means for definitively establishing the truth of any claim or the rightness of any act, nevertheless are viewed as providing us with our only hope of approaching such claims. The justification of such principles is seen as transcending any purpose more specific than that of "ascertaining the true or the right."

Against this older model stands a more recent perspective, associated with the philosophical position of pragmatism which rejects the idea of reason as adherence to a limited number of context-independent principles. Rather, it describes rationality in terms of a vast variety of ever-changing principles justified by reference to the complex and diverse purposes that humans have toward one another and to the nonhuman world. From the vantage point of this latter perspective, there is reluctance toward specifying such principles in terms that are too sweeping (i.e., in context-independent terms). Thus proponents of this perspective talk about principles of rationality in relation to particular communities. They speak of principles of natural science or of particular disciplines and emphasize the changing nature of such principles as these domains and the purposes underlying them change, but they are suspicious of attempts to elaborate a context-independent principle or set of such principles. To paraphrase the old Hegelian claim against Kant, they worry that any principle that we propose as possibly transcending contexts either will be so "thin" as to disqualify it for the tasks we want it to accomplish, such as providing the means to resolve particular problems or mediate specific conflicts, or, if it is thick enough to accomplish such tasks, it will have an implicit substantive meaning that contravenes its claims to context-independent justification.

I subscribe to the second perspective. In this essay, I advocate for its further acceptance in two ways. First, I show how rejecting the former model does not lead to "irrationality" as is sometimes claimed. The pragmatic model can be elaborated in ways that enable us to retain many of the norms of rationality that proponents of the former model worry about us losing. In short, the choice is not between a context-independent model of reason or no model at all. Second, I explore the implications of fully overthrowing the older model of reason in relation to the issue of relativism. Although fears of relativism motivate many people's allegiance to this model, such fears can be shown to be a byproduct of adherence to aspects of the model itself. When the older model is fully rejected, the issue of relativism appears in a very different and much less frightening light.

Reason Brought Home

My first major claim is that arguing against the idea of context-independent principles of rationality does not mean rejecting the idea of rationality as a means for differentiating types of judgment or argument. Thus, when those who disagree with my position say, "But, in making your argument you are yourself relying on a distinction between the reasonable and the unreasonable and on some criteria to make it," my response is, "Of course I am." That I rely on such a distinction and call on specific criteria to make it does not refute the idea that there may be contexts in which the set of criteria on which I am relying to convince the reader of the "reasonableness" of this very argument becomes open to challenge. Thus, my rejection of the idea of context-independent criteria of rationality is not a rejection of rationality per se but of a view of it as based on a single set of criteria that are defensible across contexts.

Since its first eloquent articulation by Kant, the model of rationality that I am critiquing has been put forth in a variety of versions, some closer to Kant's original formulation than others. Jürgen Habermas has articulated a powerful twentieth-century version that departs from Kant's model in certain key respects; most important, Habermas elaborates criteria of rationality in terms of discourse and understands such criteria as applying only to the procedures by which substantive claims are justified. A version by Seyla Benhabib moves even further away from the Kantian formulation. With respect to moral argument, she rejects the idea of transcendental justification. She articulates this rejection in the following:

> As opposed to Apel's strategy of *Letztbegründung* and Habermas's strategy of a "weak transcendental argument," based on the rational reconstruction of competencies, I would like to plead for a "historically self-conscious universalism." The principles of universal respect and egalitarian reciprocity are our philosophical clarification of the constituents of the moral point of view from *within* the normative hermeneutic horizon of modernity. These principles are neither the *only allowable* interpretation of the formal constituents of the competency of postconventional moral actors nor are they unequivocal transcendental presuppositions which every rational agent, upon deep reflection, must concede to. These principles are arrived at by a process of "reflective equilibrium," in Rawlsian terms, whereby one, as a philosopher, analyzes, refines and judges culturally defined moral intuitions in light of articulated philosophical principles. What one arrives at the end of such a process of reflective equilibrium is a "thick description" of the moral presuppositions of the cultural horizon of modernity.[1]

In claiming that the principles governing moral argument emerge from within a particular cultural context, Benhabib recognizes that it is conceivable that other communities might interpret "the formal constituents of the competency of postconventional moral actors," differently. Although such a reformulation opens up the way we think about reason in an important respect, the model remains closed in another way. Both in the preceding quotation and in other remarks, Benhabib appears committed to the idea that such principles, even if culturally circumscribed, can be established through philosophical analysis. Such analysis establishes the necessary conditions of moral rationality from within "the cultural horizon of modernity." Thus, while Benhabib rejects transcendental deduction in the strict sense, she adheres to what might be called a type of "cultural deduction," a form of deductive analysis made within the context of a given culture.

Benhabib's approach to the idea of rationality reminds me of how some feminists have approached the idea of "woman." Rejecting antifeminist claims that "woman" is inherently defined by a set of biological features, they recognize that the association of the concept of "woman" with, for example, the possession of a vagina is an historically contingent phenomenon. Thus, they would say that it is only from within certain cultural horizons that "possessing a vagina" defines what "woman" is. I see this kind of approach to "woman" as parallel to Benhabib's move in the above. There has emerged recently within feminism, however, a move toward understanding "woman" in an even more open-ended sense. Supporters of this move admit that "possessing a vagina" has operated as an important criterion for demarcating women from men in many societies with which contemporary scholars are familiar. But they argue that such a criterion intertwines with others, such that even within those societies where possessing a vagina operates as an important criterion for differentiating women from men, sometimes it is the case that people without vaginas, for good reasons, call themselves and/or are called by others "women." Also they claim that we cannot neatly demarcate the contexts in which "possessing a vagina" does serve as an important criterion for defining "woman" from contexts in which it does not. For example, pre–eighteenth-century societies that did not possess the concept of "vagina"—in part because they saw women's physiology on a continuum with rather than in diametrical opposition to men's—certainly understood the physical differences between women and men in ways somewhat similar to post–eighteenth-century societies. There were, however, also differences because of the dissimilarities in underlying theoretical framework.[2]

In short, such feminists are recommending that even within specific cultural contexts, we think of "woman" in Wittgensteinian terms. Thus, as Wittgenstein suggested that we think of the word "game," so are they suggesting that we think of "woman": as defined by a complex and overlapping network of criteria no one of which is necessary to its use.[3] My recommendation is that we think of "rationality" in such terms. This approach does not mean claiming that "rationality" has not had nor ought not to have criteria governing its use, any more than the above reading of "games" or "women" entailed such claims about these terms. With this reading, we can recognize both the existence and usefulness of such criteria as being open-minded or possessing a vagina to differentiate some things that we want to call respectively "rationality" or "women" from other things that we do not want to be called by those names. Problems arise only when the context and purposes of such criteria are lost in the philosophical argument that such criteria define rationality *simpliciter*, even within a specific "cultural horizon."

One way to think of the difference between Benhabib's model of rationality and mine is that my model is more sociological, more concerned with the diverse ways that "rationality" has been employed in past contexts, and more convinced of the potential for disagreement in present contexts. Some words of qualification are in order, however. In suggesting that we think of "rationality" in more sociological terms than does Benhabib, I do not mean that "rationality" should be interpreted to mean only "what the majority says it means." Thomas McCarthy takes issue with what he describes as a "sociological observer's view of justification," which he imputes to Richard Rorty:

> At the same time, however, and without any explicit acknowledgement of the shift in standpoint involved, he [Rorty] insists that whether or not an assertion is warranted is "a sociological matter to be ascertained by observing the reception of S's statements by her peers."[4] But as he himself recognizes, our norms and standards of warranted assertability are not reducible to the reception assertions in fact meet with. They typically turn on principles of evidence and argument appropriate to the domains of inquiry in which assertions arise, and they typically allow for a minority, even a minority of one, being right and the majority, even an overwhelming majority, being wrong. Consequently, Rorty will not find his sociological observer's view of justification to be the content of our engaged participant's understanding of it.[5]

Rorty could respond that McCarthy has not correctly identified the group on which Rorty is focusing his sociological eye, those who are determining the "principles of evidence and argument appropriate to the domains of inquiry in which assertions arise." In other words, Rorty's "sociological standpoint" need not be interpreted as promotion of voting over principled argument; it merely emphasizes that principles themselves need defense. Such defense can only be in light of the diverse purposes underlying the different understandings of rationality proposed by the participants in the debate.

In other words, "rationality," like "woman" and to a certain extent like "game," is a normative term, which means that few of us, as participants in a community in which the term is used, are neutral about its use. Because different uses rest on different assumptions and bring different consequences, philosophical reflection about those assumptions and consequences is important even when one rejects the philosophical enterprise as providing "*the* meaning of a term." Thus, the move toward paying greater attention to historical and social variance in the principles of rationality is intended as a guard against using deductive, even "cultural-deductive," arguments as a means to foreclose conversation about what rationality should mean. To recognize the historical and cultural messiness of concepts such as "woman" and "rationality" is to acknowledge that our moves to stipulate criteria are necessarily bound by purposes that may not be shared by those with whom we disagree. It is to recognize that the philosophical move, when it goes beyond "giving reasons for" and presumes to define through deductive arguments, risks sliding over such differences in purpose. As a consequence, it risks becoming authoritarian.

The danger of authoritarianism becomes more apparent when we turn from the word "rationality" to some of the terms that are used to define it, such as "science" and "philosophy." In the following, Benhabib uses the terms "science" and "philosophy" to locate the domain of "rationality." In this passage, Benhabib is clarifying a particular way of understanding communicative rationality cited by Rorty of Habermas:

> Habermas is, of course, concerned with specific kinds of claims to validity: namely those embedded in the rhetorical discourses of science and philosophy, and the ethical discourses of morality, jurisprudence, and the foundations of constitutional government. To use a Foucauldian terminology, these discourses are governed by the regimes of truth, justice, and democratic legitimacy. As McCarthy puts it, "Habermas's claim is that the idea of uncoerced, reasoned agreement is a pragmatic presupposition of certain types of discursive practice which are central to modern forms of life and to which we have no viable alternative."[6]

But "science" and "philosophy" are terms whose meaning has varied in the past and whose present meanings are themselves the subject of contestation. In the case of science, studies in the history of science have illustrated some of this variation and thus some of the grounds for present argument. For example, whereas some might argue that "attention to the facts of empirical observation" serves as a criterion demarcating the scientific from the nonscientific, Lorraine Daston notes how even "attention to the facts of empirical observation" has had different meanings in different contexts. As she argues, it was only in the mid-seventeenth century that "attention to the facts of empirical observation" came to mean attention to the anomalous fact as opposed to the commonplace fact. It was the latter type of "fact" that earlier natural philosophers, such as Aristotle, deemed important for their use in generating universals.[7] Our study of science is better carried out by examining the complex history of the emergence of such developments, of their similarities and differences with approaches to nature that had existed previously, and of changes in their meaning and importance in diverse activities later called "science" than through thinking of "science" as a closed system, internally consistent and easily separable from the kind of study of nature carried out by someone such as Aristotle.

Attention to the complexity, or messiness, of the criteria historically used to define "science," "philosophy," or "rationality" is useful because it undermines attempts to use tradition as a substitute for argument about why "science," "philosophy," or "rationality" should be defined in particular ways in particular contexts. Like contemporary claims that the "family" has existed as a universal throughout human history, arguments that particular criteria have always—or even within a particular "cultural horizon"—have always constituted the meaning of such activities as "science," "philosophy," or "rationality" serves as a means to avoid justifying the use of such criteria in the face of opposition by those who wish to challenge contemporary hegemonic meanings.

To be sure, arguments about *the* meaning of "rationality," like arguments about *the* meaning of the "family," are typically not only historical but also normative, resting not only on claims that particular criteria range across contexts but that they do so for good reasons. When it is assumed, however, that the "family" or "rationality" is singular in meaning across contexts, so also is it assumed that the kinds of reasons that can be advanced to justify a proposed reading are also singular across contexts. But this assumption obscures awareness that reasons have salience only in relation to purposes and that purposes not only change across contexts but also can be the subject of contestation. Thus, for example, those who argue that the "family" should exclude households in which the adult partners are homosexuals typically not only appeal to history to justify their argument but also assume a constant purpose to the "family," often that of ensuring reproduction of the species. Such arguments preclude discussion around the question of whether the "family" should include other purposes. In other words, in response to the objection that my demand for a more sociological philosophy means that I am arguing for observation over argument, I describe my demand as opening up the space for *more* argument—not only over the criteria that define a word such as "rationality" but also over the purposes that might justify any proposed criteria.

The Specter of Relativism

The preceding position raises, for many, the specter of relativism. Accepting the idea of the context dependence of the principles of judgment or discourse forces recognition that there may be times when no principle provides uncontestible means of justification. If justification for any principle must be made in relation to context or purpose, and context or purpose is always subject to conflict, then, without appeal to *some* principle that can mediate that conflict and itself be justified independent of context or purpose, how is justification for the initial principle to be provided? To be sure, conflicts over specific principles are sometimes resolvable through appeal to further principles around which consensus exists. But this possibility is only contingent. The specter of relativism emerges.

I view this specter as a consequence of fully acknowledging that the principles we have for getting on in the world, including those we use for communicating with one another, are fundamentally "human made." This acknowledgment has both discomforting and comforting aspects. The latter result from the recognition that we are not gods and that there are no guarantees that any tool that we create will necessarily fulfill the purposes we want it to, whether that be fully understanding the universe or removing all dissensus among us. The comforting aspect comes from recognizing that such principles can accomplish a great deal and, moreover, are not all that we have to rely on in moving us closer to such goals.

Let us first focus on the discomfort. The specter of relativism is often thought to involve a claim that all positions are equivalent in truth value. As noted, rejection of the idea of context-independent principles seems to open the possibility of a scenario in which objections to any given principle cannot be answered. But if that principle is being relied on to condemn Hitler's actions, for example, and if it itself cannot be assumed, then how can any moral assessment of Hitler be established? In other words, does not rejecting the idea of context-independent principles entail the possibility of scenarios in which seemingly obvious positions become no more capable of proof than those contradicting them?

Yes, it does entail such a possibility, but one needs to be careful about the implications of such an admission. It does not entail that Hitler's actions are moral or that the critic of Hitler must acknowledge them as such. It merely means that the critic cannot prove their immorality to one who does not ascribe to the second-order principles that for the critic entail the immorality of Hitler's actions. Thus, rejection of the idea of context-independent principles entails only the possibility of an inability to prove.

But to frame the worst-case scenario of the abandonment of belief in the possibility of context-independent principles *as* an inability to prove shifts the terms of the discussion about relativism. That there may be circumstances where the obvious cannot be proved becomes not the *reducto ad absurdum* conclusion of a philosophical argument but acknowledgment of potential real-life situations. Yes, there may be times when nothing we say can convince. To admit such as possibility is neither to claim such times as necessarily desirable—to endorse "epistemological relativism" as a philosophical position—nor to claim such situations as incapable of ever being overcome—to endorse "cultural relativism" as a sociological position. It is only to accept such times as real-life possibilities, sometimes within our ability to overcome and sometimes worthy of our attempts to keep trying.

That not all types of disagreement are capable of resolution through adherence to an overarching set of principles of rationality is accepted by Habermas, one of the most powerful defenders of the model of rationality that I am attacking. Habermas makes a distinction in matters of morality between justification on issues of justice and justification on issues of the good life. He argues that issues of justice are capable of resolution through adherence to the principles of rational discourse, but that issues of the good life are not—unless such resolution is conducted from within the context of a specific form of life:

> Thus the formation of the moral point of view goes hand in hand with a differentiation within the sphere of the practical: *moral questions,* which can in

principle be decided rationally in terms of criteria of *justice* or the universalizability of interests are now distinguished from *evaluative questions,* which fall into the general category of issues of the *good life* and are accessible to rational discussion only *within* the horizon of a concrete historical form of life or an individual life style. The concrete ethical life of a naively habituated lifeworld is characterized by the fusion of moral and evaluative issues. Only in a rationalized lifeworld do moral issues become independent of issues of the good life.[8]

The distinction that Habermas makes between morality aligned with justice on the one hand, and, on the other hand, the evaluative aligned with questions of the good life has been criticized from a variety of points of view. Communitarians have argued that criteria of justice, no matter how formally articulated, reflect positions on the good life.[9] Fraser has argued that Habermas's distinction philosophically reinscribes an historical division that has been particularly detrimental to women.[10] Benhabib has argued that this distinction runs against our ordinary intuitions that include "issues of the good life" as issues of morality.[11]

I focus again on Benhabib because she, unlike the other critics, wants to maintain a universalist conception of moral justification without limiting morality to the sphere of justice. I view Benhabib's attempt as interesting because it illustrates what must be abandoned for such a conception to remain even plausible.

In moving away from what she depicts as the unnecessary formalistic aspects of Habermas's theory, Benhabib makes a number of significant modifications to his position. She abandons a view of moral justification as a practice in which adherence to specific rules promotes consensus around issues of justice, instead describing justification as a practice in which emotion supplements judgment in promoting the continuation of dialogue concerning matters of the good life as well as matters of justice. The following few passages make these changes explicit:

> Communicative ethics, in my view, is a form of ethical cognitivism which has so far been presented as a form of ethical rationalism. Particularly the claim that judgements of justice constitute the hard core of all moral theory is an instance of such rationalism. . . . [T]his hard distinction between judgements of justice and those of the good life cannot be sustained even from the standpoint of the constraints of discourse theory. Neither can the privileging of moral judgements to the neglect of moral emotions and character. . . . The theory of communicative ethics more often than not seems to perpetuate the Enlightenment illusions of the rational moral self as a moral geometrician. . . . And if I am correct that our goal is the process of such dialogue, conversation and mutual understanding and not consensus, then discourse

theory can represent the moral point of view without having to invoke the fiction of the *homo economicus* or *homo politicus*.[12]

In elaborating the conditions that promote moral dialogue, Benhabib turns to Hannah Arendt and Arendt's principle of "enlarged thought." Benhabib expands the use of this principle for her own position:

> Such a capacity for judgement is not empathy, as Arendt also observes, for it does not mean emotionally assuming or accepting the point of view of the other. It means merely making present to oneself what the perspectives of others involved are or could be, and whether I could "woo their consent" in acting the way I do. . . . If, in other words, we distinguish a universalist morality of principles from Kant's doctrine of a priori rationality, then I want to suggest we must think of such enlarged thought as a condition of actual or simulated dialogue. To "think from the perspective of everyone else" is to know "how to listen" to what the other is saying, or when the voices of others are absent, to imagine to oneself a conversation with the other as my dialogue partner.[13]

Benhabib's invocation of this type of principle is illuminating for thinking about moral discourse. I agree with her assessment that discourse around value can be more or less "rational" though not as a consequence of conformity to what can be measured or definitively assessed—in other words, to a rule. The difficulty of assessing discourse about value through appeal to uncontestible means of assessment is illustrated in a question that has often been raised against utilitarianism: how does one measure the intensity of a desire? But that one cannot measure the intensity of a desire and therefore provide a means of precise, intersubjectively shared assessment does not mean that we cannot evaluate different types of argument about desire, albeit without appeal to what is incontrovertible. Although we may not be able to compare arithmetically the pain of a pinprick to that of being fired from a job, the argument of the person claiming equivalence between his or her pinprick and someone else's job loss would seem to most of us as "irrational." And, following Benhabib's suggestion, the assessment at least here would appear to rely on a judgment about this individual's lack of a "capacity for enlarged understanding."

Thus, I agree with Benhabib in her recognition that abandonment of belief in the possibility of precise rules for evaluating moral argument need not entail abandonment of belief in the possibility for all criteria. Moreover, her move from a focus on noncontradiction to communicative agreement shifts an understanding of communicative ethics in what I regard as a decidedly pragmatic direction. Where we disagree is that I would add to her focus on communicative agreement the recognition that agreement can be geared to a variety of purposes that affect and elaborate in diverse ways the principles that assess the conditions of that agreement, including such principles as those that ground her universalism, specifically "the principle of universal moral respect" and "the principle of egalitarian reciprocity."[14] Unlike Benhabib, I see the move toward understanding rationality in terms of communication and agreement as opening up an awareness of the multiplicity of contexts in which "rationality" can reside and thus the multiplicity of ways in which it can be defined. Such multiplicity in its possible definitions, of course, raises the possibility of contestation over the ranges of any stipulated definition. Therefore, our discourse about what rationality ought to mean must make explicit the purposes that motivate the differences in our proposed present candidates.

But, do not such battles over purposes, if they are not to be carried out through violence or other forms of manipulative strategies, themselves necessarily rely on shared understandings about rational argument? Yes, of course they do, but to the extent that we assume that "rationality," even moral rationality, need not be understood in singular terms, we can recognize that agreement in one context need not demand agreement in others. Thus, with some philosophical colleagues I might share certain assumptions about the criteria governing our dialogue even as we argue over how far or in what contexts such criteria should extend. Recalling Otto Neurath's metaphor, we might think of the criteria of rationality as being like multiple planks of a boat. We certainly need to stand on one plank, or one corner of a plank, as we debate its boundaries as well as whether and how we assess any of the other planks. We also, however, can move around as we carry on such debate, eventually perhaps overhauling all of our original planks.[15] It is only by assuming that rationality must be understood in singular terms that such a response becomes implausible.

"But," my critic might continue, "what happens if we have no shared understandings in any context—that is, if there exists no one plank or corner of a plank that we can stand on?" My response is that this indeed would be unfortunate but is not a dilemma from which philosophy can rescue us. If our diverse cultural histories land us in a place where no shared understandings exist, then all we have to rely on are resources such as our ability to be creative or a psychological willingness to keep trying as well as the material resources that facilitate the use of these psychological ones. And any success would be contingent. As I earlier argued, that which underlies what is frightening in the charge of "relativism" is the scenario of complete communicative breakdown or indecision about the truth of a claim or the rightness of an act. But to accept this scenario as a possible real-life situation undermines its ability to serve as a *reductio ad absurdum* conclusion to a philosophical argument.

The philosophical belief in universals seems analogous to the more popular belief in god: it is what we hope can save us when everything else we do is wrong or inadequate. We would like to believe that there are principles, whether inherent in the universe or, as Habermas has argued, in speech or, as Benhabib has argued, in the cultural horizon of modernity, that can be called on to save us from acting like sinners, animals, or the brutes of the premodern period. As the different religions have tried to give god a specific face so have different philosophers attempted to give content to such principles. The problem, however, is that although many of us feel relief at the prospect of salvation, we also want the face of our saviour or the content of our principles elaborated in accordance with our own specific values and desires. Salvation does not coexist well with diversity. At this juncture in our recognition of this conflict, I vote that we go with diversity, relying on whatever shared commitments contingently exist, combined with whatever creativity and good will we can muster, to get us through whatever conflicts they can. Relying on such contingent resources will not guarantee against communication breaking down and against our acting like brutes but, then again, neither always did the belief in salvation.

CHAPTER EIGHT

To Be or Not to Be: Charles Taylor and the Politics of Recognition

"Identity" is a much-used word these days. It comes up in debates about multiculturalism, events in the former Yugoslavia, the wisdom of single-sex schools, and the justice of affirmative action. In Charles Taylor's essay "The Politics of Recognition," he examines the historically emergent need for the recognition of identity.[1] He argues that across a wide range of contemporary social struggles, from feminism to movements of formerly colonialized people to struggles in Canada over the status of Quebec as a distinct province, can be found the demand to have recognized the distinctive characteristics of one's group. This demand comes in conflict with older traditions of liberalism that have based notions of rights on what is common among human beings. Taylor attempts a reconfiguration of liberalism that can more adequately respond to the demand for recognition than could these previous traditions.

I have a great deal of sympathy with Taylor's project for so reconfiguring liberalism. I also agree with many of Taylor's specific points about identity and the need for recognition in political life. There is, however, one aspect of his essay that I want to examine and depart from. I disagree with that element of his argument that configures the central issues of identity and recognition as generalizable across social groups and contexts. Susan Wolf, in a commentary on Taylor's essay, raises questions about the applicability of some of his central claims to feminism.[2] I believe that Wolf is right but that the problem she identifies is merely a symptom of larger issues relating to how not only Taylor but also many contemporary commentators have tended to think about the issues of identity and recognition. Certainly many of those whom Taylor is arguing against—those who argue that all acknowledgments of group specificity in public life lead to societal fragmentation and hostility—tend to think, for example, that proponents of single-sex schools have something important in common with nationalist Serbs. But even Taylor, who wishes to defend a notion of public life more open to the inclusion of group-specific goals, tends to share with such opponents the idea that we can talk about identity and the need for its recognition as issues "of modernity" whose ethical and political implications may be generalized across a wide set of social struggles. I, on the contrary, argue that even within the context of the very recent past, the meanings of identity and recognition have for understandable reasons varied widely.

My goal is not, however, just to advance a claim about the heterogeneous meaning of identity and recognition across recent social struggles. A more important purpose of this essay is to show how certain understandings of identity and recognition have emerged in the post 1960s' feminist and African American movements that take both of these concepts in directions beyond those that Taylor discusses. There have emerged demands within both of these struggles that extend the request that the distinguishing traits of both groups be acknowledged toward a request that the social practices through which the very activity of recognition takes place be changed. This different type of focus generates a way of thinking about multiculturalism and of the practices by which evaluations of worth are made that conflicts with the one advanced by Taylor in the latter part of his essay. That analysis of multiculturalism and of evaluative practices appears to follow largely from the analysis of recognition elaborated in the earlier part of his essay. In short, by questioning Taylor's analysis of the issue of recognition in contemporary social struggles, I will develop an argument that will also raise questions about Taylor's analysis of multiculturalism and how we evaluate worth.

Recognition and Modernity

Taylor argues that several features of modern life have led to the need for the recognition of oneself as a being with specific features of identity. One is the breakdown of social hierarchies, which has resulted in the replacement of an older notion of honor—one that construed recognition as necessarily attainable only by some—with a newer notion of dignity that portrays recognition as attainable by all. Taylor also credits as partly responsible for the modern need for recognition an emerging sense of authenticity—that is, the moral injunction to be true to that which sets one apart from others. This notion of authenticity emerges in relation to both the individual and the group. Taylor invokes Herder as an important spokesperson for this new ideal of authenticity and points to some of the political implications of this position in Herder's thought: "Just like individuals, a *Volk* should be true to itself, that is, its own culture. Germans shouldn't try to be derivative and (inevitably) second-rate Frenchmen, as Frederick the Great's patronage seemed to be encouraging them to do. The Slavic peoples had to find their own path. And European colonialism ought to be rolled back to give the people of what we now call the Third World their chance to be themselves unimpeded. We can recognize here the seminal ideal of modern nationalism, in both benign and malignant forms."[3]

Taylor argues that over the course of modernity many have come to realize that the process of discovering and affirming one's true identity is a dialogical process, that is, a process one engages in with others. Consequently, it has become widely understood that it is a process where the other might fail one. Thus, emergent with the modern notion of authenticity is the need for recognition, the need for the other to affirm what makes one unique. The danger here is not only that the other might, by omission, fail to affirm that which constitutes one's true self but also that the other might describe one's identity falsely (i.e., misrecognize who one is). With this awareness that the attempt to have one's identity truly recognized can and sometimes does fail emerges the politics of difference. Although this politics rests in part on the universalist grounding of morality within modernity, particularly on the idea that everyone has the right to adequate recognition, it also conflicts with such universalism in its affirmation of difference among individuals and groups. It is the conflict between the modern assumption that rights are not based on what is specific to the individual and the equally modern need for the recognition of what is specific to individuals and groups that underlies many of our contemporary conflicts of public life.

I take issue with the generalizability of this account in two ways. First, I question the wisdom of appealing to "a modern" need for the recognition of difference as a means for explaining the range of social struggles Taylor wants it to. Within modernity, for many groups and in many contexts, a recognition of difference is actively avoided. Therefore, we need a more precise analysis than such an appeal can provide for understanding why, in given contexts, difference rather than similarity is invoked. Second, even in certain contemporary struggles where an affirmation of difference is sought, the abstractness of Taylor's account obscures crucial differences among such struggles concerning how identity and recognition are understood. In other words, by claiming a common cause for many contemporary social struggles—a "modern" need for the recognition of difference—important differences in such struggles are obscured.

I see a possible cause of Taylor's overgeneralization in his focus on one particular contemporary struggle—that over the status of Quebec within Canada today. The meaning of recognition that Taylor employs—that of having one's distinguishing features acknowledged as distinctive—seems most drawn from and applicable to the highly nationalistic struggle over the status of Quebec as a distinctive province. What seems particularly characteristic of this struggle and a common feature of nationalistic struggles in general is that they are committed to the preservation of traditions, linguistic practices and modes of organizing daily life that are viewed as threatened by an alternative culture. In the context of Canada, one means perceived as possibly countering that tendency is to demand recognition by this alternative culture; another means, present here as well as in other nationalistic struggles is to demand separation from that culture. Thus, the justification of demands for separate nationhood frequently include the claim that a group united by distinctive life practices cannot flourish outside of the protection of separate state existence. My question, however, is to what extent other social struggles with which nationalistic struggles are sometimes compared are indeed similar. My contention is that whereas the demands of many of these movements may share certain similarities with this type of struggle, such similarities tend to be intermingled with differences, affecting the meaning of identity and of the demand for recognition among them.

To begin: how useful is it to appeal to "a modern" need for the recognition of difference to account for many contemporary social struggles? Within modernity, the need to have the characteristics of one's group viewed as *not* distinctive appears at least as prevalent as the need to have them viewed as distinctive. Therefore, for a given social struggle, we cannot merely appeal to the latter need; we need to understand why it has overriden the former. Karl Marx and Frederick Engels long ago pointed to a case of groups wanting to have their characteristics viewed as *not* distinctive. In discussing rising social classes, Marx and Engels claimed that such classes tended to portray their own interests and ideas as universal.[4] A more contemporary example is that, until relatively recently, crayons of a pinkish shade in the United States were labeled as "flesh-colored." Descendents of socially powerful groups in the United States have tended to depict others but not themselves as possessing "ethnicity" and men, more than women, tend to see themselves as without gender. Indeed, it has been one of the goals of the contemporary women's movement and of the contemporary African American movement to get men and white people respectively to understand elements of their own lives as reflective of a distinctive social experience rather than as reflective of the human condition in general.

For other examples, one can point to the desires of the members of many ethnic groups in the United States in the first half of the twentieth century. For many members of these groups, an important goal lay in having their distinctive cultural and religious practices be perceived as *not* distinguishing them in many areas of life, particularly in relation to wage labor outside of the home.

Such individuals pressured for the greater acceptance of the belief that they were "just like everyone else" against the belief that fundamental differences separated them from members of more culturally dominant groups. Part of the reason that many people in the United States today perceive any public recognition of group difference as dangerous is because they are aware of the problems that have stemmed from such recognition.

To a large extent, the demand to *avoid* a recognition of difference has also been a part of the African American and feminist movements of the United States. Much of the civil rights movement of the 1950s and 1960s was based on the demand that race be ignored in all arenas of life. Similarly, particularly in the early years of the rise of second-wave feminism, many were demanding that the difference of gender be ignored or gotten beyond altogether.[5] Androgeny was a significant aim of the late 1960s women's movement.

To be sure, by the mid 1970s, the goal of androgyny—or of nonrecognition of gender differences—was also having to contend with a growing tendency for feminists to demand the acknowledgment of women's differences from men. Many feminists increasingly came to believe that the goal of androgyny was premature, that women's equality with men could not really be achieved without first acknowledging and taking seriously the differences that did mark women's lives. Moreover, many came to see that equality with men often translated into women adopting hegemonic conceptions of what it meant to be male. Recognizing and celebrating women's differences began to be perceived as a more desirable outcome.

A similar change has also been an important element of the post-1960s struggle of African Americans. As U.S. feminists became suspicious of androgyny as an aim, so also did many African Americans come to perceive the limitations of the demand for the nonrecognition of racial differences. Whether it was because African Americans carried perceived physical differences with them into the political and economic world or because a different social and economic history seemed to make the American dream less achievable, disallowing differences publicly for the sake of increased political and economic opportunities began to appear problematic as a strategy. Like many feminists, many African Americans came to believe that differences might first have to be attended to before equality could be achieved.

But, even in these two cases, I question an appeal to a "modern" need for the recognition of differences as a useful explanation for the change. That explanation cannot tell us why it was only in the late 1960s and early 1970s that both the feminist and African American movements made a turn from a dominating emphasis on integration and androgyny to an increased emphasis on the acknowledgment of differences. Accounting for this change is better accomplished by focusing on the specific cultural contexts of these movements in this period.

I earlier pointed to one type of factor that may have contributed to the change: a growing disbelief within both movements of the possibility of attaining political or economic gains without attention to the differences that did mark African Americans and women. What also needs to be taken into account are changing understandings in this period of the meaning of oppression.

Whereas in the early part of the century oppression had largely been defined in political and economic terms, increasingly emerging from the middle part of the century onward was the idea that oppression also had a cultural and psychological dimension, that it affected people's sense of one another and themselves. Moreover, also developing was the sense that oppression was a social rather than merely a political phenomenon—that it extended into such areas as sexual encounters, norms of behavior, and styles of personal interaction and self-presentation. Although issues of the psyche and of "personal life" had certainly been linked to issues of political domination before the mid-twentieth century in the writings of individual scholars and thinkers, it was only around this time that such issues became a significant rallying point of large social movements. One manifestation of this change in the women's movement was the creation of the slogan "The personal is political." Post-1960s' feminists also began to talk about the distinctive and desirable traits of women in what has been called feminism's "gynocentric" turn.[6] Within the African American movement, an example of this new emphasis was the creation of "Black is beautiful" as a slogan.

This context has had implications for how "recognition" came to be understood within both the feminist and the African American movements. Because the demand for recognition emerged less from the perception that existing traditions, linguistic practices, and ways of organizing daily life were being threatened by extinction and more from the perception that oppression was manifesting itself in terms of forms of description and evaluation, the counterclaim was both "See me and recognize my distinctiveness" and, significantly, "See your activities of description and evaluation as themselves problematic."

In other words, the demand for the acknowledgment of differences within the post-1960s' feminist and African American movement has increasingly surfaced in a way that goes beyond a simple acknowledgment of differences and toward a sense of recognition that places the focus as much on the person doing the recognizing as on the person being recognized. This new focus has manifested itself in two ways. First are claims about the actual practices of recognition—how they have been made possible by imbalances of power that have enabled some to recognize and caused others to seek or avoid recognition. Second, are claims about the specific content of the affirmations or failures of recognition—how they reflect these imbalances of power in, among other ways, their claims to the universality of what are, in effect, historically specific perspectives.

Although these claims have manifested themselves throughout both of these movements—and in other post-1960s' social movements, such as the gay and lesbian movements—it is in the academy where these claims have been most thoroughly elaborated. It is here that many who have seen themselves as allied with such movements have been able to think about the epistemological implications of these new cultural understandings of oppression. Furthermore, the emergence of multiculturalism in the academy represents, in part, the consequence of the elaboration of such reflections. This point leads to the next step in my argument—the contention that Taylor's discussion of multiculturalism does not adequately address these new claims about recognition but rests too strongly on his more limited sense of what the demand for recognition is about. His discussion of multiculturalism too prominently assumes a focus on the other to be recognized and too little assumes a focus on the practice of recognition itself. Augmenting this weakness is his inclination to treat dismissively such issues as desire and power in analyzing judgment.

Although these assertions constitute the basic argument of the next section of this essay, I cannot move to them directly. Taylor's discussion of multiculturalism, which is biased in the ways I have just suggested, also contains countervailing elements that must be acknowledged. In other words, though I believe that the main thrust of his discussion of multiculturalism rests on a limited sense of what the demand for recognition is necessarily about, there are aspects of his discussion that reflect a different understanding of recognition—one that demands a focus as much on those people or institutions in a position to recognize as on those seeking recognition.

Recognition and a "Difference-Blind" Liberalism

Taylor makes a turn in the middle of his essay, after his general discussion of the emergence of recognition within modernity and before his discussion of multiculturalism. In this section, Taylor focuses on the challenges posed to our understanding of liberalism by the need for recognition. Taylor points to a charge that sometimes has been leveled at a liberalism that claims to be "difference-blind"—in other words, a liberalism that claims to "offer a neutral ground on which people of all cultures can meet and coexist."[7] Taylor forcefully points to the problems such a liberalism faces in defending itself as in fact "difference-blind." He notes that choices to relegate certain ends of life to the private sphere themselves reflect substantive perspectives on the ends of life. Thus, the division of church and state that has accompanied this form of liberalism is an outgrowth of a particular religious history. As he claims, "Liberalism is not a possible meeting ground for all cultures, but is the political expression of one range of cultures, and quite incompatible with other ranges."[8]

Taylor uses these arguments on the inconsistencies of a liberalism that claims to be "difference-blind"—also called a "procedural liberalism"—to argue for a different kind of liberalism, one that can both acknowledge collective goals and provide safeguards in the form of fundamental rights for those who do not share such goals. Here Taylor seems to be attempting to articulate a liberalism that would make it possible for Quebec to coexist with the other Canadian provinces within a liberal framework and that also would further certain substantive public goals distinctive to itself.

I support Taylor's goal in this section and agree with the arguments that he advances to develop it. It is my belief that a commitment to public secularity is a wise choice for a country with a diversity of religious beliefs or a wish to further such diversity. It does, however, represent a substantive choice. Moreover, it is not clear to what extent this kind of choice can or should be used as a model for issues other than religion. A government can, to a certain extent, choose to exclude religious commitments from its operations, but it cannot choose to have no language spoken in its courts or no curriculum mandated in its schools. I suspect that western liberal democracies have tended to understand themselves as more "difference-blind" than they are because their citizenry have been relatively homogeneous in regard to many practices about which a government must make substantive decisions, for example, the language to use on its currency. The existence of more heterogeneous populations in these democracies would more explicitly reveal the extent to which government cannot ever be purely procedural but must endorse some substantive ends, which could include decisions about the scope of government itself.[9] Taylor's model of a liberalism that can both endorse certain collective ends and protect the rights of minorities seems a liberalism more coherent with the necessary operating conditions of any potentially existent government than one claiming to endorse no ends at all.

Independent of my views on Taylor's goals in this section of his essay, I find it noteworthy that to advance his goals he resorted to a model of recognition that was really not represented in the early part of his essay. To discredit the notion of a "difference-blind" liberalism, he challenged its understanding of itself as in fact difference-blind. In other words, his justification of a liberalism oriented toward the achievement of collective goals was based not only on the need for groups within the social order to achieve recognition but also on the self-misrecognition of a liberalism claiming to be uncommitted to substantive goals. This kind of argument reflects what I have described as a different form of the demand for recognition than that earlier depicted by Taylor. Taylor not only uses this kind of argument himself; he is also explicitly aware of it as a kind of argument sometimes used by others in challenging the idea of a "difference-blind" principle of equal dignity: "The claim is that the supposedly neutral set of difference-based principles of the politics of equal dignity is in fact a reflection of one hegemonic culture. As it turns out, then, only minority or suppressed cultures are being forced to take alien form. Consequently, the supposedly fair and difference-blind society is not only inhuman (because suppressing identities) but also, in a subtle and unconscious way, itself highly discriminatory."[10]

But it is not only in his discussion of a "difference-blind" liberalism that Taylor makes the focus of recognition not those to be recognized but the recognizers themselves. In his discussion of multiculturalism, he also argues that we should adopt a stance of presumptive worth toward cultures that have existed over long periods of time. In making this argument, Taylor draws attention to the necessary limits of the value judgments of the we who should adopt such a stance: "There is perhaps after all a moral issue here. We only need a sense of our own limited part in the whole human story to accept the presumption. . . . But what the presumption requires of us is not peremptory and inauthentic judgements of equal value, but a willingness to be open to comparative cultural study of the kind that must displace our horizons in the resulting fusions. What it requires above all is an admission that we are very far away from that ultimate horizon from which the relative worth of different cultures might be evident."[11] Similarly, in an earlier section of Taylor's essay, he points out how, in studying the other, we might have to change our own standards of evaluation. In this claim, as in the preceding passage, recognition entails not a focus on the one being recognized but on the "we" who can act to recognize or not.

Recognition and Multiculturalism

The problem, however, is that these moves toward making "we" itself the focus of attention remain largely peripheral to the main focus of Taylor's argument about multiculturalism. Following from his discussion of the "politics of recognition," Taylor describes demands by the proponents of multiculturalism in terms of *a demand for recognition of the other*, in this instance, not so much of identity as of worth:

> What is new, therefore, is that the demand for recognition is now explicit. And it has been made explicit, in the way I indicated above, by the spread of the idea that we are formed by recognition. . . . The reason for these proposed changes is not, or not mainly, that all students may be missing something important through the exclusion of certain gender or certain races or cultures, but rather that women and students from the excluded groups are given either directly or by omission, a demeaning picture of themselves, as

though all creativity and worth inhered in males of European provenance. Enlargening and changing the curriculum is therefore essential not so much in the name of a broader culture for everyone as in order to give due recognition to the hitherto excluded.[12]

Certainly, it is not that Taylor is all wrong. In contemporary discussions around multiculturalism, a significant element is the demand for recognition of the worth of the contributions of women and members of certain races, cultures, and so forth. But, in describing the reason for proposed changes around multiculturalism only in terms of such demands, Taylor is ignoring some of the more challenging voices in this debate. These more challenging voices are not those saying, "Recognize my worth" but rather those saying, "Let my presence make you aware of the limitations of what you have so far judged to be true and of worth." In so far as Taylor defines the demands around multiculturalism in accord with its weaker versions, his arguments on behalf of it are less strong than they could otherwise be.

Before I expand on this point, it is necessary to elaborate more fully Taylor's argument. Taylor emphasizes that what is at stake in contemporary debates around multiculturalism is the recognition of the equal value of different cultures. The demand for recognition, implicit in other struggles, has now become explicit and it has taken a new turn: what is sought is not only recognition of cultural identity but also recognition of cultural worth.[13,14] According to Taylor, the unspoken premise behind such a demand is that we owe equal respect to all cultures. This premise can be formulated in two forms. The weaker version is based only on the presumption that further study will enable us to see the worth of all cultures. The stronger version would claim that judgments of equal worth should be attributed to all cultures as a matter of right. Taylor defends the weaker version while arguing against the stronger one.

Against the stronger version, Taylor claims that judgments of value cannot be based on principles of ethics. If judgments of value were to rest on such principles, then independent criteria for value judgments would be eliminated, and judgments of value would become indistinguishable from expressions of commitment. In other words, Taylor seems to be saying that judgments of good must be independent of judgments of right. Taylor argues that behind alternative formulations are often "subjectivist, half-baked, neo-Nietzschean theories" derived frequently from Foucault or Derrida.[15]: "The proponents of neo-Nietzchean theories hope to escape this whole nexus of hypocrisy by turning the entire issue into one of power and counterpower. Then the question is no more one of respect, but of taking sides, of solidarity. But this is hardly a satisfactory solution, because in taking sides they miss the driving force of this kind of politics, which is precisely the search for recognition and respect."[16]

But, for Taylor, rejecting the stronger version does not mean rejecting the premise altogether. Taylor defends the weaker version of the premise in the form of a presumptive starting point that should be taken to any culture that has informed a whole society over a considerable stretch of time. The claim here is not that we will necessarily end up with a judgment of positive value but that it would take "a supreme arrogance to discount this possibility *a priori*."[17] And, Taylor argues, in the process of investigating other cultures, we should leave open the possibility that the standards we employ in making our evaluations will themselves be transformed:

> But when I call this claim a "presumption," I mean that it is a starting hypothesis with which we ought to approach the study of any other culture. The validity of the claim has to be demonstrated concretely, in the actual study of the culture. Indeed, for a culture sufficiently different from our own, we may have only the foggiest idea *ex ante* of in what its valuable contribution might consist. Because for a sufficiently different culture, the very understanding of what it is to be of worth will be strange and unfamiliar to us. . . . We learn to move in a broader horizon, within which what we have formerly taken for granted as the background to valuation can be situated as one possibility alongside the different background of the formerly unfamiliar culture.[18]

In short, multiculturalism for Taylor is to be understood in terms of the demand for recognition of equal worth on the part of those groups and cultures that hitherto have been excluded from the western canon. This demand can be justifiably responded to with the presumption that any culture that has shaped a whole society over a considerable period of time has something important to say to all humans. To find out whether this presumption is justified in any given case may involve stretching outselves to the point at which our standards themselves are transformed.

My problem with this argument is not so much with the answers it generates as it is with the questions it asks. Taylor frames the topic of multiculturalism as one about how "we" should regard claims of previously excluded groups about the worth of their past contributions. But this type of framing makes central a question about the validity of only certain judgments of worth (i.e., those made by previously excluded groups). It thereby diminishes a focus on the validity of the judgments of worth made by those from socially privileged groups. Although Taylor claims that in the process of evaluating the judgments of worth of previously excluded groups "our" standards might need to be revised, he provides no description of how the awareness of that need might come to pass. The implication seems to be that it is merely through coming to know the culture of another that one gains insight into the limitations of one's own. But is this statement true? Is knowledge of another's practices and values sufficient to generate questions about one's own? Might not there also be factors about "ourselves," including our emotions or interests, that contribute to or hinder the making of that particular cognitive move?

Taylor introduces an affective element into his discussion when he notes that a stance of extreme arrogance is required to assume that a culture that has pervaded an entire society for a considerable amount of time has nothing of worth to contribute. Presumably, therefore, the absence of this particular emotional stance is required to initiate this type of inquiry. Why, however, should we assume that emotional preconditions are required at the start of this kind of inquiry but not in its midst? One problem in making such an assumption is that it assumes a "beginning" phase of inquiry that is distinctive in character from its later phases. It would be expected that any knowledge of another's culture sufficient to lead one to question one's own would be fairly extensive. But, if a certain emotional precondition is required to begin such an inquiry, why would it not also be required to sustain it along the way? The response might be that Taylor's emotional precondition is not something positive but something negative, specifically, the *lack* of supreme arrogance. Thus, to introduce this kind of precondition is not to introduce a necessary affective element in the process of inquiry but merely to require the lack of one. But does not even admitting the lack of an affective element as a precondition to inquiry require some focus on the affective state of the one who is evaluating?

Taylor, however, appears not to want to allow issues of affect or emotion to enter the discussion of multiculturalism. In this essay, when Taylor touches on the question of the "objectivity" of judgments of worth of other cultures, he quickly moves to frame will in opposition to justification and desire in opposition to judgment: "That is, if the judgement of value is to register something independent of our own wills and desires, it cannot be dictated by a principle of ethics. . . . But if these judgements are ultimately a question of the human will, then the issue of justification falls away."[19]

Like many contemporary philosophers, Taylor seems caught in the belief that either judgment has nothing to do with desire or power or that judgment is reducible to such and, therefore, all talk of standards must disappear. Certainly to pose the issue of objectivity in this way makes it easy to dismiss any talk of power or desire in discussions around multiculturalism. It is not difficult to show the philosophical limitations of a position that claims that reason is reducible to power. The question, however, is whether this mode of framing these issues is the best way of doing so.

One of the unfortunate legacies of the historical separation of the discipline of philosophy from such other disciplines as sociology and history has been the development of the subfield "epistemology" within philosophy; this subfield has not only tended to separate questions regarding the nature of knowledge from questions of historical context but has also separated cognition from other human faculties, such as emotion and feeling. The tendency to treat the study of knowing as separate from other aspects of real live humans has been undermined by many changes in post-1950s' British and North American philosophy. Developments in the subfields of "philosophy of science" and "philosophy of the social sciences" placed the study of knowledge on a much more human footing, recognizing the construction of knowledge as something that could be investigated through historical inquiry. The beliefs emerging from these subfields—that "facts" are theory laden and that values, interests, metaphors, and so forth are implicated at least in the process of theory construction—seemed to reflect this growing move toward "naturalizing" or historicizing epistemology.

Discussion has stalled over the question of whether issues of desire and power are involved not only in the process of theory construction but also in the process of justification. A common philosophical response to the acceptance of the latter possibility, a response evidenced in Taylor's essay, is to say that this latter possibility undermines the very notion of judgment because it reduces the act of judgment to one of commitment or solidarity—in other words, that it removes the faculty of reason from the analysis altogether.

But, even if one agrees with Taylor that any legitimate application of the notion of reason must assume the elimination of considerations of power or interest, we cannot divorce the issue of power and interest from discussions of multiculturalism. For even if one were to agree with the position that disagreements over judgments of worth can ideally be resolved without the presence of desire or power, the agreement itself generates no conclusions about whether past judgments of worth have been of this type or what it would take for them to be such. In other words, whatever one's position on the possibility of the rational resolution of disagreements over assessments of worth, still unresolved are the questions of whether the judgments of worth that constitute the canon of many academic institutions were reached rationally, and if they were not, how might that be changed in the future.

I am claiming that those who want to exclude talk of "power" in discussions around multiculturalism—including Taylor—on the grounds that to introduce it is to endorse "relativism" appear to rely on an unwarranted jump from "ought" statements about what judgments of worth should be (and thus, conceivably, can be) to "is" statements about the existing academic canon. An important argument of those who advocate for multiculturalism is that power *has been* a factor in the processes by which judgments of value have been made. Invocations against the mere introduction of the topic of power in philosophical discussions of multiculturalism entail deflection of inquiry away from such arguments as well as from consideration of the conditions under which power generally *can* exert itself in the making of such judgments.

One element of confusion that might attend such inquiry is the conflation of issues of interest with issues of power. It may in fact be the case that judgments of worth *are* necessarily intertwined with elements of interest. If they are, then Taylor's aspiration that judgments of worth register something independent of our wills and desires may be unrealistic. But the impossibility of separating worth and interest does not entail that reason has no place in the resolution of conflict over worth. Conflicts of interest can be rationally negotiated through a variety of means. To demand the elimination of interest as necessary to the function of reason seems to assume an overly narrow conception of reason.

There is one final objection I wish to make to the way in which Taylor has formulated the topic of multiculturalism. When the primary issue of this topic is identified as the question of the worth of the contributions of those who have been previously excluded, a distinction is assumed between the "other" who is demanding recognition of equal worth through multiculturalism and the "we" who can bestow it. Taylor does not thematize this distinction, but his assumption seems to be that this distinction is about different groups of people. But clearly there are many who straddle this distinction. As a female professor of European ancestry, I comfortably fit into both the category of the "other" who is demanding recognition and the "we" who has certain powers to bestow it. But that there are many who trouble the distinction between an "other" who is demanding recognition and a "we" who can bestow it should reinforce one of the central arguments of the preceding—that discussions around multiculturalism may often need to go beyond talk about the worth of the contributions of some groups of people in distinction from others. Merely trying to figure out which contributions fall into which groups might itself be too difficult to determine.

In conclusion, I stress that a description of the controversy around multiculturalism as primarily concerning the worth of the contributions of certain groups structures the discussion in unfortunate ways. Not only does such a description problematically assume that such contributions can be easily demarcated, but even to the extent that they can be, it also assumes that such contributions require examination in a way that those from other groups do not. I have argued that a more interesting and challenging description of the topic of multiculturalism makes the focus not the judgments of worth of any particular group but rather the process by which judgments of worth have and can be made. Such a way of describing multiculturalism would not preclude talk about power. Instead, it would begin with the recognition that we need to know more about the conditions that contribute to or undermine imbalances of power in the resolution of disagreements about worth before we can assess the degree to which past judgments *have been* free of such or the degree to which new claims about worth *can* be free of such. In short, the issue that first began to emerge from the late 1960s' social movements—that oppression may manifest itself not only in terms of direct acts of exclusion but also in the more subtle arena of judgment—needs to be acknowledged before we can even begin to adequately assess the relative worth of *all* of our contributions.

CHAPTER NINE

Emotion in Postmodern Public Spaces

In our public mode of being we speak the common language of reason, and live under the laws of the state, the constraints of the market and the customs of the different social bodies to which we belong. In our private incarnation, however, we are at the mercy of our own sense impressions and desires.

—*Roberto Mangabeira Unger* [1]

" In this passage, Unger is describing an epistemological separation between the private and the public, which he claims characterizes a liberal, modern world view. From within this perspective, reason is seen as that which brings us together in distinction from the private realm of sense impressions and desire. I believe that in this quotation Unger accurately captures one significant understanding of reason in relation to sense impressions and the passions that have been present in many societies that we would characterize as modern and liberal (i.e., the societies of western Europe and North America from approximately the eighteenth century until the early twentieth century). I also believe that this understanding, if not already broken down, has been put under considerable pressure in these societies during the twentieth century, legitimating talk about a "postmodern" reconfiguration of the association of reason with publicity and emotion with privacy. As reason has become less public—less regarded as that which brings us together—so has emotion become more public in several interesting senses: in both emerging as an explicit focus of attention in new types of public spaces and in becoming viewed as that which sometimes should override external forms of authority in decision making about personal and sometimes public life. Whereas discussion about the breakdown of reason as a faculty capable of bringing us together has been at the center of many contemporary discussions of postmodernism, relatively little has been said about the other part of this reconfiguration, the growing publicity of emotion. In this essay, I focus on the latter phenomenon, particularly as it has manifested itself in popular culture in the United States in the twentieth century.

The growing "publicity" of emotion is evident both in the creation of new forms of public spaces where emotion is the focus of attention and in the increasing acceptance of emotion as a resource for decision making over external forms of authority. These phenomena are interrelated: the growth of new forms of public spaces for the identification and analysis of emotion has both reflected and contributed to the growth of the idea that emotion is an important resource for life decisions. To illustrate these points, I focus on two types of public spaces that have flourished during the twentieth century where emotion is the explicit object of attention: 1) in the development of various forms of therapy and therapeutic movements and 2) in the transformation in certain post-1960s' political movements, where claims about inner affective states have become grounds for political demands. Both of these phenomena reflect and encourage the view that choices in life decision making are and should be informed by one's "inner feelings," at times even when such feelings conflict with rules of morality that have been handed down by institutions such as churches, schools, and the family.

My goals for this essay are not merely descriptive; I do not only want to depict certain cultural changes occurring in the twentieth-century United States. The cultural changes I describe have led to contemporary confusion and debate around the legitimacy of looking to "feelings" as a resource for personal and political decision making. Thus, as this "feeling-motivated" view of decision making has grown more popular, so also has a backlash against it. In the arguments of contemporary conservatives one can sense a growing attack on this view of decision making, which conservatives often associate with political liberalism. But even political liberals frequently attack such a view of decision making, which *they* often associate with identity politics. The argument here is that these political movements rely too heavily on group-specific feelings and too little on rational consideration of the common good. One of the purposes of this essay is to intervene in this debate, to show what is legitimate and what is not in appeals to feelings in opposition to reason or morality. Although there is much that can be criticized in the contemporary elevation of "feelings," there are also authoritarian dangers in any simple rejection of their place in personal or political decision making. Resisting these dangers requires greater attention to the changing role and meaning of "feelings" than many intellectuals have given this topic.

I begin with an historical examination of some of the conflicting ways in which emotions were viewed in the United States in the late nineteenth century. I then use the writings of Freud to illustrate some crucial differences with these earlier views. Whatever causal significance is given to Freud's writings in changing cultural attitudes, these writings can be taken as illustrative of important changes taking place in U.S. culture during the twentieth century. Such changes have resulted in what can be understood as a specifically twentieth-century understanding of "the emotions," or, as they have become increasingly thought of in the latter part of the century, as "feelings." I describe what I view as both the positive and the negative elements in this resulting construction. Finally, I use this analysis to reflect on current debates about the uses and abuses of trends in post-1960s' political movements.

Let me begin by turning to late–nineteenth-century U.S. culture. Much recent historical work has been devoted to challenging older conceptions of this culture as merely "repressive" regarding sexuality.[2] Similar moves are being made regarding attitudes within this culture toward the emotions. Contrary to seeing Victorian America as merely hostile to the emotions, historians are pointing to the many ways that nineteenth-century Americans valued emotional life. Philip Cushman, for example, points out that an appreciation for the experience of intense inner emotions is apparent during at least the latter two-thirds of the century in the development of various forms of popularly based spiritualist movements. These movements urged the experience of deep inner feelings as means of contact with the divine. For example, the highly influential movement of mersmerism counseled individuals to transcend the mundane concerns of the material world and of external opinion by making contact with their deepest inner selves. It was here that there allegedly rested a divine magnetic core.[3]

Nor is it the case that the repressive thesis works well for even more elite social groups. Certainly in European society, an appreciation for the experience of emotional intensity was prefigured as early as the late eighteenth century in the development of the romantic movement in the arts and literature. Kenneth Gergen cites figures such as Wordsworth, Shelley, Baudelaire, Keats, Goethe, Delacroix, Turner, Brahms, Schumann, Mendelssohn, Verdi, and Chopin as all looking to words, art, or music to express profound and intense inner emotions.[4] Philip Stearns points out how middle-class attitudes in the United States evidenced, by the late nineteenth century, a similar appreciation for the experience of intense inner states. Indeed, as he notes, middle-class Victorians not only viewed the lower classes with disdain for not controlling their emotions, but they also viewed the inner classes negatively for not being able to experience certain emotions, such as love and grief, with intensity.[5]

To be sure, in both Europe and the United States in the latter part of the nineteenth century, other more negative attitudes toward the emotions also existed. Certainly, the emotions could, as noted, represent the voice of the divine within each of us; however, they could also stand for the voice of nature instead. In this respect, they could be both a source of energy, inspiration, and creativity against the civilizing but dulling forces of civilization or the repository of what was most dangerous and life destroying to humans. The novels of Thomas Mann poignantly express this deep ambivalence toward the underside of reason, as that which both fuels the creativity of the artist and also threatens to destroy the life of the artist in the process.

The task then, as Mann's novels also suggest, is not merely one of eliminating the emotions; it is rather that of bringing them into balance with reason. This general idea, that the goal should be balance, is also widely found in middle-class attitudes in the United States during this period:

> At any rate, a surprisingly coherent emotional culture was purveyed to the middle class during the second half or two-thirds of the nineteenth century. The culture had two main foci: the need for control, for directing emotional fervor to appropriate ends; but also the need for intensity, for the spark necessary to a full life and to the functions essential in modern society. Emotional excess was obviously condemned, but so was emotional flaccidity. The Victorian sought, as basic ingredients of good character, the capacity for deep feeling along with the capacity to direct that feeling to appropriate targets.[6]

Fundamental changes regarding attitudes toward the emotions did begin to occur during the early part of the twentieth century in the United States and have intensified during the century. But, as the preceding quotation indicates, these changes are poorly captured in the idea that this culture became merely less "repressive" regarding the emotions. To provide a different type of explanation, let us explore further the issue of "balance" in late–nineteenth-century America. To those who were its most public defenders—middle-class Americans—though the experience of specific emotions was seen as valuable and necessary to proper human functioning, such experience is valued as a means to other ends: to a properly functioning family life, to appropriate male behavior in the realms of politics and commerce, to facilitate contact with the divine in each of us, and so forth. This understanding of the emotions, although valorizing specific emotions in certain contexts, still treats each, and their proper balance, as subordinate to ends external to the emotions. Consequently, this understanding does not fundamentally challenge Unger's view of the relationship between reason and the emotions. The determination of which emotion is appropriate in what contexts and with how much intensity is still made by what is understood as an objective reason. I view developing attitudes in the twentieth century as challenging this perspective: by making the question of emotional integration less an objective and more a subjective matter and by situating the emotions not as means to other ends but as partial constituents of the ends of human life per se.

I expand this argument by using some of Freud's texts. Whatever one believes about the causal significance of Freudian theory for affecting attitudes in the general U.S. population during the twentieth century, his writings can be used to illuminate trends that have become part of this century's thinking. Whether Freud caused many of us to believe as we do or not, his writings certainly reflect, and thus can be used as signpoints to illustrate, what those beliefs are and how they differ from earlier times.

To begin, let us briefly return to late–nineteenth-century Victorian culture. Although the experience of intense emotions was regarded as not only at times appropriate, but also indeed desirable, the question of context was crucial. It is only in specific contexts that specific emotions were valued in specific people. Thus mother love, including female feelings of compassion and empathy toward children, affection between siblings, and romantic love between spouses, all were forms of emotion seen as necessary for a properly functioning family life.[7] Anger and fear were viewed as acceptable when they appropriately motivated male action or led to the development of male courage.[8] As these examples indicate, emotions were highly gender coded. Whereas the issue of balance pertained to both women and men, the emotion to be experienced, the context in which it was to be experienced, and the degree to which it was to be experienced all were gender specific. This gender specificity points to the important role that the idea of proper social functioning played regarding the experience and expression of emotions. Women were to feel motherly love in certain amounts and in certain contexts because without it the natural functioning of the family would fall apart.

Freudian theory, however, provides an interesting contrast to this stance. One can say that in relation to many aspects of his theory, Freud was relatively unconcerned about who was to feel what in specific contexts. Although Freud certainly included the issue of gender in his narratives of childhood development, his basic structures of the mind were both highly gender neutral and highly vague in general in regard to specific emotional content. Thus, Freud generalized the antithesis of reason into the generic concept of sexuality or into the dual concepts of sexuality and aggression. These very generally described drives were thought to depict the antithesis of reason for both women and men.[9]

In other words, Freud's goal appears less that of furthering a particularly ordered society (though aspects of his theory may in fact have contributed to that) than of understanding and working toward a general balance within the individual between socially given ends and individual libidinal drives. Freud certainly articulated ideas about the ends of psychic and social balance at various points in his life; he wrote, for example, about the maintenance of civilization or the construction of the nonneurotic individual. Particularly interesting about these ends was that they were very general and vaguely formulated. Their vagueness means that they did not provide much content beyond the idea of balance itself. Thus, for Freud, a civilized society was not much more than one that has successfully channelled potentially destructive drives into productive means; a nonneurotic individual was one who had been able to achieve a balance between childhood sexual drives and responsible adult functioning. In Freud's theory, balance itself became the end rather than a means to a further, more specifically defined and socially given end.

The dispacement of specifically defined and socially given ends by a more generic notion of balance has an interesting corollary: within the Freudian world view, the ego supercedes the superego as standard bearer for the role of reason. The superego, rather than the means of determining "the right thing to do," becomes one more element, along with the id, and the constraints of contemporary reality, in constituting the demands that the ego must balance in formulating decisions about reasonable action. The following passage makes this point clear. "Thus an action by the ego is as it should be if it satisfies simultaneously the demands of the id, of the superego and of reality, that is to say if it is able to reconcile their demands with one another."[10]

To be sure, a certain ambiguity exists within Freud's thinking regarding what constitutes "reasonable action." At one level, the superego remains the voice of reason in that it dictates the ideal toward which imperfect creatures, such as human beings, should strive. Given the psyche's need for happiness and inclination toward aggression, however, the demands of the superego must be considered ultimately unreasonable: "Exactly the same objections can be made against the ethical demands of the cultural super-ego. It too, does not trouble itself enough about the facts of the mental constitution of human beings. It issues a command and does not ask whether it is possible for people to obey it. On the contrary, it assumes that a man's ego is psychologically capable of anything that is required of it, that his ego has unlimited mastery over his id. This is a mistake; and even in what are known as normal people the id cannot be controlled beyond certain limits."[11] Thus the ego, as balancer of the demands of the id, the superego, and present reality, is ultimately a more "rational" faculty than the superego, which remains blind to such other demands. And the ego, as arbiter of the conjunction of specific demands made by the id, the superego, and present reality, is a faculty of the individual. Subjective rationality supercedes objective reason.

It is not, however, just that the ego supercedes the superego as the ultimate voice of reason within the Freudian world view. In this act of supercession, the role of the emotions also undergoes transformation. As noted, one important consideration in determining whether an act by the ego is rational is whether the id has been given its due. But, consequently, the desires of the id become not a means to other ends but a constituent ingredient of the endpoint of human functioning itself. Thus Freudian theory can be said to have strengthened the role of the emotions, although not because he, unlike the Victorians, merely admitted their existence or even their potential strength. It is rather that, for Freud, unlike for many in late–nineteenth-century America, the demands that the emotions make must be taken as a given irrespective of what they do or do not make possible for proper human functioning or a well-run social order. Although balance is crucial in both the Freudian and the Victorian world views, the endpoint of balance has shifted: from ends external to the self to the internal ordering of the self itself.

There are other ways in which Freudian theory ultimately strengthened an understanding of the role of the emotions in psychic life. Previously I noted how Freud's theory contributed to a more gender-neutral theory of the mind than had previously been dominant. The generality of his structural theory, however, established not only a gender-neutral but also a class- and ethnic-neutral theory of the psyche. This generality also meant an extension both of the range of specific emotions considered potentially present among human beings and of the population believed to be subject to emotional imbalance in general. For example, whereas the negative emotions of anger and fear had been primarily ascribed to men, within the more gender-neutral terms of Freudian theory, they could also be attributed to women. Freud's invocation of a generic "sexuality" undermined the gender, class, and ethnic coding of sexual feelings. In so far as women in general and members of lower social class and ethnic groups had been perceived as more likely to achieve emotional imbalance, the emphasis in Freudian theory of such imbalance as a possibility for all contributed to extending the potential range of this state. Eli Zaretsky also points to this gender, class, and ethnic neutrality of Freud's theory of the psyche and how it extended the domain of emotion's reach:

> Specifically, his work showed that the "problems"—passivity, lack of control, dependency—that Victorians had linked to women, to the working class, or to "inferior" or "uncivilized" people were universal. The logic of the distinction between those in control (male professionals) and those in need of control (women, homosexuals, Jews, "backward" peoples) began to break down. In a sense, Freud can be described as "outing" the white, gentile male professional's dependency. In so doing, however, he threatened a whole system by which identity and social place were being maintained.[12]

The "democratization" of the possibility of emotional imbalance was furthered in another way in Freudian theory—in his undermining of the distinction between the "mad" and the rest of us. Freudian theory began with a focus on the mentally odd; but, in a turn common to directions twentieth-century psychology in general was taking, it increasingly explained the mentally odd in ways that had relevance for the mentally not so odd. By situating the origins of abnormalities in common life situations and struggles, Freudian theory contributed to a growing view of mental health as being along more of a continuum with rather than in stark opposition to mental illness. Zaretsky, again, makes a similar point: "Psychotherapy was at the center of mass culture. Whereas nineteenth century psychiatry had functioned by excluding and isolating the so-called "mad," the forms of psychotherapy that emerged in the late nineteenth century stressed the universality of a "subconscious," a secondary or subliminal self, in which, one could transcend the conflicts and travails of everyday existence."[13]

To be sure, people who visited psychoanalysts in the early part of the twentieth century in the United States tended to have very severe problems. It has been only in the post–World War II period that there developed a view of "mental health" and of therapy in general as applying to the masses and to those who are not "crazy." Thus, it has been only in the second half of the century that the democratic implications of Freudian theory have been realized. Certainly, such democratic implications have manifested themselves in forms of therapy—Jungian therapy, gestalt therapy, and twelve-step programs, to name only a few—whose theoretical connections with Freudian theory are thin. But all of these types of therapy share with Freudian theory certain basic essentials. Specifically, they all assume that it is part of the human condition to possess emotional elements that have the power to disrupt our lives or contribute to our functioning and that forestalling such disruptions or maximizing such contributions requires paying attention to these elements in some way.

These therapeutic movements manifest important cultural shifts in a variety of ways. For one, their existence has meant the creation of new forms of public space where emotion is given attention. The phenomenon of increasing numbers of individuals going to see therapists in their offices, to church, school, or YMCA basements to attend twelve-step programs, or to expensive resorts to engage in weekends of mass psychic rejuvenation has meant that it has become increasingly acceptable to focus on one's emotions in the company of virtual strangers. All of these events constitute new kinds of public spaces, those that are explicitly devoted to the analysis of emotion.

The growth of these movements constitutes new forms of public spaces and signifies new understandings of the proper grounds for decision making about private life. Certainly, in previous centuries, people sometimes went outside of the family for advice on life decisions; but doing so meant going to some "authority," such as a religious figure or an etiquette advisor, for a position on the "right" thing to do. Consulting with a therapist about whether to end a marriage is very different from consulting with a minister. In the latter case, one is looking for information about the rules of "good" behavior, the rules that will enable one to remain acceptable in the eyes of god. In the former case, one is looking for help in decoding one's own emotions—in estimating what they are and in deciding which will or will not provide satisfactory bases for action. The differences between these two types of consultation is that, in the latter but not in the former case, one's emotional states are viewed as requiring serious reflection before any life decision can be made.[14]

It is not just that emotions are understood as having to be factored into any decision one makes: it is also that the decision itself has become viewed as more individual and less generalizable. In part because individual emotions are seen as a necessary contributor to the outcome and in part because the general circumstances involved in decision making are understood as more unique, decisions about "the right thing to do" have become viewed during the twentieth century as highly personal. Again, as was noted in the earlier discussion about Freud, reason has become understood in more subjective and less objective terms; but the conjunction of this more subjective conception of reason and the greater weight given to affective elements as a factor in the decision-making process has resulted in a specifically twentieth-century psychic construction—"feelings." In popular discourse, the term "feeling" has come to signify a conjunction of the affective and the subjectively cognitive, indicating a personal cognitive orientation to the world that contains an affective element. Whereas in older social constructions of the basic elements of the psyche, reason stood firmly separated from "the passions" and later from "the emotions"; in contemporary popular understanding," "reason" and "the emotions" have become fused into "feelings."

Many twentieth-century intellectuals have written extensively and persuasively about the negative aspects of this cultural turn. Writers such as Philip Rieff, Christopher Lasch, Joel Kovell, T. J. Jackson Lears, Philip Cushman, and Warren Susman have linked it to the development of a consumeristic, individualistic, narcissistic self who cares more about managing the impressions that others have of him or her than of doing good, who desires fame more than respect, and who is caught in the hopelessly self-defeating cycle of trying to fill up a fundamentally empty interior life with more and more commodities.[15] Although these critiques offer much that is important and insightful, they are sometimes expressed in ways that leave the reader feeling hopeless about contemporary culture. To avoid generating that conclusion, I review these critiques for the express purpose of separating those aspects of this turn that have led to ugly developments in contemporary society from those that have had more positive consequences. From this more nuanced analysis, we are in a better position to develop modes of intervention that could affect future trends in positive ways.

A first step in this direction, however, does involve focusing on the negative. The kinds of criticisms that have been leveled against what might be called "the therapeutic turn" can be roughly divided into three different types. First, this turn has been criticized for contributing to the construction of a self that accepts perpetual desire as a legitimate aspect of who it is. Earlier I pointed to the very general ways in which Freudian theory depicted the underside of reason, in terms of the encompassing category of sexuality or of sexuality and aggression. Such vague formulations were compatible with thinking of the underside of reason in terms of the generic concept of desire. Although Freud himself thought of the healthy psyche as one that learned how to integrate such desire with external social demands, the overall legitimation that his theory and other twentieth-century therapeutic theories have accorded this aspect of the psyche has been said to facilitate the construction of a consumer culture in which desire in an endless variety of forms is continually courted. Thus early promotional campaigns for cigarette smoking claimed that the suppression of sensual gratification led to the development of neurosis.[16]

Second, "the therapeutic turn" has been said to contribute to a commodity like conception of self. The optimistic, pragmatic reading of Freud popularized in the United States led to an idea of psychological therapy as a new and powerful form of "self-help." In this respect, it could join the burgeoning diet, cosmetics, and, of course, advertising industries in furthering a view of the self as endlessly malleable. The "therapized" self could become as confident or as charming as was necessary to make it a successful player in the market of commerce or romance. Certainly one might say that this reading of Freud represented a distortion of his ideas, particularly those regarding what psychoanalysis could reasonably hope to accomplish. But the very vague and open-ended way in which Freud formulated the ends of therapy—again, also present in therapeutic theory after Freud—could be said to facilitate an interpretation of therapy in such terms. As I have claimed, the sense of balance between socially given ends and individual libidinal desires that Freudian theory attributes to the properly functioning psyche is specified in relatively vague and open-ended ways. But the theory's open-ended understanding of the meaning of psychic health made it, and the theories that followed, susceptible to furthering the idea of the endlessly improvable self that American capitalism was simultaneously working hard to construct.

The idea of the self as both filled with insatiable desire and endlessly malleable can be seen as manifestations of a more encompassing problem in U.S. culture that "the therapeutic turn" has been said to accentuate—its extreme individualism. To focus on the desires or the malleability of the self means that one is looking to the self as that which must be satisfied or changed. The focus moves from "individual in relation to world" to individual psyche alone. Again, one can say that such an individualistic turn represents a distortion of

Freud's ideas and also that his theory was in accord with such a move. The theory was concerned with integrating given instinctual demands with demands made by the external world on the psyche. In this sense, his theory can be seen as no more individualistic than other late–nineteenth-century prescriptive theories that sought to bring the individual's emotions into line with socially given expectations. There are, however, aspects of Freudian theory that shifted this similar aim in more individualistic directions. Previously, I have addressed the ways in which Freudian theory constituted the ego rather than the superego as the voice of reason as internal psychic balance superceded external social acceptability as the goal of proper human functioning. But this process means that the passions are no longer to be deployed for the sake of what society decrees; rather, the decrees of society need to be brought into balance with them. Individual internal harmony instead of external social acceptability becomes the point of the therapeutic process and of the good life itself. The question, "How do I feel?" takes priority over other types of questions as a motivator for human action.

I claimed earlier that I would focus not only on what has been negative about "the therapeutic turn" but also on its social benefits. In this regard, I turn to the democratic possibilities made possible by this turn. Intertwined with the individualistic aspects of this turn is its legitimation of the idiosyncratic, or of that which is *not* yet recognized by the social whole. In part, the modern conception of an "emotion" is distinguished from other psychic phenomena because it represents the relatively nonlinguistic; it is also distinguished by its subjective intensity.[17] The word has been used to depict contexts where we sense something strongly and yet do not quite possess the language for it. This suggestion of a more tenuous connection with language than is, for example, true of "beliefs" has also been carried into the meaning of "feelings." Consequently, what are called emotions or feelings can represent forms of resistance to what can be said. Certainly not everything that is described as an "emotion" or a "feeling" is rebellious against the existing social order. What we cannot easily put into words, such as visceral forms of revulsion to homosexual acts, may represent mimetic responses to what is all around us and may operate to sustain the given. But, in so far as emotions or feelings do stand for reactions that exist more than other psychic phenomena outside of language, to legitimize them is also to provide space for the at least potentially disruptive. Alison Jaggar conveys a similar point when she talks about the phenomena of "outlaw emotions"—emotions that resist socially accepted orientations to the status quo.[18]

Moreover, an increased focus on the question of "what I feel" means that forms of social integration that rest on the disparagement or devaluation of certain individuals or groups become more open to challenge. A focus on individual feelings can provide an important source of critique to versions of social rationality whose psychological consequences for specific social groups are harmful.

In short, "the therapeutic turn" cannot be evaluated in simply negative or positive ways. Implicit in the cultural changes connected with it are both aspects that many would agree are negative and others that must be regarded as positive. Understanding the turn in this complex way enables us to develop more nuanced understandings of some of the societal changes associated with it than have often been offered. To elaborate this point, I focus on a societal change that can be linked to this turn: the emergence of new directions in post-1960s' social justice politics.

The Psyche Is Political

There is a story among some white, male leftists that views the period from the late 1960s to the present as one of unadulterated decline. According to this story, the 1960s was a period when women, black people, and white males worked together around a common vision of social justice. By the end of the 1960s, this unified movement began to break down as African Americans increasingly abandoned the politics of civil rights in favor of the politics of black nationalism and as the women's movement also became more separatist in orientation. As these two movements became less focused on what humans share in common, so did there also proliferate new social groups—such as groups devoted to gay liberation and the needs of the physically challenged—whose politics were similarly group-specific rather than universal in orientation. The end result according to the story, is that the left has become so fragmented today that it is unable to challenge the steady ascendency of the right.

This story has elements of truth to it. Changes did take place in left politics toward the end of the 1960s that challenged some of the universalist assumptions of the earlier left. These changes did undermine some of the unity that had existed on the left, but they also greatly expanded the left's understanding of the meaning of social justice. It is because many feminists, African Americans, gay people, and others recognize the importance of this expansion that the previous story is one found rarely outside of the thinking of some white, male leftists. Less widely recognized is the connection between this expansion and the changes in U.S. culture that I have identified as "the therapeutic turn." Making this connection more explicit helps us not only to better understand the history of the left in the post-1960s period but also to clarify some of the positive as well as negative aspects of "the therapeutic turn."

To tell this story, I return to the 1960s and briefly to the women's movement of that period. As many historians of this movement have noted, the women's movement that surfaced in the United States during the 1960s was composed of two different types of social activists. There were those who started to talk about "women's rights" in the early part of the 1960s. Participants in this part of the women's movement focused on female identity primarily to draw attention to the illegitimacy of its use as a criterion to deny access to what otherwise would be publicly available opportunities. Activists in the 1950s and 1960s civil rights movement similarly focused on the illegitimacy of using race as a criterion of identity to limit publicity of access.

Neither the 1950s and 1960s civil rights movement nor the early "women's rights movement" appear importantly affected by "the therapeutic turn." Indeed, the demands of both movements seem not qualititatively different from demands pressed by nineteenth-century versions of both of these movements: in, for example, the movement for women's suffrage rights or in nineteenth-century movements geared toward the advancement of African Americans.

The type of politics represented in the civil rights and women's rights movements was expanded during the 1970s and 1980s as other social groups constituted movements on similar bases. People with physical disabilities, gays and lesbians, and members of other ethnic groupings began to make claims about their rights to opportunities they were denied as a consequence of these identities. Beginning in the 1960s, however, there also developed from within the women's movement, the civil rights movement, and elements of these other movements, types of political organizing in which identity began to occupy a different role. Specifically, certain segments of these movements began to focus on the implications of gender, race, ethnicity, sexual orientation, and so forth, not only in terms of denial of access to otherwise publicly available opportunities but also in terms of the wide-scale social manifestations and psychic effects of these categories. Women's liberationists in the late 1960s began to think about the consequences of gender on housework. They also began to question the effects of practices such as national beauty contests on women's sense of themselves. African Americans began to claim "Black is beautiful" in opposition to the undermining effects of alternative notions of beauty on the self-esteem of black people. In short, identity began to matter not only as a means to ferret out specific forms of exclusion but also as a means to evaluate the social manifestations and psychic consequences of the categories of race and gender. Norms and customs associated with these categories, previously viewed as "natural" or necessary, began to be subject to discursive evaluation.

From where did this increased focus on the norms and customs associated with gender and race come? On the one hand, it merely came from thinking about issues such as gender and race in more sustained ways than had sometimes earlier been the case. Many of those who participated in the 1960s' civil rights and women's movement were students and writers who had opportunities to think about the deep-seated consequences of gender and race in ways available only to isolated individuals in earlier times. In this respect, the writings that began to emerge about these issues in the 1960s continued traditions of thought—as can be found, for example, in the works of such figures as W. E. B. Dubois, Charlotte Perkins Gilman, Alain Locke, Elizabeth Cady Stanton, Virgina Woolfe, and Malcolm X. On the other hand, the ways of thinking that differentiated women's liberation from women's rights and the black power movement from the civil rights movement had to do with the new ways of connecting issues of social justice with the psyche that were surfacing in a variety of ways during the 1960s. An example is the New Left. One of the ways in which the New Left was different from the left of the 1930s was in its concern with issues of consciousness. It looked at oppression not only in economic and political terms but also in terms of how people felt about themselves. A concern with feeling states affected many aspects of the New Left, often making problematic, for example, the boundaries between "politicos" and "hippies." But the concern with feeling states was not just the province of the New Left. By the 1960s, many Americans had become accustomed to thinking about the effects of societal practices not only on their material well-being but also on their psyches. As earlier noted, the locution "I feel" was beginning to occupy a prominent place in ordinary language. It is not surprising that many of those who were beginning to think about women's issues or issues of race in deep ways should also have begun to think about the psychological impact of race and gender.

Both the negative and the positive aspects of "the therapeutic turn" were manifest in this new direction in post-1960s' political movements. Understanding the negative aspects requires some care for these are not as they are often presented. According to the white, male leftist story of what supposedly went wrong in the 1960s, the civil rights and women's movement became too focused on group-specific issues and too little focused on the problems humans share. But this story ignores the point that these groups and others, in looking at the implications of gender, race, sexuality, and other aspects of identity in deeper ways than had previously been the case, were also uncovering group-specific forms of oppression that needed to be addressed. Women had to think about the gender-specific consequences of social practices as housework and sexuality to end the ways in which women's work in the domestic sphere or women's pleasures from sexuality were not equal to men's. African Americans had to think about the race-specific consequences of prevailing versions of U.S. history if black children were to have a sense of their ancestry equal to that of white children. Prevailing notions of "what humans have in common" tend often to be insufficient in addressing social injustice simply because prevailing notions of "commonality" often assume unjust social patterns. So it is not the group-specific focus of these movements' transformation in the 1960s that I would describe as negative. Rather, I would look at other aspects of these movements.

In an earlier discussion of "the therapeutic turn," I wrote about the individualizing aspect of this turn. A focus on "what I feel" places emphasis on phenomena around which shared understandings may be difficult to achieve. In recognition that social customs do psychically affect groups differently, many members of post-1960s' political movements have sometimes reacted with claims that only those physically marked in ways that make them subject to differentially negative experiences can understand or be motivated to challenge social practices that perpetuate such differentiated experiences. It is *this* aspect of post-1960s' political movements that I view as more problematic than the group specificity of the goals they have sought. Thus, I believe that it is with *this* argument that the left must cogently deal if it is to successfully move forward.

One way some leftists are beginning to deal with this argument is by pointing out how, though it does contain important elements of truth, it tends to view psychic identity in more homogeneous and static ways than the evidence from social reality often warrants. For example, Judith Butler has argued that none of us are simply "men" or "women" in seamless ways.[19] Gender identity in each of us is always a bit of a mismatch between socially assigned labels and psychic needs. Similarly, "the souls of white folk" are not as homogeneous or seamless as some African American separatists have sometimes depicted them. Although white people do not have the same experiences as black people, the intersection of some white people's identities, such as with being liberal or compassionate, facilitates a greater openness toward recognizing the reality of the reported experiences of black people than others without that identity. In sum, a focus on psychic orientation is problematically individualizing only in so far as it is accompanied by the belief that it is impossible to communicate the meaning or affective "feel" of such states to others.

Sometimes people have responded to the separatist tendencies of post-1960s' political movements with the demand that we abandon such politics altogether and return to an earlier, supposedly better, type of politics in which only the needs we share in common are allowed to be articulated. As I have argued, however, "the needs we share in common" are generally too "thin" to address the forms of oppression present in a society and rather tend to presuppose many of those forms. "The therapeutic turn," *because* of its individualizing, or at least anticommunitarian tendencies, provided us with ways of moving beyond such a politics.

As I have earlier suggested, the focus on the psychological consequences of social categorization enormously extended the range of phenomena viewed open to critique and thus change. By focusing on the psychic as well as the material consequences of social categorization, African Americans, for example, could stretch the discourse of political oppression beyond issues of political and economic exclusion and talk about how a white culture made them feel about their culture, their history, and their physical appearance. Feminists were able to claim subjects such as women's feelings about their bodies, food, work, and sexuality as legitimate topics of political discourse. Early consciousness-raising groups represented a new union of the therapeutic and the political. They were therapeutic in the sense that they encouraged examination of inner emotions about daily existence. Unlike most traditional therapeutic encounters, however, they operated on the assumption that the circumstances that generated these feelings were socially shared among many women and were historically contingent. Similarly, many of the ways in which the gay and lesbian movements developed into movements addressing the needs of many sexual minorities were greatly abetted by the new legitimization of inner feelings.

In sum, one can say that "the therapeutic turn" contributed to making U.S. culture more democratic than it had previously been by extending the range of claims that could be made on the body politic. Taking seriously this contribution means recognizing the necessity for the continued existence of spaces where difference can flourish as a creative source of challenge to whatever ideas of unity we have so far managed to create. Consequently, however, any contemporary move beyond "identity politics" has to preserve some of the kinds of spaces identity politics has worked hard to construct.

Certainly, those spaces need not necessarily be conceptualized in quite the same ways as they have sometimes been in the past. As earlier suggested, some previous versions of identity politics have conceptualized psychic identity as problematically homogeneous and static. These ways of understanding identity have denied the multiple, intersecting, and shifting nature of identity in all of us. In consequence, the politics emerging out of such understandings, such as those based on being a "woman," though powerful in elaborating certain antihegemonic perspectives, have also been limited to those for whom this aspect of identity criss-crosses only with certain other, primarily more hegemonic, aspects of identity, such as being white or of the middle class. Moreover, without an understanding of identity as multiple and shifting, we have difficulty conceptualizing an idea of a politics in which different groups occasionally come together around partially shared needs or visions.

But if the understandings of identity informing a politics of the future must be different from notions of identity informing certain forms of identity politics of the past, group-specific identity will still have a space in such a politics of the future. The current phrase of choice to describe such a future politics is "coalition politics." One reason for the popularity of this phrase is that it joins the idea of possible alliance making with an intent to keep open spaces for identity formations. It also suggests that both the alliances created and the identity groups of which such alliances are composed should be understood as subject to perennial contestation and shift. Both the issues constituting such alliances and the groups constituting the alliances themselves would be understood as subject to change. Partly as a consequence of the legitimation of idiosyncrasy that "the therapeutic turn" brought to U.S. culture, any unity we can create must be recognized as only a temporary resting point. "The therapeutic turn" has left a powerful and importantly democratic imprint on the shape of our politics.

Notes

Acknowledgments

Many of the essays included in this volume, although edited in many degrees, have been published previously, and I extend my thanks to the first publishers for permission to reprint them. The following are the original publication sites:

"Women, Morality, and History." *Social Research* (Autumn 1983):514–536.
"Feminism and Marx: Integrating Kinship with the Economic." *Praxis International* 5 (January 1986):367–381.
"Feminist Theory: The Private and the Public." In *Beyond Domination: New Perspectives on Women and Philosophy,* edited by Carol Gould, 221–230. Totowa, N.J.: Rowman and Allanheld, 1984.
"Interpreting Gender." *Signs: Journal of Women in Culture and Society* 20 (Autumn 1994):79–105.
"The Myth of the Traditional Family." In *Feminism and Families,* edited by Hilde Nelson, 27–42. New York: Routledge, 1997.
"To Be or Not to Be: Charles Taylor and the Politics of Recognition." *Constellations* 3, (April 1996):1–16.
"Emotion in Postmodern Public Spaces." In *Emotion in Postmodernism,* edited by Gerhard Hoffman and Alfred Hornung, 1–25. Heidelberg, Germany: Universitätsverlag C. Winter, 1997.

Introduction

For inspiring through conversation and for commenting on drafts of this essay, I thank Alison Jaggar, Ted Koditschek, and Steve Seidman.

1. Two important collections inflencing feminist theory of that period were Rayna R. Reiter, ed., *Toward an Anthropology of Women* (New York: Monthly Review Press, 1975) and Michelle Zimbalist Rosaldo and Louise Lamphere, eds., *Woman, Culture, and Society* (Stanford, Calif.: Stanford University Press, 1974).

2. Carol Gilligan, *In a Different Voice: Psychological Theory and Women's Development* (Cambridge: Harvard University Press, 1982).

3. Lawrence Kohlberg, *The Philosophy of Moral Development: Moral Stages and the Idea of Justice* (San Francisco: Harper & Row, 1981).

4. Susan Buck-Morss, "Socio-Economic Bias in Piaget's Theory and its Implications for Cross-Cultural Studies," *Human Development* 18(1975):38.

5. The problem of Gilligan's silence about the historical parameters of her claims was augmented by her use of a model of female moral development (a model that showed how girls and women progress in their moral decision making). Such a model of moral development, because it, like Kohlberg's theory, is based on the idea of progress, presupposes an ahistorical means of assessment.

1: Women, Morality, and History

1. Lawrence Kohlberg, "The Future of Liberalism as the Dominant Ideology of the West," in *Moral Development and Politics,* eds. Richard W. Wilson and Gordon J. Schochet (New York: Praeger, 1980), 59.

2. *Ibid,* 60.

3. *Ibid.*

4. Lawrence Kohlberg, "A Reply to Owen Flanagan and Some Comments on the Puka-Goodpaster Exchange," *Ethics* 92 (April 1982):518.

5. Carol Gilligan, *In a Different Voice: Psychological Theory and Women's Development* (Cambridge: Harvard University Press, 1982), 9–10.

6. *Ibid,* 18.

7. Kohlberg, "A Reply to Own Flanagan," 517–518.

8. *Ibid,* 514–516.

9. Lawrence A. Blum, "Kant and Hegel's Moral Rationalism: A Feminist Perspective," *Canadian Journal of Philosophy* 12 (1982):287–288.

10. *Ibid,* 298–299.

11. Roberto Mangabeira Unger, *Knowledge and Politics* (New York: Free Press, 1975), 27.

12. *Ibid,* 45.

13. Bill Puka, "An Interdisciplinary Treatment of Kohlberg," *Ethics* 92(April 1982):475, n. 13.

14. For more on this point, see Linda Nicholson, "Women and Schooling," *Educational Theory* 30 (Summer, 1980):225–233.

15. This argument that it would be impossible to find people today unaffected by the separation of private and public parallels an argument Eleanor Leacock makes. She argues for the impossibility of finding a contemporary society that does not evidence gender oppression because western imperialism brought gender distinctions with it in its contact with nonindustrial cultures. Eleanor Leacock, "Women in Egalitarian Societies," in *Becoming Visible,* eds. Renate Bridenthal and Claudia Koonz (Boston: Houghton Mifflin, 1977), 17.

16. Kohlberg, "A Reply to Owen Flanagan," 518.

17. *Ibid,* 524.

18. Susan Buck-Morss, "Socio-Economic Bias in Piaget's Theory and its Implications for Cross-Cultural Studies," *Human Development* 18(1975):38.

19. *Ibid*, 42.

20. Kohlberg, "The Future of Liberalism," 57.

21. Gilligan, 2.

22. *Ibid*, 74.

23. Kohlberg, "A Reply to Owen Flanagan," 518.

24. Gilligan, 173–174.

2: Feminism and Marx: Integrating Kinship with the Economic

1. Karl Marx and Frederick Engels, *The German Ideology* (Moscow: Progress Publishers, 1968), 39. Emphasis added.

2. Jürgen Habermas has made a similar objection to Marx's work. Habermas notes that although Marx does claim to incorporate the aspect of symbolic interaction, understood in the concept of "relations of production," within his theory, this aspect is ultimately eliminated within Marx's basic frame of reference. This point replicates feminists' criticism in that in both cases Marx is cited for an ambiguity in his concept of "production." In the problems pointed to by Habermas there is an ambiguity in Marx's inclusion under "production" of either both "the forces and the relations of production" or of only "the forces of production." In the problems cited by feminists, there is an ambiguity concerning even what is included in "forces of production." In all cases, such ambiguity is made possible by Marx's movement away from broader to more narrow meanings of production. For Habermas's critique, see *Knowledge and Human Interests*, trans. Jeremy Shapiro (Boston: Beacon Press, 1972), 25–63.

3. Karl Marx, *A Contribution to the Critique of Political Economy*, (New York: International Publishers, 1920), 20–21.

4. Marshall Sahlins, *Culture and Practical Reason* (Chicago: University of Chicago Press, 1976), 212.

5. Karl Polanyi, *The Great Transformation* (Boston: Beacon Press, 1957), 60.

6. *Ibid*, 66.

7. As Polanyi argues, the absence of some regulation does not mean the absence of all regulation. On the contrary, he claims that markets and regulation grew together.

8. Polanyi, 20.

9. *Ibid*, 171.

10. *Idem*.

11. *Ibid*, 57.

12. Mary O'Brien, "Reproducing Marxist Man," in *The Sexism of Social and Political Theory*, eds. Lorenne M. G. Clark and Lynda Lange (Toronto: University of Toronto Press, 1979), 107.

13. *Ibid*, 102, 11.

14. *Ibid*, 105.

15. Karl Marx, *The Poverty of Philosophy* (New York: International Publishers, 1963), 180.

16. This point of the progression from kinship to state and to market has been made often in Marxist literature. See, for example, Frederick Engels, *The Origin of the Family, Private Property and the State*, (New York: International Publishers, 1972), 72–73.

17. O'Brien, 114.

18. Ann Ferguson and Nancy Folbre, "The Unhappy Marriage of Patriarchy and Capitalism," in *Women and Revolution* ed. Lydia Sargent (Boston: South End Press, 1981), 318.

19. Iris Young, "Beyond the Unhappy Marriage of Patriarchy and Capitalism: A Critique of Dual Systems Theory," in *Women and Revolution*, ed. Lydia Sargent (Boston: South End Press, 1981), 52.

20. *Ibid*, 49.

21. *Idem*.

22. Georg Lukács, *History and Class Consciousness*, trans. Rodney Livingstone (Cambridge: MIT, 1971) and Habermas, 42.

3: Feminist Theory: The Private and the Public

1. Rosalind Petchesky, "Dissolving the Hyphen: A Report on Marxist-Feminist Groups 1–5," in *Capitalist Patriarchy and the Case for Socialist Feminism,* ed. Zillah R. Eisenstein (New York: Monthly Review Press, 1979), 376–377.

2. Iris Young, "Socialist Feminism and the Limits of Dual Systems Theory," *Socialist Review* 10 (March–June 1980):169–188. See especially pages 179–181.

3. *Ibid,* 169–168.

4. Michelle Zimbalist Rosaldo, "The Use and Abuse of Anthropology: Reflections on Feminism and Cross-Cultural Understanding," *Signs* 5 (Spring, 1980):389–417.

5. See, for example, Karl Marx, *The Poverty of Philosophy* (New York: International Publishers, 1963), 180. Mary O'Brien cites other examples in "Reproducing Marxist Man," in *The Sexism of Social and Political Theory,* eds. Lorenne M. G. Clark and Lynda Lange (Toronto: University of Toronto Press, 1979), 107.

6. For a discussion of some of these differences, see Mary Lyndon Shanley, "Marriage Contract and Social Contract in Seventeenth Century English Political Thought," *Political Quarterly* 32 (March 1979), 79–91; and Gordon Schochet, *Patriarchalism in Political Thought* (Oxford: Basil Blackwell, 1975).

7. Marilyn Arthur, "'Liberated' Women in the Classical Era," in *Becoming Visible,* eds. Renate Bridenthal and Claudia Koonz (Boston: Houghton Mifflin, 1977), 67.

8. Hannah Arendt, *The Human Condition* (Chicago: University of Chicago Press, 1958), 24.

9. Lawrence Stone, *The Family, Sex and Marriage in England 1500–1800,* abridged ed. (New York: Harper & Row, 1979), 99–100.

10. *Ibid,* 111.

11. Arthur, 69.

12. This controversy, with its respective adherents, is noted by Sarah Pomeroy, *Goddesses, Whores, Wives and Slaves: Women in Classical Antiquity* (New York: Schocken Books, 1975), 58–60.

13. Arthur, 43.

14. Pomeroy, 57–92.

4: Interpreting Gender

This essay has been in the making for several years; consequently, it has a long and complex genealogy. For this reason I cannot begin to thank all of the people who have read or heard some ancestor to the present essay and who contributed a little or a lot to the birth of the present version. Many people will find much of this familiar. A few special thanks are, however, necessary. I thank the Duke–University of North Carolina at Chapel Hill, Center for Research on Women, for providing me with a Rockefeller Foundation Humanist in Residence Fellowship for 1991–1992. That fellowship, combined with a University at Albany, State University of New York, sabbatical gave me a year to think about many of the ideas in this essay. I also want to thank Steve Seidman for reading every draft and for intervening in the development of this essay at several crucial points.

1. Joan Scott, *Gender and the Politics of History* (New York: Columbia University Press, 1988), 2.

2. Gayle Rubin, "The Traffic in Women," in *Toward an Anthropology of Women*, ed. Rayna R. Reiter (New York: Monthly Review Press, 1975), 159.

3. Elizabeth Spelman, *Inessential Woman: Problems of Exclusion in Feminist Thought* (Boston: Beacon Press, 1988), 128.

4. Although the growth of a materialist metaphysics may have contributed to the growth of that strong sense of individualism that many writers have linked to modern, western conceptions of the self, it would be a mistake to see such individualism merely as a result of the growth of such a metaphysics. Some writers, such as Charles Taylor, have pointed to an emerging sense of "inwardness," one aspect of such an individualism, as early as in the writings of Augustine. See Charles Taylor, *Sources of the Self: The Making of the Modern Identity* (Cambridge: Harvard University Press, 1989), 127–142. And, according to Colin Morris, such a turn to a language of inwardness represents a widespread twelfth-century phenomenon. He notes the decline of this tendency in the mid-twelfth century followed by a gradual resurfacing culminating in the late fifteenth-century Italian Renaissance. Colin Morris, *The Discovery of the Individual* (London: SPCK, 1972). Moreover, even in the period after the emergence of a materialistic metaphysics, social transformations other than the growth of such a metaphysics have contributed to the development of such a sense of individualism differently among different social groups.

5. For the reference to Filmer, see Gordon Schochet, *Patriarchalism in Political Thought* (Oxford: Basil Blackwell, 1975), 151, 137. For Locke, see John Locke, *Two Treatises of Government* (New York New American Library, 1965), 364.

6. Ludmilla Jordanova, *Sexual Visions: Images of Gender in Science and Medicine Between the Eighteenth and Twentieth Centuries* (Madison, University of Wisconsin Press, 1989), 25–26.

7. *Ibid*, 27.

8. For discussions of this point, see Winthrop Jordan, *White Over Black: American Attitudes Toward the Negro, 1550–1812 (Chapel Hill:* University of North Carolina Press, 1968) 217–218; Cornell West, "Towards a Socialist Theory of Racism," in *Prophetic Fragments*, ed. Cornell West (Grand Rapids, Mich.: Africa World Press, 1988), 100; Lucius Outlaw, "Towards a Critical Theory of Race," in *The Anatomy of Racism*, ed. David Theo Goldberg (Minneapolis: University of Minnesota Press, 1990), 63; and Michael Banton and Jonathan Harwood, *The Race Concept* (New York: Praeger, 1975), 13.

9. Jordan, 3–98.

10. Thomas Laqueur, *Making Sex: Body and Gender from the Greeks to Freud* (Cambridge: Harvard University Press, 1990), 148.

11. *Ibid*, 36–37.

12. *Ibid*, 35–36.

13. *Ibid*, 40. Laqueur's reference is to Galen, *Peri spermatos (On the Seed)*, ed. Thomas Kuhn 622.

14. Laqueur, 35.

15. *Ibid*, 149–150.

16. Londa Schiebinger, "Skeletons in the Closet: The First Illustrations of the Female Skeleton in Eighteenth Century Anatomy," in *The Making of the Modern Body: Sexuality and Society in the Nineteenth Century*, eds. Catherine Gallagher and Thomas Laqueur (Berkeley: University of California, 1987), 42.

17. *Ibid*, 42.

18. Michel Foucault, *Herculine Barbin*, trans. Richard McDougal (New York: Pantheon, 1980), vii.

19. Laqueur, 151–152.

20. Any elaboration of this opposition requires a book-length discussion. That a full-scale materialism was not easily endorsed in the very early period is most obviously indicated in the dualism of one of the most outspoken advocates of such a materialism, René Descartes. But even Descartes's position was considered much too radical by "The Cambridge Platonists." In the minds of many of these figures, a complete materialism left no room for god. For an informative discussion of religious tensions around the adoption of materialism during the modern period, see John Hedley Brooke, *Science and Religion: Some Historical Perspectives*

(Cambridge: Cambridge University Press, 1991). In the late nineteenth century, other non-religious arguments emerged against the utility of scientific modes of explanation in accounting for human behavior and social laws. This movement was pronounced in Germany and is represented in the writings of Wilhelm Dilthey.

21. It was as a consequence of reading Chandra Talpade Mohanty's very insightful discussion of Robin Morgan's introduction to *Sisterhood Is Powerful* that I thought of looking to Morgan's essay as a useful exemplar of biological foundationalism. See Chandra Talpade Mohanty, "Feminist Encounters: Locating the Politics of Experience," in *Destabilizing Theory*, eds. Michele Barret and Anne Philips (Cambridge, England: Polity, 1992), 74–92. I see the intent of Mohanty's analysis as overlapping with mine.

22. Robin Morgan, "Introduction/Planetary Feminism: The Politics of the 21st Century," in *Sisterhood Is Global: The International Women's Movement Anthology*, ed. Robin Morgan (Garden City, N.Y.: Doubleday, 1984), 4.

23. *Ibid*, 6, 8.

24. Janice Raymond, *A Passion for Friends: Towards a Philosophy of Female Affection* (Boston: Beacon Press, 1986), 21.

25. Janice Raymond, *The Transsexual Empire: The Making of the She-Male* (Boston: Beacon Press, 1979).

26. *Ibid*, 100.

27. *Ibid*, 114.

28. One radical feminist theorist who explicitly endorsed biological determinism in the late 1970s is Mary Daly. In a 1979 interview in the feminist journal *off our backs*, Daly responded to the question of whether men's problems are rooted in biology that she was inclined to think they were. See *off our backs* 9 (May 1979), 23. This interview was brought to my attention by Carol Anne Douglas, *Love and Politics: Radical Feminist and Lesbian Theories* (San Francisco: ism Press, 1990). For other instances of this tendency within radical feminist theory during the 1970s, see Alison Jaggar's useful discussion of biology and radical feminism in *Feminist Politics and Human Nature* (Totowa, N.J.: Rowman and Allanheld, 1983), 93–98.

29. Iris Marion Young, "Humanism, Gynocentrism and Feminist Politics," in *Hypatia: A Journal of Feminist Philosophy*, 3, a special issue of *Women's Studies International Forum* 8 (1985):173–183.

30. Carol Gilligan, *In a Different Voice: Psychological Theory and Women's Development* (Cambridge: Harvard University Press, 1984); Nancy Chodorow, *The Reproduction of Mothering: Psychoanalysis and the Sociology of Gender* (Berkeley: University of California Press, 1978).

31. Judith Lorber, in faulting Chodorow's work for not paying enough attention to social structural issues, explicitly raised questions about the class biases of *The Reproduction of Mothering*. Her more general points, however, would also apply to race. See her contribution to the critical symposium on *The Reproduction of Mothering* in *Signs* 6 (Spring, 1981):482–486. Elizabeth Spelman focuses on the ways in which Chodorow's account insufficiently addresses race and class in *Inessential Woman*, 80–113; Adrienne Rich notes the lacuna in Chodorow's analysis regarding lesbianism in "Compulsory Heterosexuality and Lesbian Existence," *Signs* 5 (Summer, 1980):635–637. Audre Lorde has raised issues of racism in relation to Mary Daly's *Gyn/Ecology*, in "An Open Letter to Mary Daly," in *This Bridge Called My Back: Writings by Radical Women of Color*, eds. Cherrie Moraga and Gloria Anzaldúa (Watertown, Mass.: Persephone Press, 1981), 94–97. Spelman also looks at the ways in which Daly's analysis tends to separate sexism and racism and make the latter secondary to the former in *Inessential Woman*, 123–125. The separatism of radical lesbian feminist separatism has been criticized as ignoring issues of race. See, for example, The Combahee River Collective, "Black Feminist Statement" in *This Bridge Called My Back: Writings by Radical Women of Color*, eds. Cherrie Moraga and Gloria Anzaldúa (Watertown, Mass.: Persephone Press, 1981), 210–218. The class and race biases of Gilligan's work have been pointed to by John Broughton in "Women's Rationality and Men's Virtues" *Social Research* 50 (Autumn, 1983):634. I also develop this issue in my article in that same volume, "Women, Morality, and History," 514–536. "Women, Morality, and History" is also included in this volume.

32. On the ways in which the Native American berdache undermine European notions of gender, see Walter I. Williams, *The Spirit and the Flesh: Sexual Diversity in American Indian Culture* (Boston: Beacon Press, 1986), and Harriet Whitehead, "The Bow and the Burden Strap: A New Look at Institutionalized Homosexuality in Native North America," in *Sexual Meanings: The Cultural Construction of Gender and Sexuality,* eds. Sherry B. Ortner and Harriet Whitehead (Cambridge: Cambridge University Press, 1981), 80–115. For a useful discussion of the phenomenon of female husbands, see Ifi Amadiume, *Male Daughters, Female Husbands: Gender and Sex in an African Society* (Atlantic Highlands, N.J.: Zed Books, 1987). Igor Kopytoff, "Women's Roles and Existential Identities," in *Beyond the Second Sex: New Directions in the Anthropology of Gender,* eds. Peggy Reeves Sanday and Ruth Gallagher Goodenough (Philadelphia: University of Pennsylvania, 1990), 77–98, provides an extremely provocative discussion of the relation between the phenomena of female husbands and broader issues concerning the nature of self-identity.

33. Raymond, *The Transsexual Empire,* 28–29.

34. *Ibid,* xxiii–xxv.

35. This general weakness in arguments that employ the concept of "false consciousness" was suggested by Marcia Lind.

36. Of course, the demand for particularity is always relative. As such, any demand for particularity cannot be interpreted in absolutist terms but only as a recommendation for a greater move in such a direction.

37. Ludwig Wittgenstein, *Philosophical Investigations,* trans. G. E. M. Anscombe (New York: Macmillan, 1953), 31e–32e.

38. The tapestry metaphor was first used in an article I co-authored with Nancy Fraser. See Nancy Fraser and Linda Nicholson, "Social Criticism Without Philosophy: An Encounter Between Feminism and Postmodernism" in this volume.

5: The Myth of the Traditional Family

For their generous and insightful help with this article, I thank Nancy Fraser, Hilde Nelson, Philip Nicholson, Steven Seidman, and Eli Zaretsky.

1. The categories we have for sorting families include more than "traditional" and "alternative." There are also categories such as "deviant" and "unnatural." Indeed, the category "alternative" represents a more tolerant attitude toward non-"traditional" families than do the latter categories. I use the category "alternative" instead of these more derogatory categories as the contrast category to "traditional" only because I can thereby illustrate more clearly some of the privilege that is still accorded "traditional" families even in the context of the increased acceptance of non-"traditional" ones.

2. The variability in how kinship is defined has caused some anthropologists to question its utility as a cross-cultural analytical concept. The issue has been raised as to whether contemporary anthropologists have read into the concept assumptions of their own culture, such as the centrality of the mother/child bond, biological connections in general, or the separation of "domestic" and "public" life. For a discussion of these issues, see David Schneider, *A Critique of the Study of Kinship* (Ann Arbor: University of Michigan Press, 1984) and Jane Fishburne Collier and Sylvia Junko Yanagisako, eds., *Gender and Kinship: Essays Toward a Unified Analysis* (Stanford, Calif.: Stanford University Press, 1987). Kath Weston also discusses the difficulties of using the concept of "kinship" in *Families We Choose: Lesbians, Gays, Kinship* (New York: Columbia University Press, 1991), 33–41.

3. See Peter Laslett, *The World We Have Lost* (New York: Scribner's, 1965) and Peter Laslett, ed., *Household and Family in Past Time* (Cambridge: Cambridge University Press, 1972).

4. Wally Seccombe, *A Millenium of Family Change: Feudalism to Capitalism in Northwestern Europe* (London: Verso, 1992), 121.

5. The precise figures on this are the following. The village contained 62 households and a total population of 277 individuals. Of these households, 33 were composed of members of the lower social classes and averaged in size just under 3. These demographics made for a population of the lower social classes of 99 or approximately 35 percent of the total population. The rest of the population (i.e., 179 individuals or 65 percent of the total) lived in 29 households that averaged approximately 6.2 people per household. See Jean-Louis Flandrin, *Families in Former Times: Kinship, Household and Sexuality,* trans. Richard Southern (Cambridge: Cambridge University Press, 1979).

6. *Ibid,* 5.

7. *Ibid.*

8. Michael Mitterauer and Reinhard Sieder, *The European Family: Patriarchy to Partnership from the Middle Ages to the Present,* trans. Karla Oosterveen and Manfred Hörzinger (Oxford: Basil Blackwell, 1982), 6.

9. Lawrence Stone, *Family, Sex, and Marriage in England, 1500–1800* (New York: Harper and Row, 1979).

10. Natalie Zemon Davis, "Ghosts, Kin, and Progeny: Some Features of Family Life in Early Modern France," *Daedalus* 106 (Spring 1977):87–91.

11. Randolph Trumbach, *The Rise of the Egalitarian Family: Aristocratic Kinship and Domestic Relations in Eighteenth-Century England* (New York: Academic Press, 1978), 130–131. Many aspects of Trumbach's description are in accord with Stone's *The Family, Sex and Marriage* as well as with Edward Shorter's *The Making of the Modern Family* (New York: Basic, 1975). Although certainly there are interesting differences in many of the specifics depicted in each of these works as well as in their respective explanations for the changes, in broad outlines each describes a strikingly similar transformation.

12. Alan MacFarlane, *Marriage and Love in England: Modes of Reproduction 1300–1800* (Oxford: Basil Blackwell, 1986), 174–208. MacFarlane cites literature that documents the importance of love and the tying of love to marriage as far back as the time of Chaucer. Even if MacFarlane is right, this observation would not invalidate the thesis of the transformation among the upper classes from a patriarchal to a more egalitarian notion of marriage for love does not entail either equality or partnership.

13. The emphasis here is on western as opposed to eastern Europe. In eastern Europe, large family households including multiple generations and married siblings was the more common form. See Shorter, 35–37.

14. *Ibid,* 31–35.

15. Seccombe.

16. Shorter, 26–27.

17. Trumbach argues that the more egalitarian structure among the lower classes was a result of the aristocratic adoption of patrilineal kinship structures around the tenth century. Other groups continued with more ancient forms of cognatic, kinship principles, relating children to kin on both the mother's and the father's sides. Trumbach argues that such principles tended to promote greater equality between women and men. See Trumbach, 16.

18. Shorter, 44–46.

19. *Ibid,* 46–50.

20. *Ibid,* 218–22.

21. *Ibid,* 265.

22. *Ibid,* 243.

23. Stephanie Coentz, *The Way We Never Were: American Families and the Nostalgia Trap* (New York: Basic, 1992).

24. *Ibid,* 130–137.

25. *Ibid,* 136.

26. For an elaboration of those factors that made the creation of a certain ideal of family life possible for many in the 1950s, see Coontz, 23–41.

27. *Ibid,* 26.

28. *Ibid,* 27–28.

29. *Ibid,* 27.

30. Kenneth T. Jackson, *Crabgrass Frontier: The Suburbanization of the United States* (New York: Oxford University Press, 1985), 290–291.

31. Robert Lekachman *The Age of Keynes* (New York: Random House, 1966), 190; Michael Harrington, *The Other America* (New York: MacMillan 1962), 31–32.

32. Lekachman, 190. This quote was first brought to my attention in Arlene Skolnick *Embattled Paradise: The American Family in the Age of Uncertainly* (New York: Basic, 1991), 55.

33. Obviously, many non-blacks in this period were also poor and most blacks before this period had been poor. What made this period unique, however, was that many non-blacks who had been poor, unlike many blacks, were now able to become not poor.

34. Harrington, 31.

35. Henry A. Walker, "Black-White Differences in Marriage and Family Patterns," in eds. Sanford M. Dornbusch, and Myra H. Strober *Feminism, Children and the New Families,* (New York: Guilford, 1988), 87–116 and Coontz, 242–243.

36. Kingsley Davis, "Wives and Work: A Theory of the Sex-Role Revolution and its Consequences," in *Feminism, Children, and the New Families,* eds. Sanford M. Dornbusch and Myra H. Strober (New York: Guilford, 1988) 67–86.

37. Coontz, 32.

38. Davis, 79.

39. For an excellent discussion of this movement by gays and lesbians and of how it has opposed prior trends to place gays and lesbians outside of kinship see Weston.

40. Carol B. Stack, *All Our Kin: Strategies for Survival in a Black Community* (New York: Harper & Row, 1974). It should be emphasized that Stack's study is of a particular community at a particular point in time. The degree to which her study was generalizable to other poor black communities in the late 1960s and to which it can be found within any community today are open questions.

41. *Ibid*, 91.

42. *Ibid*, 106–107.

43. For an excellent study of this issue, see Arlie Hochschild with Anne Machung, *The Second Shift: Working Parents and the Revolution at Home* (New York: Viking, 1989).

6: Social Criticism Without Philosophy: An Encounter Between Feminism and Postmodernism

This essay has previously appeared in *Communication* 10 (1988) 345–366; *Theory Culture and Society* 5, (June 1988):373–394; *Universal Abandon? The Politics of Postmodernism*, ed. Andrew Ross (Minneapolis: University of Minnesota Press, 1988), 83–104; and *Feminism/Postmodernism*, ed. Linda J. Nicholson (New York: Routledge, 1990), 19–38, as well as in many other places. We are grateful for the helpful suggestions of many people, especially Jonathan Arac, Ann Ferguson, Marilyn Frye, Nancy Hartsock, Alison Jaggar, Berel Lang, Thomas McCarthy, Karsten Struhl, Iris Young, Thomas Wartenberg, and the members of SOFPHIA. We are also grateful for word processing help from Marina Rosiene.

1. Exceptions are Jane Flax, "Gender as a Social Problem: In and for Feminist Theory," *American Studies/Amerika Studien* (June 1986), 193–213; Sandra Harding, *The Science Question in Feminism* (Ithaca, N.Y.: Cornell University Press, 1986) and "The Instability of the Analytical Categories of Feminist Theory," *Signs* 11 (1986), 645–664; Donna Haraway, "A Manifesto for Cyborgs: Science, Technology, and Socialist Feminism in the 1980s," *Socialist Review* 80 (1983), 65–107; Alice A. Jardine, *Gynesis: Configurations of Women and Modernity*

(Ithaca, N.Y.: Cornell University Press, 1985); Jean-François Lyotard, "Some of the Things at Stake in Women's Struggles," trans, Deborah J. Clarke, Winnifred Woodhull, and John Mowitt, *Sub-Stance,* 20 (1978):9–17; Craig Owens, "The Discourse of Others: Feminists and Postmodernism," *The Anti-Aesthetic: Essays on Postmodern Culture,* ed. Hal Foster (Port Townsend, Wash. Bay Press, 1983), 57–82.

2. Jean-François Lyotard, *The Postmodern Condition: A Report on Knowledge,* trans. G. Bennington and B. Massumi (Minneapolis: University of Minnesota Press, 1984).

3. *Ibid.* Cf. Jean François Lyotard and Jean-Loup Thebaud, *Just Gaming* (Minneapolis: University of Minnesota Press, 1987); also Jean François Lyotard, "The Differend, the Referent, and the Proper Name" *Diacritics* 14 (Fall 1984), 4–14.

4. See, for example, Michel Foucault, *Discipline and Punish: The Birth of the Prison,* No. 3 trans. Alan Sheridan (New York: Vintage Books, 1979).

5. Michael Walzer, *Spheres of Justice: A Defense of Pluralism and Equality* (New York: Basic, 1983).

6. It should be noted that, for Lyotard, the choice of philosophy as a starting point is itself determined by a metapolitical commitment, namely to antitotalitarianism. He assumes erroneously that totalizing social and political theory necessarily eventuates in totalitarian societies. Thus, the "practical intent" that subtends Lyotard's privileging of philosophy (and that is in turn attenuated by the latter) is anti-Marxism. Whether it should also be characterized as neoliberalism is a question too complicated to be explored here.

7. See, for example, the essays in *Discovering Reality: Feminist Perspectives on Epistemology, Metaphysics, Methodology, and Philosophy of Science,* eds. Sandra Harding and Merrill B. Hintikka (Dordrecht, Holland: D. Reidel, 1983).

8. Shulamith Firestone, *The Dialectic of Sex* (New York: Bantam, 1970).

9. Gayle Rubin, "The Traffic in Women," *Toward an Anthropology of Women,* ed. Rayna R. Reiter (New York: Monthly Review Press, 1975), 160.

10. Michelle Zimbalist Rosaldo, "Woman, Culture, and Society: A Theoretical Overview," *Woman, Culture, and Society,* eds. Michelle Zimbalist Rosaldo and Louise Lamphere (Stanford, Calif.: Stanford University Press, 1974), 17–42.

11. These and related problems were soon apparent to many of the domestic/public theorists themselves. See Rosaldo's self-criticism, "The Use and Abuse of Anthropology: Reflections on Feminism and Cross-Cultural Understanding," *Signs* 5 (1980), 389–417. A more recent discussion, which points out the circularity of the theory, appears in Sylvia J. Yanagisako and Jane F. Collier, "Toward a Unified Analysis of Gender and Kinship," in *Gender and Kinship: Essays Toward a Unified Analysis,* eds. Jane Fishburne Collier and Sylvia Junko Yanagisako (Stanford, Calif.: Stanford University Press, 1987).

12. Nancy Chodorow, *The Reproduction of Mothering; Psychoanalysis and the Sociology of Gender* (Berkeley: University of California Press, 1978).

13. A similar ambiguity attends Chodorow's discussion of the family. In response to critics who object that her psychoanalytic emphasis ignores social structures, Chodorow has rightly insisted that the family is itself a social structure, one frequently slighted in social explanations. Yet, she generally does not discuss families as historically specific social institutions whose specific relations with other institutions can be analyzed. Rather, she tends to invoke the family in a very abstract and general sense defined only as the locus of female mothering.

14. Ann Ferguson and Nancy Folbre, "The Unhappy Marriage of Patriarchy and Capitalism," in *Women and Revolution,* ed. Lydia Sargent (Boston: South End Press, 1981), 313–338; Nancy Hartsock, *Money, Sex and Power: Toward a Feminist Historical Materialism* (New York: Longman, 1983); Catharine A. MacKinnon, "Feminism, Marxism, Method, and the State: An Agenda for Theory," *Signs* 7 (Spring 1982), 515–544.

15. Carol Gilligan, *In a Different Voice: Psychological Theory and Women's Development* (Cambridge: Harvard University Press, 1982).

16. Cf. *Ibid,* 2.

17. Marilyn Frye, *The Politics of Reality: Essays in Feminist Theory* (Trumansburg, N.Y.: The Crossing Press, 1983); bell hooks, *Feminist Theory from Margin to Center* (Boston: South End Press, 1981), 91–107; Audre Lorde, "An Open Letter to Mary Daly," in *This Bridge Called My*

Back: Writings by Radical Women of Color, eds. Cherrie Moraga and Gloria Anzaldúa (Watertown, Mass.: Persephone Press, 1981), 94–97; Maria C. Lugones and Elizabeth V. Spelman, "Have We Got a Theory for You! Feminist Theory, Cultural Imperialism and the Demand for the Woman's Voice," *Hypatia: A Journal of Feminist Philosophy,* a special issue of *Women's Studies International Forum* 6, (1983), 578–581; Adrienne Rich, "Compulsory Heterosexuality and Lesbian Existence," *Signs:* 5 (Summer 1980), 631–660; Elizabeth Spelman, "Theories of Race and Gender: The Erasure of Black Women," *Quest* 5 (1980/81), 36–62.

18. See, for example, Hélène Cixous, "The Laugh of the Medusa," trans. Keith Cohen and Paula Cohen, in *New French Feminisms,* eds. Elaine Marks and Isabelle de Courtivron (New York: Schocken Books, 1981), 245–261; Hélène Cixous and Catherine Clément, *The Newly Born Woman,* trans. Betsy Wing (Minneapolis: University of Minnesota Press, 1986); Luce Irigaray, *Speculum of the Other Woman* (Ithaca, N.Y.: Cornell University Press, 1985) and *This Sex Which Is Not One* (Ithaca, N.Y.: Cornell University Press, 1985); Julia Kristeva, *Desire in Language: A Semiotic Approach to Literature and Art,* ed. Leon S. Roudiez (New York: Columbia University Press, 1980) and "Women's Time," trans. Alice Jardine and Harry Blake, *Signs* 7 (Autumn 1981), 13–35. See also the critical discussions by Ann Rosalind Jones, "Writing the Body: Toward an Understanding of I'Ecriture Féminine," *The New Feminist Criticism: Essays on Women, Literature and Theory,* ed. Elaine Showalter (New York: Pantheon Books, 1985) and Toril Moi, *Sexual/Textual Politics: Feminist Literary Theory* (London: Methuen, 1985).

7: Bringing it All Back Home: Reason in the Twilight of Foundationalism

Those who read drafts of this essay and provided useful reactions were Mark Berger, Felmon Davis, Nanette Funk, and Berel Lang. Steve Seidman's comments about an earlier draft caused me to make substantial revisions. A conversation with Nancy Fraser and Eli Zartetsky in the early stages of my writing of this essay was helpful in enabling me to clarify some of my more general claims. I appreciate Seyla Benhabib's careful attention to this essay and the conversations we have had about it. Her comments precluded even greater misunderstandings of her position than might remain. My understanding of these issues was also strengthened through reading Alison Jaggar's essay, "A Feminist Perspective on Discourse Ethics," a paper presented at a conference on "Angewandte Ethik als Politicum" ("Applied Ethics as Politics") in Essen in December 1995. I also thank Alison for her very close reading of a draft of this essay. Her judgment on issues of style and content were, as usual, invaluable.

1. Seyla Benhabib, *Situating the Self: Gender, Community and Postmodernism in Contemporary Ethics* (New York: Routledge, 1992), 30.

2. For the most elaborated discussion of this issue, see Thomas Laqueur, *Making Sex: Body and Gender from the Greeks to Freud* (Cambridge: Harvard University Press, 1990).

3. I suggest this way of thinking about "woman" in my essay, "Interpreting Gender," which is printed in this volume. Cressida Hayes elaborates more extensively a Wittgensteinian "take" on this concept in her manuscript, *Essentialism in Feminist Theory and Practice: A Wittgensteinian Approach.* For Wittgenstein's discussion of the word "game," see Ludwig Wittgenstein, *Philosophical Investigations,* trans. G. E. M. Anscombe (New York: MacMillan, 1953), 31e–32e.

4. Richard Rorty, "Putnam and the Relativist Menace," *Journal of Philosophy* 90 (September 1993), 449.

5. Thomas McCarthy, "Philosophy and Critical Theory: A Reply to Richard Rorty and Seyla Benhabib," *Constellations* 3 (April 1996), 96.

6. Seyla Benhabib, "The Local, the Contextual and/or Critical," *Constellations* (April 1996), 88–89. The quotation from McCarthy is from David Couzens Hoy and Thomas McCarthy, *Critical Theory* (Cambridge: Basil Blackwell, 1994), 245.

7. Lorraine Daston, "Baconian Facts, Academic Civility, and the Prehistory of Objectivity," in *Rethinking Objectivity*, ed. Allan Megill (Durham, N.C.: Duke University Press, 1994), 37–63.

8. Jürgen Habermas, "Moral Consciousness and Communicative Action," in *Moral Consciousness and Communicative Action*, trans. Christian Lenhardt and Shierry Weber Nicholsen (Boston: MIT Press, 1990), 178. This passage from Habermas was brought to my attention by Benhabib, *Situating the Self*, 182.

9. For example, Charles Taylor has argued that liberalism, with its assumption of a separation between politics and religion, represents not a neutral ground with respect to culture but a particular cultural perspective. See Charles Taylor, *Multiculturalism and the Politics of Recognition: An Essay* (Princeton: Princeton University Press, 1994), 62.

10. Nancy Fraser, "What's Critical about Critical Theory? The Case of Habermas and Gender," in *Unruly Practices: Power, Discourse and Gender in Contemporary Social Theory* (Minneapolis: University of Minnesota Press, 1989), 113–143.

11. Benhabib, *Situating the Self*, 182–190.

12. *Ibid*, 51–52.

13. *Ibid*, 137. The reference that Benhabib makes to Arendt in this passage is to Hannah Arendt, "Crisis in Culture," in *Between Past and Future: Six Exercises in Political Thought* (New York: Meridian, 1961), 221.

14. See Benhabib's description of these principles in her chapter, "In the Shadow of Aristotle and Hegel" in *Situating the Self*, 23–67.

15. Otto Neurath, "Protocol Statements," in *Philosophical Papers 1911–1946*, ed. and trans. R. S. Cohen and M. Neurath (Dordrecht: D. Reidel, 1983), 92.

8: To Be or Not to Be: Charles Taylor and the Politics of Recognition

I thank Mark Berger, Nancy Fraser, Alison Jaggar, Berel Lang, and Steve Seidman for their comments on earlier versions of this essay.

1. Charles Taylor, *Multiculturalism and the Politics of Recognition: An Essay* (Princeton: Princeton University Press, 1994). Taylor also examines the emergence of the need for recognition in *The Ethics of Authenticity* (Cambridge: Harvard University Press, 1991). Because my concern with his discussion of this topic is regarding its relation to the question of multiculturalism discussed in the later book but not in the earlier one and because the earlier book does not appear to introduce any ideas relevant to multiculturalism that are different from those of the later one, my focus in this essay is only on the later book.

2. Susan Wolf, "Comment" in Taylor, *Multiculturalism and the Politics of Recognition*, 76–77.

3. Taylor, *Multiculturalism and the Politics of Recognition*, 31.

4. Karl Marx, and Frederick Engels, *The German Ideology* (Moscow: Progress Publishers, 1968), 62.

5. This point is related to one that Susan Wolf makes in her "Comment" on Taylor's essay. Wolf notes, "The predominant problem for women as women is not that the larger or more powerful sector of the community fails to notice or to be interested in preserving women's gendered identity but that this identity is put to the service of oppression and exploitation" (p. 76).

6. Iris Marion Young, "Humanism, Gynocentrism and Feminist Politics," in *Hypatia: A Journal of Feminist Philosophy*, a special issue of *Women's Studies International Forum* 8 (1985), 173–183.

7. Taylor, *Multiculturalism and the Politics of Recognition*, 62.

8. *Ibid.*

9. Nancy Fraser, "Politics, Culture, and the Public Sphere: Toward a Postmodern Conception," in *Social Postmodernism*, ed. Linda Nicholson and Steven Seidman (New York: Cambridge University Press, 1995), 287–312. Fraser notes the ways in which the power to draw the line between private and public was differently distributed between the supporters of Anita Hill and Clarence Thomas in the 1991 debates over Thomas's confirmation for the Supreme Court. Fraser's discussion highlights the point that claims about where this line should be drawn reflect substantive, political acts. I also talk about the historically changing meanings of "public" and "private" in Linda Nicholson, *Gender and History: The Limits of Social Theory and the Age of the Family* (New York: Columbia University Press, 1986).

10. Taylor, *Multiculturalism and the Politics of Recognition*, 43.

11. *Ibid*, 73.

12. *Ibid*, 64–66.

13. *Ibid*, 64.

14. *Ibid.*

15. *Ibid*, 70.

16. *Ibid.*

17. *Ibid*, 73.

18. *Ibid*, 66–67.

19. *Ibid*, 69.

9: Emotion in Postmodern Public Spaces

For their extensive comments on earlier drafts of this essay, I thank David Kahane, Ted Koditschek, Berel Lang, and Steve Seidman. I received useful reactions from the participants in a variety of conferences, including the conferences on "Postmodernism and the Emotions" held at Mainz, Germany, in January 1996 and on "Social Construction, Culture and the Politics of Identity" at The New School for Social Research in April 1996. Mary Gergen, Dan P. McAdams, David Woolwine, and the members of the University of Wisconsin at Madison community reacted to an earlier version of this paper in March 1996. This essay has been previously published in *Emotion in Postmodernism*, eds. Gerhard Hoffman and Alfred Hornung (Heidelberg: Universitätsverlag C. Winter, 1997), 1–25.

1. Roberto Mangabeira Unger, *Knowledge and Politics* (New York: Free Press, 1975), 59.

2. Michel Foucault's *The History of Sexuality* (New York: Pantheon, 1978) is most famous for arguing against the repressive thesis as a mode of understanding Victorian attitudes toward sexuality. For another analysis of the problems of the repressive thesis, particularly for understanding attitudes in the United States, see Steven Seidman, *Romantic Longings: Love in America, 1830–1980* (New York: Routledge, 1991).

3. Philip Cushman, *Constructing the Self, Constructing America: A Cultural History of Psychotherapy* (Reading, Mass.: Addison-Wesley, 1995), 123–131.

4. Kenneth J. Gergen, *The Saturated Self: Dilemmas of Identity in Contemporary Life* (New York: Basic, 1991), 20–27.

5. Peter N. Stearns, *American Cool: Constructing a Twentieth Century Emotional Style* (New York: New York University, 1994), 42.

6. *Ibid*, 42.

7. *Ibid*, 48–49.

8. *Ibid*, 37–46.

9. The gender neutrality of Freudian theory becomes more straightforward in later therapeutic theories as Freud's specific theories of childhood development become eliminated or given a more minor role.

10. Sigmund Freud, *An Outline of Psychoanalysis,* trans. James Strachey (New York: W. W. Norton, 1949), 16–17.

11. Sigmund Freud, *Civilization and Its Discontents,* trans. and ed. James Strachey (New York: W. W. Norton, 1961), 108–109.

12. Eli Zaretsky, "Bisexuality and the Ambivalent Legacy of Psychoanalysis" Unpublished paper, p. 13.

13. *Ibid*, 17.

14. This increased public focus on the emotions does not mean that Americans have become more emotionally expressive in public spaces in the twentieth century than they were previously. Clearly, there are important class, gender, and ethnic issues involved here, but Peter Stearns has argued that at least one dominant trend in U.S. popular culture during the twentieth century has been in the direction of decreasing, not increasing, the public expression of emotion.

15. See Cushman. See also Joel Kovel, "The American Mental Health Industry," in *Critical Psychiatry: The Politics of Mental Health,* ed. David Ingleby (New York: Pantheon, 1980), 72–101; Christopher Lasch, *The Culture of Narcissism: American Life in an Age of Diminishing Expectations* (New York: W. W. Norton, 1979); T. J. Jackson Lears, "From Salvation to Self-Realization: Advertising and the Therapeutic Roots of the Consumer Culture, 1880–1930" in *The Culture of Consumption: Critical Essays in American History, 1880–1980,* eds. Richard Wightman Fox and T. J. Jackson Lears (New York: Pantheon, 1983), 1–38; Philip Rieff, "Reflections on Psychological Man in America," in *The Feeling Intellect,* ed. Philip Rieff (Chicago: University of Chicago Press, 1990), 3–10; Philip Rieff, *Freud: The Mind of the Moralist* (New York: Viking, 1959); Warren I. Susman, *Culture as History: The Transformation of American Society in the Twentieth Century* (New York: Pantheon, 1973).

16. Cushman, 155.

17. These points were suggested by Sidney Callahan, who claims that "emotions differ from cognitions in their subjective intensity, specificity, and nonverbal richness." See Sidney Callahan, "The Role of Emotion in Ethical Decisionmaking," *Hastings Center Report* (June/July 1988):9–14. Callahan references Douglas Derryberry and Mary Klevjord Rothbart, "Emotion, Attention and Temperament," in *Emotions, Cognition and Behavior,* eds. Carroll E. Izard, Jerome Kagan, and Robert B. Zajonic (Cambridge: Cambridge University Press, 1984), 17–37.

18. Alison M. Jaggar, "Love and Knowledge: Emotion in Feminist Epistemology," in *Gender/Body/Knowledge: Feminist Reconstructions of Being and Knowing,* eds. Alison M. Jaggar and Susan R. Bordo (New Brunswick, N.J.: Rutgers University Press, 1989), 145–171.

19. Judith Butler, "Imitation and Gender Insubordination," in *Inside/Out: Lesbian Theories, Gay Theories,* ed. Diana Fuss (New York: Routledge, 1991), 13–31.

Index

Feelings, 13–14, 146–147, 153, 155, 158–159, 160
Feminine/femininity, 18–20, 27, 72, 110
Feminism/women's movement, 2, 99–100, 114–115, 130, 132–134, 156–158, 160
    feminism, postmodern, 100, 113–115
    feminism, psychoanalytic, 113
    feminism, radical, 67–68
    a feminism of difference, 67, 70–72
Feminist theory, 2–3, 7, 10, 30, 43, 46–47, 68, 106–109, 111–114
Ferguson, Ann, 39, 111
Firestone, Shulamith, 107–108
Flandrin, Jean Louis, 80
Folbre, Nancy, 39, 111
Foucault, Michel, 4, 61–62, 104, 138
Foundationalism, 9–11, 100–106, 117
Fraser, Nancy, 125
Freud, Sigmund, 146, 149, 150–155
Frye, Marilyn, 113

Gay and lesbian
    households, 89–90, 95
    movement, 135, 156–157, 160
Gender, 3, 7, 17–20, 36–45, 50, 53–57, 66, 69, 71–72, 100, 103–104, 109–110, 114, 149, 151, 157–159
Gergen, Kenneth, 147
Gilligan, Carol, 3–5, 18–21, 26–28, 67–68, 71
Gilman, Charlotte Perkins, 158
Gynocentrism, 112, 134

Habermas, Jürgen, 42, 119, 122, 124–125, 127
Harrington, Michael, 88
Hartsock, Nancy, 111
Hegel, G.W.F., 5, 21, 102, 118
Hermaphroditism, 61–62
hooks, bell, 113

Identity, 129–132, 158–161
    politics, 146, 160–161
Individualism, 154–155, 159
Irigiray, Luce, 68

Jackson, Kenneth, 87
Jaggar, Alison, 155
Jordan, Winthrop, 60
Jordanova, Ludmilla, 59
Joseph, Gloria, 113
Justice, 25–26, 102–104, 124

Kant, Immanuel, 21–23, 118–119, 126
Kinship, 5–6, 29, 36, 38–39, 41, 44, 48–50, 79, 82, 89, 92–93

Kohlberg, Lawrence, 3–5, 18–21, 23–28, 112
Kovell, Joel, 153

Labor, 5, 34–36
Laqueur, Thomas, 60–62
Lasch, Christopher, 153
Laslett, Peter, 80
Lears, T.J. Jackson, 153
Lekachman, Robert, 87
Lesbian, 2, 66, 68, 77, 112
    See also Gay and lesbian households; and Gay and lesbian movement
Lever, Janet, 20
Liberalism/liberal theory, 45–47, 50–51, 129, 135–137, 146
Linnaeus, Carolus, 60
Locke, Alain, 158
Locke, John, 5, 46–47, 51, 59
Lord, Audre, 113
Lugones, Maria, 113
Lukács, Georg, 42
Lyotard, Jean François, 9–10, 100–105, 113–114

MacKinnon, Catharine, 111
Mann, Thomas, 148
Marx, Karl, 5–6, 29–33, 37–41, 45, 63–64, 102, 132
Marxism, 2, 8, 36–42, 45, 47, 103, 105, 107
Marxist feminism, 39, 44
Masculine/masculinity, 18–21, 27 ,72, 110
McCarthy, Thomas, 121–122
Metanarrative, 102–107, 109, 111–113
Mitterauer, Michael, 81
Modernity, 9, 10, 14, 130–132
Morality, 17, 20 ,22, 121, 125, 131, 146
    moral argument, 119, 126
    moral development, 3–4, 18–20, 25, 27–28, 112
    moral theory, 17–18, 22, 24–25
Morgan, Robin, 65–67
Morss, Susan Buck, 4, 25
Mothering, 109, 111, 114
Multiculturalism, 12, 129–130, 135, 137–142

Neurath, Otto, 127

Objectivity, 106, 117, 140
O'Brien, Mary, 37–38
Oppression, 134, 143

Patriarchal societies/patriarchy, 45, 66, 73, 82–84
"The Personal Is Political," 47, 51, 134